POLITICAL MOBILIZATION OF THE VENEZUELAN PEASANT

Written under the auspices of the Center for International Affairs, Harvard University

Political Mobilization of the Venezuelan Peasant

JOHN DUNCAN POWELL

Harvard University Press, Cambridge, Massachusetts, 1971

DEDICATED TO THE SOCIAL AND ECONOMIC
EMANCIPATION OF ALL PEASANTS

ACKNOWLEDGMENTS

The Land Tenure Center of the University of Wisconsin financed and supported my field work in Venezuela in 1964 and 1965–66. In particular, I would like to express deep appreciation to Raymond J. Penn, the first director of the Land Tenure Center, for his continued personal interest in my work; and to Peter Dorner, current director of the center.

The Inter-American Committee on Agricultural Development (CIDA) financed the survey of local peasant union leaders in Venezuela early in 1966, and furnished interviewers from its agrarian reform evaluation staff. For this support, I am grateful to Thomas F. Carroll and the late Michael Sund. During this same period John R. Mathiason of the University of Washington was of particular help and, in addition, generously shared the data generated by his own research.

The Center for International Affairs at Harvard University provided part-time support over the past several years, while I was rewriting and refining the manuscript. Special thanks go to Samuel P. Huntington for his sponsorship of my work at the center.

For providing invaluable editorial assistance, I an indebted to Marina Finkelstein, publications editor of the Center for International Affairs, and Philip B. Taylor, Jr., director of Latin American Studies at the University of Houston.

Finally, I would like to thank my wife, Linda, without whose loving but firm prodding all my years of effort on this book might not have come to fruition.

CONTENTS

FIGURES

TABLES

POLITICAL MOBILIZATION OF THE VENEZUELAN PEASANT

Frequently Used Abbreviations

AD   Acción Democrática—Democratic Action party

BAP   Banco Agrícola y Pecuario—Agriculture and Livestock Bank

COPEI   Comité de Organización Política Electoral Independiente—known by its acronym, also as Social Christian party

CTV   Confederación de Trabajadores de Venezuela—Confederation of Venezuelan Workers

FCV   Federación Campesina de Venezuela—Peasant Federation of Venezuela

FND   Frente Nacional Democrática—National Democratic Front party

IAN   Instituto Agrario Nacional—National Agrarian Institute

ITIC   Instituto Técnico de Inmigración y Colonización—Technical Institute for Immigration and Colonization

MAC   Ministerio de Agricultura y Cría—Ministry of Agriculture and Livestock

MEP   Movimiento Electoral del Pueblo—People's Electoral Movement

ORVE   Movimiento de Organización Venezolana—Movement for Venezuelan Organization

PDN   Partido Democrático Nacional—National Democratic party

URD   Unión Republicana Democrática—Democratic Republican Union party

INTRODUCTION

> The peasant begins to see that among the causes of *la miseria*
> are the interests of men who are not essentially different from
> himself and certainly not outside of his own field of action. As
> he accepts, thus, the possibility of eventually overcoming the
> human causes of *la miseria,* he begins to participate in the
> making of history.
>
> —F. G. Friedmann[1]

The passage of a peasant class from being objects of national
events to being participants in their direction has been taking place
in Venezuela since 1936. This process is not yet complete, nor
are the forms of participation so established and consolidated that
the Venezuelan peasantry may yet be regarded as makers of history.
But the course of the journey has been so swift, so dramatic, and
so significant to the development of a political democracy in that
important nation as to require the telling.

Peasants, broadly defined as rural agriculturalists of extremely
low socioeconomic and political status, have been studied by the
scholarly community from a number of viewpoints.[2] The most common perspective is that defined by the peasant's own horizon, focusing on his kinship groupings, neighborhood and community groupings, and occasionally on the larger world as it operates on and
is perceived by him.[3] Another important context is the peasant's
struggle for power at the national level, in which he functions
as an actor on the political stage—either as an active participant
or as a relatively passive factor to be taken into account and dealt
with by others.[4] Recently, a number of efforts have been made
to analyze the peasantry in a context of sociopolitical development.[5]
In what may become a contemporary classic on political development, Samuel P. Huntington's *Political Order in Changing Societies,*
appears a provocative analysis of the potential role of the peasantry

in the political processes of developing areas.[6] Particular stress is given to what Huntington calls "the Green Uprising," a peasant mobilization in which, under certain developmental conditions, the peasantry is incorporated into the political process through alliance with an urban-based political elite. That such an alliance can occur, which thereby mobilizes the peasantry, is particularly clear in the case of Venezuela. To examine the formation of the Venezuelan alliance and its subsequent functioning is the primary concern of this study.

The formation of a peasant-urban alliance almost always results from an initiative by the urban partner. This is not to suggest a lack of interdependence but to emphasize that the timing and circumstances for such an alliance are primarily determined by events in the national political arena. The impulse for the alliance arises when an urban elite, engaged in a struggle for power at the center, perceives the need for a massive base of support and determines that such a base is available in the peasantry in return for agrarian reform. As Elias Tuma puts the matter in a history of agrarian reform:

> Though the objectives of reform are varied, the primary ones are usually political regardless of who initiates reform. The reformers use reform to win the support of specific groups, to create or restore political stability, to legitimize their own political positions, or to create what they consider to be democracy. The timing and extent of the reform are determined more by political pressure than by the genuine social and economic needs of the rural population. Furthermore, land distribution is closely associated with revolution and change in the regime in power. A new elite tends to distribute the land both to win the support of the peasantry and to weaken its opponents, in contrast to the continuing elite or ruling class who try to prevent reform as long as possible, and when it comes, to preserve as much of the old structure as possible.[7]

Although one would expect a difference in the degree of peasant mobilization and in the distribution of land reform benefits, it seems that both a new elite seeking legitimacy and an established elite trying to preserve it can employ agrarian reform as a means to mobilize a peasant base of support. One recent study of eight developing countries advances the following three hypotheses on the relationship between agrarian reform and political elites: (1) a perceived need for legitimacy—whether to strengthen a new regime, or to permit an incumbent regime to resist drastic change—is the factor that prompts a political elite to initiate reform; (2) the relationship between the initiating elite and the landed class determines the nature of the reform undertaken; and (3) the political commitment to reform—a willingness and readiness of the political elite to mobilize significant available resources—determines the extent of the reform actually carried out.[8] What is of particular significance in the Venezuelan case is the fact that the urban partner of the alliance was not in power at the time it formulated an appeal for agrarian reform, but built and utilized the alliance in order to obtain governmental power. Once power was achieved, the agrarian reform program was used to consolidate the peasant base of support.

One significant context in which to analyze an agrarian reform is thus its utilization by, or its effect on, an aspiring political elite engaged in a struggle for power at the national level. The use of the reform issue is—or under certain conditions may be—highly instrumental in deciding not only who governs but also the social base and degree of his legitimacy, the direction and pace of socioeconomic and political change among the rural masses, and perhaps the very structure of society itself. But in analyzing the use of the agrarian reform issue as an instrument in the struggle for national political power among competing elites, one should not lose sight of the fact that agrarian reform, as an issue, is not necessarily decided at the level of elitist maneuverings, but often at the level of mass political behavior. That is, competing elites do not win or lose power by arguing the pros and cons of agrarian reform, but by mobilizing instrumental patterns of political behavior among masses of peasants.

An analytical distinction must be made between the issue that is the basis for mobilizing mass political behavior among the peasantry, and the political mobilization phenomenon per se. The British sociologist J. P. Nettl distinguishes between two functions of the mobilization process: authority legitimation and interest articulation.[9] In a peasant mobilization based on agrarian reform, as shown with particular clarity in the Venezuelan case, these two functions are interdependent. For the urban partners of the alliance, the objective is to acquire the legitimacy to govern: they offer agrarian reform to the peasants as an inducement to support their claim to legitimacy, as through the electoral process. For the peasant partners to the alliance, the objective is the articulation of interests and their accomplishment through an agrarian reform program: they offer their legitimating support to the urban elite in return for such a program. The political leadership of a peasant mobilization thus enters into a collaborative arrangement with peasant supporters to seek authority legitimation, while the peasants support the leaders in order to seek interest articulation. In the case of Venezuela, this interdependent relationship is a dynamic process, requiring high levels of political skill and imagination to maintain an appropriate balance between the two functions during shifting political circumstances.

A general explanation for the mobilizing capacity of those who champion the concept of agrarian reform among the peasant masses lies in the nature of peasant life—in particular, in the traditional land tenure systems which are the framework for that life. The appeal of agrarian reform, which promises a drastic alteration in land distribution, derives both from the intrinsic quality of peasant life, and from characteristic facets of traditional land tenure systems—facets familiar to peasants in other times and places than twentieth-century Latin America.[10] Certainly one of the most critical factors characterizing peasant life is the asymmetrical nature of the relationship between landed elites and peasant cultivators. The essence of this relationship is the extraction of an agricultural surplus from the peasantry. In discussing the arrangement, which he takes to be a consequence of the peasant's position in society and polity, Henry A. Landsberger argues that essentially, the person who extracts a surplus from the peasant "does so beyond any service he or his class has performed, and that he is able to exact his appropriation through control of the political system—the state, the law, and ultimately, force."[11]

The nature of this asymmetrical relationship is explained by the interaction of two intimately related factors: concentration of land ownership and atomization of the labor force. As a result, socioeconomic and political power is tied to land ownership, while socioeconomic and political weakness is tied to labor. In the case of Latin America, the present forms of concentration of land ownership and the subordination of labor in agriculture can be traced directly to the Spanish conquest. The encomienda system, as practised by the Spanish crown, consisted of distributing grants to conquistadors and other loyal subjects, "delegating to them the substance of seigneurial power, with rights to exact compulsory labour (*servicios personales*) and tribute from the Indian populations entrusted to them." Andrew Pearse characterized this practice as a political system of "indirect rule." By the end of the sixteenth century, control and possession of lands formerly in the encomienda system had become the basis of a private property system. Other crown lands, the *resguardos*, were held aside for the Indian populations, but these lands were conditioned by the institution of the repartimiento, a labor tribute that the new landowning class could extract from the Indians living on them. The resguardo holdings were gradually encroached upon through a systematic policy of attrition by landowners, in collaboration with local officials. According to Pearse's analysis, both "power and . . . prestige could be maintained directly by the acquisition of labour power and its application to the land without deep involvement in market relationships." Although the seizure and maintenance of control over land and labor have been the twin pillars of Latin American society, the land-labor institutions have evolved through several historic stages, beginning with the use of naked force over the native population, followed by a system of legally-defined labor duties and the introduction of African slaves. During the republican period, coercive state power was used against laborers by means of the legal contrivance of debt, combined with the monopolistic occupation of lands and the consequent expulsion of an adequate number of peasants from independent subsistence. Ultimately, an agrarian labor market was created, which permitted the buying of labor from the landless or land-poor peasant in a buyer's market.[12]

The more recent pattern of land tenure systems, a consequence of these historic trends, is known as the latifundia-minifundia complex. This complex comprises two interdependent components: the large landholdings or latifundia, concentrating much land in a few hands, with the mass of the rural population either depending on the latifundia lands for income opportunities or subsisting on a fragment of the remainder of the available land, alloted in microparcels or minifundia. Although the two components are dependent on one another, the overwhelming importance of the large landholdings is clear. Recent field studies in Argentina, Brazil, Chile, Colombia, Ecuador, and Guatemala have revealed that the proportion of farm families owning or operating estates ranged from 1.6 percent in Guatemala to 14.6 percent in Brazil, and that the amount of land controlled by these families ranged from 51.9 percent of the farm land in operation in Argentina to 93.5 percent in Brazil. In mean figures, 6.4 percent of the farm families controlled 74.6 percent of the land in farm operations. Equally important is the total proportion of farm families dependent or living on these estates: the figures ranged from a low of 28.6 percent in Guatemala to a high of 76.5 percent in Brazil, with an average figure of 45.6 percent. Given the enormous population of Brazil, which would skew total absolute numbers upward, one can conservatively estimate that half of all farm families in Latin America are peasants dependent or living on large estates, and that these families probably represent one-fourth of the total population of the area.[13] These are the people for whom an agrarian reform is of greatest significance.

The social organization and land-labor relationships on the large landholdings vary greatly in detail, but certain characteristics stand out sharply. First, as suggested by Pearse, land is exploited as an economic production factor, but neither so intensively nor so rationally as is labor. This imbalance stems from the fact that the owners of the primary means of production—land and modest capital inputs—do not combine them with labor in a rational mix calculated to maximize agricultural production, and hence monetary profit, but rather in a manner designed to maximize social status for the owners of land. The resulting status position may be turned to monetary profit through politics or other economic pursuits, but rarely through agricultural enterprise. The arena of prestige for a landowner transcends the local community that he dominates, where it is expressed in elaborate forms of deferential behavior. A high value on rural landownership is part of the national value system of the traditional elites, and is often incorporated into the value system of new, upwardly mobile elites.[14]

The second characteristic feature of the large-landholding system in Latin America is that a number of ways have been developed to bond a quasipermanent labor force to the land. This has been accomplished in order to insure a ready supply of labor at the times of greatest need, since much of the productive work is of a seasonal nature. The most common pattern is one of service-tenancy, in which a peasant farmer is given a plot of land and some sort of housing for his family in return for a certain amount of labor on the landowner's operation. In times of peak activity, the resident labor force is often supplemented, either with local minifundistas anxious to supplement their subsistence income or with migrant labor.[15]

The third characteristic of this land tenure system is the complex and subtle nature of the system-maintenance pattern. It is a blend of sanctions and rewards, which functions at both latent and manifest levels. At the level of manifest sanctions, the means employed by landowners may range from direct violence to the person of the peasant, to eviction and inscription on a tenant's blacklist. More indirect means are the contrivance of debt, through over-crediting the landlord's contributions to the tenancy relationship (inflating the cost of housing, food, tools, short-term credits, goods at the "company store") or undercrediting the peasant tenant's contributions (deflating the measurement of the quantity produced or the assessment of its market value at time of sale).[16] Manifest rewards, like manifest sanctions, are selectively applied to individual peasants and their families in order to structure preferred forms of behavior and deference. Thus, much the same as in the case of the black American in the South, the man who knows his "place" can use this knowledge to his advantage, even within a system of general exploitation. Individual tenants may be rewarded with better plots or housing; they may be granted special favors, such as medical care or schooling for a child; they may eventually be made overseers if they know their place well enough and strive for rewards within its limits. On a general level, this pattern of rewards is known in Latin America as the *patrón* system. It enjoys deep cultural roots of Hispanic origin and is therefore supported on the local scene by many sociocultural elements in the national society.

At the latent level, the system of sanctions and rewards generates defensive patterns in the peasant subculture. Thus, personal anxieties, which anticipation of the sanction system generates, themselves function as sanctions against deviation from approved forms of behavior. For example, it is reported that on a Brazilian fazenda a peasant was recently stigmatized with the initials of the landowner

8

for joining a peasant league.[17] This punishment undoubtedly increased the anxieties of other tenants about taking similar action. Conversely, there are great psychological rewards for the individual who adopts a model of submissiveness and idealization of the patrón. His internal values are thus supported by and congruent with both the system of manifest sanctions and rewards, and the value system of the higher culture. From the perspective of mental health, one might argue that peasant submissiveness, at least in the short run, is clearly a functional defense mechanism.

The system of sanctions and rewards, often backed up by the state and manipulable by the landlords, and the cultural adaptations made to that system by the peasantry, form a potent combination which has functioned to maintain the basic social patterns of the landed estates over a long period of time. That is, as a form of social organization and control, the classic latifundia system is predictably stable in its internal arrangements, and the probability of initiatives for change emerging from within the system is of a very low order. For this reason, the key element in changing the system is the entry of leadership from outside the peasant subculture, dedicated to precipitating change through mobilization of the subculture.

The initiation of a peasant-urban alliance, based on an appeal of agrarian reform, satisfies these conditions for change. In the absence of an outside challenge to traditional elites and their incorporated value system, there is little likelihood that the land-labor relationship will be challenged from within by the peasants themselves. On the occasions when such a challenge has occurred, the resulting violence has been relatively unstructured, noninstrumental, ad hoc, and short-lived. The local landlord has been able to rely on the support of the governing elites to maintain the favored status quo. However, when the governing elites are themselves undergoing a serious challenge, the opportunity may arise for an effective challenge to the traditional land tenure system by means of agrarian reform. This opportunity occurs when a challenging elite both perceives the possibility of forging a peasant base of support and commands the organizational skills and persistence required to break through the resistance of the landlords and the submissiveness of the peasantry in order to consummate the alliance. To the degree that changes have already been occurring in the peasant subculture and breaking down traditional patterns of acceptance of the ongoing system, the precipitating leadership will find a responsiveness to its mobilizing appeal.

Perhaps one of the most important factors leading to changes in the peasant subculture is the attempted commercialization of traditional agriculture, not because of the role played in the process by the peasantry, but because of the consequences for the peasantry of the role played by traditional and new landed elites. Barrington Moore argues that the success or failure of the landed upper class in taking up commercial agriculture has a tremendous influence on the probability of a peasant-supported revolution and, consequently, on the nature of the political arrangements within a given society. In the case of Venezuela, the following three propositions might be offered. (1) If the traditional forms of estate management spread geographically or increase in number, the resulting enserfment of an increasing proportion of the peasantry is likely to lead to peasant unrest and responsiveness to urban leadership. (2) If the traditional forms of estate management are transformed into rudimentary commercial forms by a further squeezing of the labor force and by a depersonalization of and reduction in the paternalistic services of the traditional patron, peasant unrest and responsiveness to urban leadership are likely to increase. (3) If rudimentary forms of commercial organization spread geographically or increase in number, while seeking both to maximize production by squeezing labor and minimizing ownership obligations and to enjoy the personal status of the traditional landowning elite, peasant unrest and responsiveness to urban leadership will increase. Thus, a number of forces for change and destabilization in the peasant subculture may be at work in a given situation, all tending to increase responsiveness to an urban leadership that promises a broad program of agrarian reform.

This study of peasant mobilization and agrarian reform focuses on two levels: the concrete reality of the Venezuelan case, and certain abstract behavioral generalizations that this case might test, challenge, or amplify. An effort is also made to go beyond the confines of the particular case in order to consider relationships among peasant mobilization, agrarian reform, urbanization, commercialization of agriculture, and the politicization of the peasant masses in other developing areas of the world. The choice of Venezuela for such a study was fortuitous in several ways. In 1961, when I began the field work in Venezuela, it was known that an important, large-scale agrarian reform was underway as a result of the election of a reformist government, but it was not then known that the election of that government was the result of a previous political mobilization of the peasantry by the reformist party of Rómulo Betancourt. Similarly, it was known that for some time commercial agriculture in Venezuela had been stagnant and inadequate, but it was not then known how this stagnation related to the mobilization potential of the peasantry. Finally, Venezuela was known to have been undergoing drastically modernizing political changes since the mid-1930's, but it was not then known how closely related these changes were to the failure of commercial agriculture, the political mobilization of the peasantry, and the different phases of agrarian reform that had occurred under several reformist governments. It is my hope that the insights into the development process that have emerged from a careful analysis of the Venezuelan case will prove stimulating, applicable, and fruitful in the study of political change and ferment in other agrarian or peasant-based societies of the world.

Part One   Political History of the Mobilization

I

THE STRUGGLE FOR POWER, 1928–1945

The present political system of Venezuela is the outcome of a struggle for power at the national level that began in 1928. A national political system was remarkably late in developing in Venezuela, stabilizing into a predictable pattern only at the end of the nineteenth century. From the time of its independence in 1830 until its stabilization and consolidation under General Juan Vicente Gómez (1908–1935), Venezuela was an extremely primitive nation, controlled but not governed by a succession of narrowly based, competing elites.

In Venezuela, as in the other Spanish colonies, land and dependent labor were the pillars of elite power. The repartimiento and encomienda systems in Venezuela concentrated from early times on cattle, cacao, coffee, and sugar operations. The most extensive of these operations were the great cattle ranches or *hatos,* situated on the upper Orinoco rain plains called llanos. Land concentration was heaviest in the cattle industry, owing to the nature of climatic and soil conditions in the llanos, which required that operations be extensive rather than intensive. Thus, by the late 1700's about thirty cattle-owning families had appropriated approximately one and one-half million acres in what are now the states of Apure, Guárico, and Cojedes.[1] Concentration in more traditional hacienda patterns also occurred but was limited by the frequent changes in ownership that resulted from elite involvements in the unending struggle for power. Concentration into classical latifundia on a grand scale occurred only after the struggles among the white, aristocratic, landed elites had run their course through the nineteenth century.[2]

The shifting patterns of ownership of hacienda holdings began with the Wars of Independence (1810–1823), during which loyalist and revolutionary landed elites struggled for each other's property as well as for determination of the formula for governance. The landed elite was enlarged at the termination of the wars when speculators acquired large blocs of land bonds from veterans who had received them as compensation for serving Bolívar and other independence leaders. The bonds, or land bonuses, had been a chief instrument in recruiting and maintaining the armies, but after the wars it became apparent that the new Republican governments were reluctant to make good on them. However, after speculators had acquired large blocs from impoverished veteran foot soldiers at a fraction of their value, the bonuses were honored by the Congress.[3] Although the landed elite was apparently further enlarged during the course of the nineteenth century, agricultural production failed to keep up with the needs of the populace, and by 1855 Venezuela had become an importer of food, which it remains today.[4]

Throughout most of the century—in fact, from 1830 to 1900—Venezuela was "governed" by a series of regional caudillos or bosses, who challenged one another with their private armies for possession of Caracas, the center of culture and of the rudimentary foreign trade system that had developed.[5] Although these struggles were often small affairs, involving only a few thousand troops on either side, they prevented stable relationships from developing within economy and polity. Most frequently launched from the great cattle ranches, the campaigns of aspiring caudillos were carried out by peasant soldiers, recruited on the basis of booty. Looting and disorder were thus the hallmarks of a campaign for political control. More important than the acquisition of personal property, however, was the acquisition of real estate, for the promise of land ownership was an important incentive to foot soldier and caudillo alike. The lands of enemy hacienda owners were usually awarded to the loyal lieutenants of a successful regional caudillo, and less frequently were divided among the peasant foot soldiers, though often promised to them.

Temporary patterns of order emerged from time to time during the course of the century. Most important was the regime of Antonio Guzmán Blanco (1870–1888), which followed the Federal Wars of 1858–1864. Guzmán's regime incorporated traditional Latin American notions of economic policy favored by liberal parties and was supported by the most advanced sectors of national society, principally the Caracas traders and merchants. During Guzmán's rule a start was made on creating an economic infrastructure for the liberal state, including construction of public works of various kinds, railroads, piers, and roads, most of which enhanced Caracas as the center for domestic and international trade. A beginning was also made on development of a municipal educational system. But the advances toward state-building under Guzmán were limited in nature and restricted in impact. As one historian noted: "though Guzmán Blanco's rule had positive aspects, on balance his was a regime that brought few lasting benefits to the nation . . . For a decade after the death of Guzmán Blanco, the Venezuelan state foundered in new political chaos. For four years civilian elements tried to re-establish responsible, representative government. In 1892, the military, led by General Joaquín Crespo, took power by force. Crespo, though he ruled for six years, was not destined to assume Guzmán Blanco's dictatorial mantle for long. Instead this was to pass to caudillos from the Andean state of Táchira." [6]

By the end of the nineteenth century, there were four distinct subsocieties in Venezuela, with no clearly established pattern of stable interdependence among them. They included the urban population, amounting to a very small percentage of the total populace; the cattle ranchers, representing only a small number of the population, who concentrated much land in few hands and were the fountainhead for the destabilizing quests for national power; the owners of the haciendas, growing in number but, owing to the vicissitudes of the struggle for national power, limited in the land and rural populace under their control and in the degree of effectiveness of that control; and the remainder of the population, the vast majority, who were marginal, impoverished peasants living as slash-and-burn subsistence farmers, known as *conuqueros*. No Venezuelan government had emerged to regulate and stabilize the relationships among these four subsocieties. Indeed, an even more elementary task, that of developing integrative relationships among them, had barely been addressed. The Guzmán Blanco regime had taken the first step in this direction by beginning a communications network, designed to serve, possibly, as the basis for a national exchange economy between city and hinterland. But until some pattern of political integration could be achieved, the integration of the national economy was unlikely, if not impossible. The first successful steps toward national political integration were taken by early caudillos from Táchira, who supplied a series of dictators for Venezuela up to 1945. The first of the rulers from this backward Andean region, General Cipriano Castro (1899–1908), is known primarily for his international adventures involving in particular the British-Venezuelan boundary dispute over Guiana. But most important for the integration of the polity was the rule of his chief lieutenant and successor, the indomitable Juan Vicente Gómez.[7]

THE GÓMEZ ERA, 1908–1935

Being a military man, Gómez moved first on the problem of achieving a monopoly on effective violence for the national government. By reorganizing and modernizing the national army, Gómez deprived regional caudillos of the capability of marching on the capital and seizing, or even disrupting, the power of the central authorities. Gómez further integrated the nation by means of an economic infrastructure, building roads, railroads, and port facilities. In establishing a sound communications base for the national economy, his various administrations sought and attracted foreign investment, especially in petroleum after 1914. In fact, Gómez was fortunate enough to rule at a time when increased state revenues—primarily from petroleum concessions and royalties—could be used to support

18

policies of building economic infrastructures without sacrificing the other interests in the society. One can read the career of Juan Vicente Gómez as a minor-key echo of a similar Latin American state-builder, Mexico's Porfirio Díaz, under the influence of his *científicos*.[8] But the parallels deceive, for unlike Díaz, Gómez did not identify with the captains of commerce and industry, even though his policies supported them. He identified with the Andean *hacendado,* the *llanero* cattle rancher, and the latifundista from the central states. It seems that the great "Tyrant of the Andes" was just a country boy at heart.[9]

Symbolic of this identification, Gómez moved the business of the federal capital from Caracas, its historic site, westward to Maracay—a small, lovely, and thoroughly traditional provincial town. From there he ruled, not in splendor but in the dignity and style of a colonial landowner. His rural and provincial conservatism was marked, deriving from his caudillo background, which even today excites the comment of historical analysts: "After 1900 the cattle and ranching *caudillo* became the primary political power of Venezuela; he supplied the substance and direction for the issues of the day. Andean conservatism—hidebound, strong, and determined—was based upon closed folkways rather than upon open democracy. It was certainly nonintellectual. The political terms it laid down were indeed harsh, one-sided, and not open to debate. After a century's struggle over federalism, liberty, and greater regional expression, there emerged just the opposite: a strong, central power and one-man rule."[10]

However one may evaluate the process of national consolidation under Gómez, there is general agreement that it in fact occurred. Struggles among various competing elites seem to have subsided, perhaps because with increasing government revenues, the interests of one elite did not have to be sacrificed for the interests of another. The situation with regard to several upper-class elites has been described as follows: "It seemed as though the only beneficiaries of the Gómez system, besides the oil firms, were himself, his family, the military officers, and his Táchira friends in high government positions. Gómez ran the nation as the private preserve of his own family and the army. Through various kinds of graft, particularly speculation in dealing in oil concessions, and through confiscating the properties of his opponents, he became the nation's largest landholder. His accumulated fortune in cattle, coffee plantations, industrial plant, and real estate was estimated at over $200 million. His associates enriched themselves with the residue."[11]

Two important aspects of the situation emerge. First, there was a great deal of personal enrichment among several elite groups—friends and family of Gómez, military and bureaucratic elites, and their friends. Though no extensive evidence is at hand on this point, these elite circles, expanded by familial and friendship ties, probably included all or most of the upper-class ruling elites in Venezuela. For despite harsh repressions of newly challenging elites during this period, it seems that, unlike the nineteenth century, there was no restless struggle for power among established elites. Gómez seems to have found both the political formula and the additional sources of revenue to satisfy all those who were already established as "influentials." Gómez' political formula was one of personal rulership, or patrimonialism, in Weberian terms. In such a rule, as practiced in Venezuela from 1908 through 1935—and in lesser degree since that time—the power of the leader rests on a system of material incentives and rewards rather than on a belief in the ruler's unique qualifications to rule, as in a traditional patrimonial system. Rather than a Sun God, one is a Boss—the leader of a clique, machine, or faction. In Venezuela, he is the leader of the "Tachirense circle," as the groups around the dictators from Táchira were called. In describing such systems in today's emerging nations, Guenther Roth reports that "there exists what is imprecisely known as 'corruption': 'connections' count, favoritism prevails, and for the few there is abundant profit in real-estate dealings." And in discussing such states in general, Roth casts light both on the nature of the Gómez regime and on one of the possible reasons that it has excited the disapprobation of so many commentators: "In terms of traditional political theory, some of these new states may not be states at all but merely private governments of those powerful enough to rule; however, this only enhances the applicability of personal rulership (in the sense of detraditionalized, personalized, patrimonialism). Such personal governance easily evokes notions of opportunism and corruption from the perspective of charismatic or legal-rational legitimation."[12]

The second point of peculiar importance is the identification of the Gómez regime with the consolidation of latifundismo in Venezuela. There is overwhelming agreement among writers on the agrarian question in Venezuela that land concentration reached its most extreme degree during the reign of Gómez. The establishment of public order and the end of armed competition for control of the state may in themselves have provided a sufficient basis for the consolidation and expansion of large landholdings in the rural areas. But the fact is that Gómez during his long rule played an active role in the process of consolidation of landed power into fewer and fewer hands. Gómez himself became possibly one of the greatest landowners in all of Latin American history. Though estimates of the acreage and value of his personal and family holdings vary, they were probably in the range of almost twenty million acres, worth approximately $50 million.[13] Members of the Gómez regime and their friends benefited from their positions by receiving grants of land from the government. Although data on this development are sketchy, one reliable historical source notes that local cohorts of the dictator were ceded large blocs of public lands and gives specific figures for several years—more than 50,000 acres in 1917, over 105,000 acres in 1920, and more than 50,000 again in 1921.[14] There is reason to believe that this process occurred on a fairly regular basis, although definitive evidence is not available. In any case, by the mid-1920's, in addition to the Gómez holdings concentrated in the central states of Aragua and Carabobo, there were several other spectacular holdings, such as the latifundio

Pimentel. The most precise estimate as to the size of this latifundio is that "it used to take five or six days' travel by horseback to reach the far side of it."[15] Another gigantic holding, in the Lander District in the state of Miranda, was the Hacienda Mendoza, which one analyst of latifundia estimated as covering some seven hundred and ten thousand acres.[16]

The data on land concentration toward the end of the Gómez era are more satisfactory. In 1932 a partial cadastral survey by the

Table 1. Distribution of exploitations according to size, 1937.

Size (hectares)[a]	Percentage of total units	Percentage of total area
0–1	1.88	0.02
1–4.9	33.6	0.3
5–9.9	22.4	0.4
10–19.9	14.8	0.6
20–49.9	10.5	0.9
50–99.9	4.3	0.9
100–499.9	6.0	4.0
500–999.9	1.9	4.0
1,000 and up	4.8	89.0

Source: Agrarian Reform Commission, *Reforma Agraria* (Caracas: Editorial Arte Sucre, 1959), IV, 221.
a. One hectare equals 2.47 acres.

Ministry of Agriculture in the central states provided hard evidence of extreme concentration. But the Gómez holdings, which were scattered throughout the central states, were not included in the survey, since this was "truly taboo."[17] Finally in 1937 the first nationwide Agricultural Census was conducted, yielding unmistakable evidence of extreme concentration of landholding in the latifundia-minifundia complex.

In terms of owners rather than farm units, the 1937 Census

disclosed that 4.4 percent of rural property owners, the *latifundistas,* held 78 percent of the land surveyed, while 95.6 percent of the owners, the *minifundistas,* held the other 22 percent of the land. Of the rural dwellers classified as peasants or campesinos, 10.6 percent owned land, while the other 89.4 percent worked on the land of other persons.[18] It makes a difference whether the expansion of large landholdings was of a traditional type, which enserfed the peasantry but provided paternalistic benefits within an overall exploitative relationship; or whether it was an expansion in the number and size of rudimentary, commercially oriented farm operations, in which a common formula was the squeezing of the peasant labor force accompanied by a depersonalization and reduction of the goods and services provided by the landowner. Both forms of expansion lead to peasant unrest, but the latter seems more likely to lead to overt conflict.

THE TURN TOWARD COMMERCIALIZATION

To evaluate the success of the landed elites in adapting to commercial agriculture, it is necessary to determine which type of large landholding arrangement increased in Venezuela during the Gómez era. Although the evidence is not conclusive, the answer seems to be that both types of large estate operations spread: the traditional, paternalistic, noncommercial type, in which landowner status was emphasized; and the rudimentary, market-oriented type, in which the owner exploited traditional privileges while neglecting traditional obligations. Nevertheless, the rudimentary or commercial type appears to have spread more rapidly and significantly than the traditional type. Since the regime of Gómez was in fact a ruralist one, dominated by the cattle rancher, the coffee hacendado, and the latifundista, it remains to be determined whether these rural elites were commercializing their operations, and the degree of their success or failure. The evidence, while mainly circumstantial, seems to lead to the conclusion that the landed elites which came to hold increasingly large amounts of land under Gómez were market-oriented but failed to make a success of commercial farming. Since this is such an important issue, both in terms of subsequent developments in the Venezuelan agrarian reform, and of the general theoretical perspective of peasant mobilization, it seems worthwhile to deal with.

During the initial period of the nation's consolidation under the Andean caudillos, that is, from 1900 to 1920, agricultural exports from Venezuela increased 40 percent in volume. This was the same period during which Gómez was making large cessions of land to his followers. Though there is no evidence that those lands were utilized for export production, certainly the incentives were there, for during the same twenty-year period the prices on Venezuelan agricultural exports rose 131 percent. Rural entrepreneurship by members of the various Gómez administrations would certainly have been consistent with their policies of building up the rudimentary liberal state through infrastructure projects, such as port facilities, roads, dams, and irrigation projects. However, regardless of whether they were actually members or friends of the Gómez regime, numbers of landowners in the rural areas of Venezuela were producing more and more for the world agricultural market.

As shown in Figure 1, the high value of export products provided ever-increasing incentives through World War I. The composition of exports changed, however, following the blockade of Germany, which was Venezuela's primary high-grade coffee market. While coffee production dropped off, other crops were produced and shipped to maintain an overall increase in export volumes, which again suggests the presence of a growing entrepreneurial responsiveness in the agricultural sector. However, by the early 1920's, the value of exports was already beginning to drop sharply. Once again, though the coincidence may only have been circumstantial, it was during the same period, in 1924, that the Chamber of Commerce first publicly broached the idea of the creation of an agricultural mortgage bank to provide credits for farm entrepreneurs. As prices and values of exports continued to drop through the 1920's, rural interests succeeded in forcing the government to create an Agriculture and Livestock Bank (BAP) in 1928.[19]

Primarily concerned in its first years of operation with shoring up the coffee industry, the agricultural bank was in 1936 reorganized to provide credits for most cash-crop producers. Ironically, however, as Figure 1 illustrates, the viable market for such produce had been disastrously weakened by the world depression. In an

Figure 1. Venezuelan agriculture exports. Adapted from Gustavo Pinto, *Agricultura y Desarrollo: El Caso de Venezuela* (Maracaibo: Sociedad Venezolana de Ingenieros Agrónomos, 1966), p. 7.

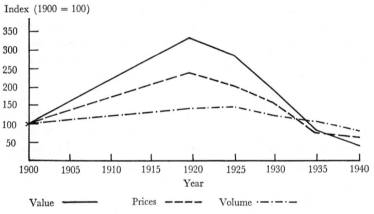

almost classic case of cultural lag, farm entrepreneurs continued to mortgage their farms to the bank for credits long after market incentives to produce had disappeared. By 1937, the portfolio of properties held by the Agriculture Bank as mortgage collateral was valued at 22 percent of the total value of all farm properties, as estimated in the 1937 Agricultural Census. The ultimate irony lay in the outcome of this economically irrational attempt to keep producing in the face of market disincentives. During the late

1930's and early 1940's, continuing marketing losses, plus the carrying charges of the bank's mortgage-credit program, resulted in a series of farm failures and foreclosures by the bank. Thus, by 1945, the Venezuelan government's attempts to save commercial agriculture had succeeded only in making the government a major holder of arable land. Two potent forces were at work in the distribution of entrepreneurial talents among the various sectors of the economy: failures in agriculture were pushing entrepreneurs out, and the booming petroleum industry with its satellites were pulling entrepreneurs into new sectors.[20]

The general conclusion to be drawn from this evidence is that the concentration of land in fewer and fewer hands during the Gómez regime was accompanied by a surge of effort to produce more and more for the world market—an effort that failed. There is no conclusive evidence that the type of large landholding which increased during this time was exclusively the traditional type. Nor is there evidence on which to conclude that it was exclusively a rudimentary-commercial type of operation. Both types spread, and particularly the latter. Further, the Agricultural Census of 1937 indicates that the most highly productive states—Aragua, Carabobo, and Miranda—had the highest degree of tenancy as opposed to wage labor, which one would expect to find in rationalized capitalistic enterprises. Since there is good reason to believe that there was a corresponding reduction in the quality and amount of the landowner's contributions to the tenancy relationship, caught as he was in a declining market situation and increasing indebtedness, his behavior in these central states may have been extremely destabilizing, in that labor was squeezed, traditional landowning contributions were reduced, and at the same time, traditional status privileges were insisted upon by the landowning class. Such behavior may be surmised from a number of facts. First, this area was the heartland of the Gómez holdings and of the Pimentel and Mendoza latifundia, and thus the most likely area for an extreme style of privileged landlord behavior. Moreover, it is known that Gómez kept troops on some of his holdings during this period, owing to "peasant unrest." Apparently there was also some sort of embryonic guerrilla warfare in the Carabobo Mountains at this time. And finally, these three states ultimately became the scene of the most intensive peasant response to the organizational efforts begun in 1936.

THE GENERATION OF '28

While the traditional elites—landed, religious, and military—had been pacified by the Gómez formula of governance, new groups were emerging in the slowly differentiating Venezuelan society. These groups, which occupied positions in the social structure nearer to the traditional elites than to the masses, had for some time been quietly groping for a fuller realization of elite status. As one analyst observed, the new groups included:

> . . . the mass of white collar and skilled service workers, small tradesmen and farmers, as well as elitist groups of professionals, intellectuals, industrialists, and university students. These new elites were relatively deprived groups in the sense that significant positions of political authority and power were denied them. Although lacking a pronounced class consciousness, their swelling numbers—a consequence of rapidly paced urbanization—gave them a sense of internal unity, and, above all, a sense of mission. Their members regarded themselves as the phalanx of modernity. Politically, they claimed to speak for *all* Venezuelans, except the oligarchs. This stance assured them of popular support.[21]

What was generally lacking among these groups was any organized interaction. Among the groups, only the university students had engaged in an organizational effort producing important long-range political consequences, and their activity had resulted in

1912 in the closing of the Central University by Gómez for eleven years.[22] However, the students seemed to be the most likely group in which organizational initiatives could develop. Beyond the normal interactions in which university students are generally involved, students at the Central University operated a student federation (FEV) which was reorganized in 1927 after having been for some time prohibited by Gómez. In addition, the university being a marketplace of ideas, student leaders (unlike many other aspiring leaders) were exposed to numerous ideas and insights concerning social organization and development. As one analyst observed: "Leaders of the opposition were the students at the Central University in Caracas. Ideologically influenced by the First World War, the Mexican Revolution of 1910, and the Russian Revolution of 1917, it was they who first saw that Gómez was more than a national despot, that he was also the instrument of foreign control of the Venezuelan economy. For them the battle cries became democracy, economic nationalism, and social justice."[23]

Marxian and neo-Marxian ideas on capitalist exploitation fitted nicely with an emphasis on national independence, for by the late 1920's the foreign petroleum companies had clearly emerged as the single most important factor in the Venezuelan economy, and the Gómez regime's encouragement of further concessions and privileges (through which the members of the government personally enriched themselves) promised an almost limitless penetration of foreign interests.[24]

An outburst of sentiment and activity against the state of the nation under Juan Vicente Gómez occurred during Student Week in 1928. Traditionally a festival involving cultural activities, speeches, and the presentation of original works of literature and poetry, Student Week in 1928 took on a different, political character, highly critical in nature and explicit in opposition to Gómez. Among its leaders were Rómulo Betancourt, Raúl Leoni, Jóvito Villalba, and many other present-day notables, who were to become known as "The Generation of '28." As the week progressed from

February 6 through 12, and as the news of its activities circulated around Caracas, excitement and tension mounted. The Gómez police cracked down on the student leaders. However, both antagonists were apparently surprised when several massive, spontaneous street demonstrations erupted among the general populace of the city. As Betancourt later recorded: "I had the first concrete revelation that the popular mass was beginning to intervene in Venezuelan history as a new factor. The student movement had initially been wrapped within its own pride. We students considered ourselves . . . as chosen to transform the country. Then our people suddenly made known their presence; and without leaders, without action committees or strike funds, the people organized a massive demonstration in Caracas."[25]

The Gómez reaction against the students had been sharp. But the public showing of sympathy for them resulted in their release from prison and thereby fostered an indelible blueprint for organizational action among the Generation of '28. For if the masses could affect political action "without leaders, without labor and political organizations, without action committees and strike funds," what might they do with them? Rómulo Betancourt, in particular, seemed struck with this vision of the "masses without intellectual chiefs, and the intellectual chiefs without masses."[26] He and the others of '28 determined to unite the two forces.

The attempt by the challenging elites to forge an instrument of mass support for political action was thwarted, however, until after the death of Gómez in 1935. Following the Student Week upheaval in 1928, Betancourt and others among the more radical student leaders took part in an attempted putsch by young army officers.[27] Hunted by the Gómez police, the members of the Generation of '28 fled into exile. Betancourt escaped to Curaçao, thence to Santo Domingo, and finally to Costa Rica in 1931. Until their return to Venezuela in 1936, he and his exiled colleagues were active with the kind of grandiose projects that are typical of the Latin American radical left in exile. Specifically, Betancourt helped in the initial formation of the Costa Rican Communist party and was later instrumental in founding a broader, more nationalist leftist front, the Agrupación Revolucionaria de la Izquierda (ARDI). Traveling to Colombia, members of this group of young radicals formulated the noted Barranquilla plan, a Marxian sociological analysis of the developmental problems of Venezuela that called for an end to the dominant role of foreign capital and the personal rule of Gómez. During this period there was apparently an attempt to initiate guerrilla warfare in the mountains of Lara, Trujillo, Miranda, and Portuguesa states but it was unsuccessful.[28]

Meanwhile, in the twilight of the career of Juan Vicente Gómez, the domestic factors pressing for the incorporation of upwardly mobile, modernizing elites were growing. The agricultural foundation of the Venezuelan state had been replaced by the petroleum industry and its manufacturing and servicing satellites, with the result that new elite groups, not privy to the inner councils of decision and influence as established and protected by Gómez, increasingly sought means of access to the political process. As long as "the czar of Maracay"[29] lived, however, the rural-based traditional elites he favored maintained a privileged, though increasingly vulnerable, position. With the death of the old man on December 17, 1935, the struggle between established and challenging elites broke into the open.

The essential issue in this struggle, which was to continue for the next decade, was the establishment of a political system in which the electoral process would play a central role. The challenging elite groups, spearheaded by intellectuals, and most conspicuously by the Generation of '28 student leaders, were dedicated to the transformation of the Venezuelan system from a patrimonial, personal government to one more in line with the rational-legal models of the Western democracies. This transformation involved three elementary tasks: dislodging or somehow overcoming the established elite groups that had become entrenched during the Gómez period of consolidation through patrimonial rule; the development of a system of electoral procedures and enforceable norms to ensure that the electoral process, expanded and reformed, would in fact become a major determinant of who governed; and finally, the building of an electoral base of organized support for the modernizing policies of the challenging elites, so that they could, through the electoral process, acquire hegemony in the governmental decision-making process. This decade from 1936 to 1946 was the most critical in Venezuelan political history, for the desired transformation was ultimately accomplished: the patrimonial elites were dislodged, a significant, broadly based electoral process was established, and a multiparty system was developed.

Upon the death of Gómez at the end of 1935, his minister of war, General Eleazar López Contreras, assumed control of the state and became the new steward for the Tachirense circle. But the passage of Gómez proved unsettling to the political subculture of Caracas. Constitutional guarantees, such as they were, were suspended in February 1936. This action was followed in short order with a protest campaign sparked by the national student federation and continued in the press, a governmental crackdown on the press, a strike in protest of the crackdown, a demonstration by some 25,000 persons in the Plaza Bolívar, and a volley of rifle fire into the crowd, killing eight and wounding about two hundred people. The shooting was swiftly followed by a tempestuous march on Miraflores Palace, led by student and labor leaders, which brought about a personal appearance of General López Contreras and his acquiescence to the demands for restoration of political rights. Once again, as in 1928, partially organized mass demonstrations had proven effective political instruments in restraining the government's treatment of the opposition.

In the period of political tolerance that followed, new groups working for a variety of reforms flourished. The exiled members of the Generation of '28 returned. Embryonic political movements sprouted from all points on the ideological spectrum, led by young entrepreneurs, members of the "liberal bourgeoisie," professional

31

Communists, and "'Romantic Jacobins" like Rómulo Betancourt. While López Contreras spoke of reforms in public health, education, fiscal and commercial policy, immigration and agricultural colonization, the challenging elites presented prescriptions for universal suffrage, improved land use, career civil service, the protection of workers, and judicial autonomy. By March of 1936 several of the key groups among the opposition had merged into a political front known principally by its acronym, ORVE.[30] After several permutations, this organization became the institutional forerunner of the leading democratic leftist party of the present day, Acción Democrática (AD).

In April 1936 opposition demands became crystallized for presentation to the session of Congress called to ratify the accession of López Contreras to the presidency. Under the Gómez electoral system, a highly circumscribed electorate voted for municipal councils and state legislative assemblies. These, in turn, elected the members of the national Congress, which elected the president. The opposition called on the Congress (which, being a creation of Gómez and the Tachirense circle, had no trouble in elevating López Contreras) to authorize constitutional and statutory reforms in the old system to permit the contested election of a constitutional president, a new Congress, and new municipal and state representatives. The Congress was not responsive to these contemplated changes, and an overambitious and abortive general strike, sponsored by the opposition early in June, served to strengthen the hand of the right in Congress and elsewhere.

By August of that hectic year, Rómulo Betancourt had become secretary general of ORVE; and by October, looking forward to the congressional and municipal elections of January 1937, ORVE merged with several other key labor and political fronts to found a political party, the Partido Democrático Nacional (PDN), with Betancourt in the key position of secretary of organization. The struggle now shifted to obtaining legal status for the party, so that it might test its electoral muscle in the January contest. When this status was withheld by the courts, opposition candidates, including those active in the PDN effort, ran independently, winning more than a dozen seats. But López' policy of tolerance for the opposition was drawing to a close. He had permitted opponents of the regime to attend the First Labor Congress in December 1936 and to express strong support of the petroleum workers' strike begun earlier that month; but a few days before the election, he abruptly ended the strike with a show of force. A few days after the election, several opposition winners were jailed without explanation, and shortly thereafter the courts nullified the election of all but one opposition candidate, the poet Andrés Eloy Blanco.[31]

López Contreras let the resulting furor carry on for almost a month and then struck the leadership of the political opposition a sharp blow by banning all political organizations and exiling forty-seven "Communist" leaders, who happened to be the leaders of every major opposition movement, group, front, or embryonic political party.[32] However, by shifting the struggle of the challenging elites underground, the decree of March 13, 1937, may have had a decidedly beneficial effect on its eventual outcome. Since the initial effort to dislodge the established elites had under the existing electoral regime proved fruitless, and since that electoral regime could not be changed so long as the established elite remained in control of the government, the challenging elites were forced to rethink their priorities.

In their one frenetic year of freedom to oppose the government publicly, the challenging elites had engaged essentially in maneuvers, intended only to influence the established elites and to participate in governmental power through the electoral process. These maneuvers had failed. Though the Congress had written a new constitution, it preserved the highly indirect system of elections designed by Gómez and restricted the suffrage even more than under the prior constitution.[33] What was lacking in the challenge of the new urban elite groups was an organized political-resource base from which, and with which, to wage their struggle. The problem of "the masses without intellectual chiefs, and the intellectual chiefs without the masses," diagnosed by Rómulo Betancourt many years before, remained the major problem of the new elites, for with land, wealth, and the power of the church and the army in the hands of the established elites, the only unorganized base of political resources available was the great mass of the Venezuelan people. The problem of party-building—the construction of an organized infrastructure of mass support for the challenging elites— was the fundamental task, outranking all others. Being driven underground or into exile by López Contreras, the opposition turned from elitist maneuverings to the arduous task of cadre organization.

Among the list of forty-seven "Communists" who were exiled by the decree of March 1937 was one major figure who, characteristically, was in the interior of the country organizing local cadres when it was promulgated, by which he avoided immediate arrest and exile. He was Rómulo Betancourt, then secretary of organization of the PDN. The underground organizational effort consisted of two basic phases: the establishment of local party cells, and the organization by leaders of each cell of an occupational branch that would draw in more members. Most of these branches were syndicates, or unions, established along the general lines stipulated in the Labor Code of 1936, which permitted labor to unionize under carefully regulated conditions. While the most immediate success in the establishment of these occupation-derived party branches took place in the petroleum industry, organizational efforts soon penetrated the construction, transportation, and service industries. The effort also penetrated the agricultural sector, which, though rapidly falling behind the petroleum sector as the economy's mainstay, still occupied the majority of the population.

By the end of 1937 the PDN had experienced considerable internal conflict over the nature of its constituency. The Communists, who up to this point were effective participants in the cadre-building process, wanted a clearly identified, single-class orientation. The "moderate" radicals, led by Betancourt, believed in a multiclass organization. Basically, the dispute seemed to be whether to include "small" intellectuals, such as schoolteachers, and members of the growing petty bourgeoisie on the margins of the urban service industries, such as small shopkeepers, artisans, and white collar workers, or to concentrate exclusively on the industrial and rural proletariat. When this internal struggle burst into the open, despite the fact that party membership was still a clandestine activity, Betancourt took the lead in expelling the Communists from the PDN in February 1938. From that time on, the PDN, although reduced to a pool of six to eight hundred leaders, was clearly established as a future-oriented, electoral-building effort, aimed at broad strata of the middle and lower classes in urban and rural Venezuela.[34]

The impression should not be left that the only party-building effort going on in Venezuela during this period was the PDN, though it turned out to be the most successful. There was a similar but short-lived party called the Partido Demócrata Venezolano (PDV), a Communist party (PCV), and even an effort by the established elites to form a partylike grouping. This last effort, initiated by López Contreras, consisted of organizing notables into "cultural" groups. Later they were to become a nationwide system of informal caucuses of established elites, called the Bolivarian Civic Groups.[35] Quite clearly, the trend throughout the Venezuelan social structure was toward the formation of institutions in one way or another explicitly designed to involve large numbers of participants in the governmental decision-making process. This trend, while not identical, was certainly compatible with the development and legitimation of a broader-based electoral process within the political system.

During the remainder of the López Contreras regime, ending in 1941, the PDN organizers busied themselves in the interior of the country, establishing party nuclei. Until his capture and exile in 1939, Betancourt led this effort personally. In addition to his organizational efforts, Betancourt contributed significantly to the growing public dialogue over Venezuela's developmental problems in his role as a columnist for the Caracas daily, *Ahora* (Now). Written for the financial and economic section of the paper, his columns constituted a reasonably sophisticated and thorough analysis of the problems that faced the country, particularly in the agricultural sector.[36]

As the end of the López Contreras tenure approached, he named his fellow Tachirense and minister of war, General Isaías Medina Angarita, as his successor, expecting the nomination to be ratified automatically by a vote of Congress, since under the indirect election system, Congress would elect the next president. At this point the leadership of the PDN decided to "run" a symbolic candidate in opposition to the governmental choice. They chose Rómulo Gallegos, the respected novelist (*Doña Bárbara*) and a teacher. Gallegos, who had been the mentor of many of the opposition leaders during their student days at the Andrés Bello High School in Caracas, was also an established, if minor, public figure. He had been a member of Congress and had even served briefly as minister of education under López Contreras. Gallegos was respectable enough, and the repressiveness of the López Contreras regime restrained enough, to permit him to conduct a public speaking campaign, which focused on the developmental problems confronting the nation and the unsatisfactory nature of continued governmental control by the traditional elites through the Tachirense circle. Although the "campaign" was unsuccessful, with Medina Angarita receiving one hundred and thirty congressional votes to Gallegos' thirteen, it did bring to the surface the broad, general theme of increased participation for the growing number of pluralistic interests within Venezuela's steadily differentiating and modernizing society. This was clearly an idea whose time had almost arrived.

Early indications of the timeliness of opening up the political process came from the new president from Táchira, Medina Angarita. When it became known that he did not view responsible opposition parties as necessarily antithetical to his concept of public order, an application for the legalization of the PDN under a new name, Acción Democrática (AD), was submitted. Action was completed on the legalization process on September 13, 1941, with Venezuela's most distinguished leaders in attendance after years of exile, and thus a new political force in Venezuelan politics was formally born.

But the next few years were to demonstrate the inadequacy of an electoral thrust for governmental power under the existing rules. The highly proscribed electorate plus the indirect system of presidential elections removed two steps from popular participation meant that it was a practical impossibility to challenge the incumbent elites through the electoral process. In the Venezuelan system, as is the norm in almost every Latin American system, governmental power was concentrated in the chief executive; state and local governments had extremely limited powers of taxation and therefore few disposable political resources that did not come to them by decision of the central authorities. Through a conscious manipulation of sanctions and rewards, the president in such a system remained almost beyond challenge, so long as he could satisfy the traditional elites whom he represented. The newer, upwardly mobile elites in Venezuela were attempting to bring a new political resource to bear on the decision-making process: the ability to organize a massive registration of support for new policies through the electoral process.[37] They were attempting to build this resource through a party system. But as long as the established elites were able to set the rules of the game, the challenging elites never seemed able to bring this resource into play. Without universal suffrage and the direct, secret election of the members of Congress and especially the president, the ability to organize a massive showing of public support could not dislodge the established elites.

With voting limited to literate males and further conditioned by age, residency, and property and tax qualifications, the enfranchised electorate was on the order of 5 percent of the population—

about what it was in the United States at the time George Washington was elected president. The opposition parties in Venezuela tried to operate within these limitations but soon realized how little could be accomplished. In the municipal and state elections of 1942, government candidates were successful in 981 of the 1,405 Municipal Council races that they contested, and in 286 of the 302 state Legislative Assembly contests. Although AD managed to elect four of its ten candidates for the Caracas Municipal Council, it was clear that the January 1943 elections for Congress were already decided by the composition of the state assemblies. AD determined to "abstain" from the congressional elections since they were so far removed from popular control.[38]

The growing urge for increased political participation was, however, recognized within the governing elite, at least by Medina Angarita and his closest political advisors. Medina perceived two political facts: that the elite's version of broader political participation, the Bolivarian Civic Groups, was not only a very narrow base of public support but an inept instrument in showing that support as well; and that the leaders of the challenging elites had apparently found, in the multiclass political party formula, a potentially effective instrument for attracting and organizing large numbers of people as political supporters. Accordingly, in April 1943 President Medina took steps to create a new party for governmental support, the Partido Democrático Venezolano (PDV), which was henceforth to represent the Tachirense circle's interests behind the facade of a national political party. This step suggests strongly that, within Venezuelan society and polity, pressures were steadily growing for electoral legitimacy as a determining factor in who was to govern and how. As a formula for governing the nation, patrimonial rule or personal governance were gradually coming into discredit among increasing numbers of actors in the political system or on its margins. A legal-rationalistic set of rules of political conduct was steadily becoming a tenet of the political culture.

The problem facing the Venezuelan nation in the mid-1940's was how to make the transition from one form of rule to the other. The solution, in brief, was for a leading element of the challenging elites—AD—to combine with a dissident element in one of the established elites—the army—to overthrow the incumbent government by force and establish an entirely new basis for the acquisition and transfer of governmental power. Thus, in Venezuela, a democratic electoral process was brought into being by the use of force.

OPENING THE DOOR TO POLITICAL PARTICIPATION

President Medina's attempt to overcome the inadequacies of the Bolivarian Civic Groups by setting up his own political party, the PDV, in 1943, was an early indication of a schism developing within the heart of the incumbent elites, the Tachirense circle. The basis of the schism was the issue of how far it was necessary to go in responding to pressures from below for increased political participation; that is, how to deal with the challenging elites. Upon assuming the presidency, López Contreras had immediately relaxed the policies of suppression maintained by Gómez, and he had permitted opposition organizational efforts to flourish for a time. But in the end, López had cracked down on all of his opponents as "Communists."

Similarly, shortly after assuming office, Medina Angarita had relaxed the suppressive policies pursued by López, permitting opposition political parties such as AD to function legally. But Medina, as it turned out, was to go much further than López in accommodating the opposition. In fact, in Venezuela he is often regarded as a rather exemplary chief executive, considering the fact that he was put in power by the Tachirense circle. Medina's relatively progressive policies were perhaps a measure of the man, and certainly a measure of the growing legitimacy of the opposition's demands for increased popular participation in decision-making and a thorough modernizing reform of the nation-state. Two convincing indications of Medina's progressiveness late in his term were his successful sponsorship of female suffrage and of a modest agrarian reform act. These reforms, which formed partial goals of AD and other opposition parties, were ill-fated from the start. They went far enough to induce the opposition to cooperate with Medina but not far enough to make them his dependable allies; and they went far enough to arouse suspicion among the established elites but not so far as to precipitate an immediate and open revolt. The consequence was a gradual unraveling of consensus among the incumbent elites, and the onset of a period of maneuvering and ferment among conservative forces, focused on the question of whom to entrust with the Tachirense stewardship at the end of Medina's term. That is, who was to be the next president?

In 1944 the ranks of the government party were strained by the announcement of ex-President López Contreras that he was ready to resume the duties to which he had once been called, in order to redress what he considered a clearly deleterious trend toward rapid political change. The right wing of the government party began to coalesce around López, diminishing the cohesion of the Andean conservatives. But Medina, still in control of the party apparatus, convoked the PDV convention in mid-summer of 1945 and nominated his own choice for a successor, Diógenes Escalante, the politically moderate Venezuelan ambassador to Washington. This choice was meant both to diminish dissatisfaction within Medina's own party—since Escalante, though a civilian, was a Tachirense—and to maintain the cooperation of the opposition in moving cautiously but steadily toward progressive reforms for the country.

AD, which had previously announced that it would once again abstain from the election of a new president by the Congress, because such an election was twice removed from popular participation, reassessed its position and sent two emissaries to Washington to hold talks with Escalante. The two AD representatives, Rómulo

Betancourt and Raúl Leoni, returned with the announcement that they were satisfied with the prospect of Escalante as the new president. Betancourt has since written that Escalante had agreed with their conditions for support, establishment of universal suffrage and the direct election of Congress and the president.[39]

But if Escalante was the key to holding both conservative and progressive opposition forces within a sphere of manageable political activities, he proved a tragically short-lived solution. Several weeks after his return from Washington, the former ambassador suffered a nervous breakdown, which took him from the scene only a few months prior to the presidential election. With his centripetal influence removed, the boundaries of political action were breached in several directions by the centrifugal forces of the challenging and incumbent elites. The right rallied strongly behind López Contreras once again, and President Medina tried as before to forestall the thrust of reaction by naming a new candidate of his choice, the colorless minister of agriculture, Angel Biaggini. This time his effort failed, and rumbles began to be heard among the army generals of the old school.

In the meantime, AD also found Biaggini unacceptable as the candidate arbitrarily imposed by Medina.[40] One last effort was made, however, to reconstruct the basis on which they had been willing to support Escalante. Rómulo Gallegos was sent to negotiate personally with President Medina an arrangement under which the new president would be elected for a one-year interim term, during which constitutional reforms would be made to bring about universal suffrage and direct elections. Then another congressional and presidential election was to be held under the new system. Medina, his political support within his own movement strained to the utmost by the López thrust, declined to take on the task of trying to accomplish what AD had requested. As a consequence, the leaders of AD felt that they had exhausted all legal remedies for the redress of their political grievances.[41]

By virtue of one of those historical coincidences of timing and appropriateness, an extralegal remedy for redress had, a few months earlier, been presented to the leaders of AD. It seems that the revival of the possibility of a López Contreras presidency, favored and supported by the old-line army generals of the Tachirense circle, had exacerbated tensions between a group of younger military officers and the old generals. The army, as it had been organized and consolidated under Juan Vicente Gómez early in his career, was the stepchild of his patrimonial formula of governance. That is, the higest honors went to those who, through demonstrations of personal loyalty, family connections, wealth, or a combination of all these factors, proved useful in the maintenance of the ruler. Conversely, those rewarded with positions of power were able to use them for their personal benefit and that of their family and chosen friends and followers. Such was the nature of a patrimonial regime. This formula for advancement to and the use of power clashed sharply, however, with the norms of professionalism that were being inculcated in the younger members of the officer corps by the Military Academy. The Venezuelan military, through exposure to professional training in foreign countries and the adoption of such standards in their own, had bred a generation of younger officers for whom the old system of promotions and assignments appeared disastrous from a professional military point of view, and the military quality of the ancient generals from Táchira seemed ridiculous. Some of these younger officers formed a secret group, the Patriotic Military Union (UPM), to organize efforts for reform. To this group, the threat of a return to power by López Contreras meant a reinforcement of the old system and a probable increase in the power of the old-line generals to resist changes. While primarily focused on military reforms, they recognized that only within a progressive, modernizing nation-state could a professional military establishment be developed and supported. That is, they recognized the general inadequacies of the older formula of patrimonial governance for the building of a modern nation-state. What they needed, they felt, was a professional ally in the political field with whom they could work for a more effective, modern Venezuela.

AD was chosen by the young leaders of the embryonic military coup. In a series of exploratory conversations, selected leaders were approached in June 1945. The leadership of AD held back from commitment to an extralegal change of government, which was antithetical to its value judgments concerning democratic political processes. With the collapse of the Escalante candidacy, however, the military men viewed the challenge of López Contreras with increasing alarm; and with the collapse of the Gallegos negotiations for an interim presidential commitment from Medina and Biaggini, the AD leadership decided that the time for drastic action had arrived.[42]

When the military officers of the Patriotic Military Union made their move on October 18, 1945, their ranks were joined by the leaders of AD. It seems ironic that this military coup was to prove essential to the achievement of a rough electoral democracy in Venezuela, but then, it was a different kind of coup. By bringing a rapidly growing, mass-based political party into the ranks of the new regime, the military leaders of the coup achieved a kind of instant vertical integration in the polity. Thus, the process of national integration, begun by Juan Vicente Gómez through the horizontal integration of regional, traditional elites, was complemented by what is known in Venezuela as the Revolution of October 1945. This is not to suggest that the vertical integration of the masses was completed in the act of successfully overturning the Medina regime and bringing a popularly based party into the new government. After all, AD was only one party, and it had not organized the entire bulk of the potential but disenfranchised electorate. But the mobilization base that it had organized had been strategic, in terms both of electoral considerations at the time and of a future peasant mobilization and agrarian reform in Venezuela.

II
BUILDING THE MOBILIZATION BASE, 1936–1945

When Acción Democrática (AD) was swept into power by the events of October 1945, it brought with it the organizational base of potential electoral mobilization that it had been building since 1936. Although this mobilization base was not instrumental in the overthrow of the incumbent governing elite system, it was instrumental in the selection of AD as the civilian partner of the military leaders of the coup. Quite clearly, the value of that mobilization system as a means of demonstrating, consolidating, and expanding popular support for the new system of government was perceived by the revolutionary leaders. With the Revolution of October 18, a breakthrough by the new, urban-based, upwardly mobile, challenging elites into the innermost chambers of political power was achieved.

However, the Revolution of 1945 went beyond enlarging the governing elite; it set in motion a large-scale vertical integration of subelites and masses of common citizens. A consideration of the nature of that mass following which AD brought with it on achieving access to governmental power raises a number of questions. What kind of subelites and base members were recruited, and how? What were their goals and aspirations? How did these relate to the political programs and policies advocated by the leaders of AD? What organizational strategies and tactics were followed by the AD cadre-builders, and how did these function to shape and channel the potential forms of political participation that could be expected from the mass base once the party had broken through into political power?

In organizing a massive base of political and electoral support, the challenging urban elites had followed a logical course. First, leadership cadres were established in the larger urban centers, and then gradually in the provincial towns. Within the urban centers, functional branches, that is, trade unions, were established in the construction and transportation industries, and among service industries and other white collar workers. In the petroleum camps, where a skilled labor force existed in confrontation with a highly organized, wealthy, and foreign employer, the trade unions flourished. But ultimately, if the mass of the Venezuelan population were to be penetrated and organized, political leaders had to leave the cities and towns and go into the villages and scattered rural settlements where almost 70 percent of the population lived.[1] To organize the mass of the population in 1936, one had to organize peasants. And under the personal leadership of Rómulo Betancourt, the leadership cadres of ORVE, PDN, and AD proceeded to do just that.

THE RURAL SITUATION

The other side of the coin of land concentration under Gómez had been the gradual enserfment of the Venezuelan peasantry. Prior to the advent of Gómez and the consolidation of latifundia and the nation-state, the vast majority of peasants had been slash-and burn migrants, called conuqueros, having no clearly established relationships with the large landowners, exploitative or otherwise. As more and more land came to be held by fewer and fewer, the total amount of land held in the predial estates increased also, mainly through encroachment onto governmental lands.

Two patterns of estate organization became more common: a rudimentary commercial type and the traditional latifundia. As the area of controlled land resources increased, the number of peasant families living within these realms of private authority also increased. There is specific evidence, for example, that rudimentary lumbering operations in Sucre state spread onto governmental lands through the activities of friends of the Gómez regime. Peasant woodcutters and charcoal-makers who had lived and worked in these areas for years became enserfed; that is, they were drawn into an entangling contractual relationship with those who claimed control of the land and were forced to turn over the fruits of their labor, as well as their labor itself.[2]

In the coffee and cacao industries, a special combination of enserfment and property-expansion had taken place even before Gómez; undoubtedly it continued as market conditions improved during the early Gómez period. This expansion tended to engross existing latifundia and was tied to what is known as the *colono* system, which enserfed peasant labor through an induced indebtedness and expanded the boundaries of coffee properties through peasant proxies. The process has been described in these terms:

> Following the abolition of slavery, the problem for coffee and cacao plantations was the varying seasonal requirements for labor. They had to have workers available without paying them for the entire year. Thus was developed the system of colonos or medianeros—being for the most part a combination of seasonal salaried work with additional unpaid work obligations and sharecropping. The owner would furnish a plot of land, usually in the hilly or outlying parts of the plantation. There the peon cultivated articles for consumption, and planted coffee and cacao. One half of the latter plantings would go, when entered into production, to the owner, and the other half had to be sold to him at his option. While the coffee and cacao plants were not yet producing, the worker drew against his eventual earnings with advances from the owner, against the day when the plants would enter production. Clearly there is something of servitude in this situation, which is logical, since historically the slave tends to be replaced by the servant. This system was a notorious factor in the expansion of the coffee and cacao plantations. Thus the farms were enlarged, at the expense of public lands, which upon being cultivated, were automatically "incorporated" into the farm.[3]

Traditional estate holdings, or nonproductive latifundia, also expanded the area of their control during the golden days of the Gómez regime. Thus, many lands after 1920 were engrossed through a process of extending loans to peasant small-holders on the perimeters of the latifundia, entangling them in increasing indebtedness, and finally taking over their parcels in payment. Similarly, moneylending was used to draw propertyless conuqueros into peonage as labor for the estate operations.[4] It is extremely difficult to decide whether such expansion constituted a very weak commercializing impulse in action or merely indicated that an expansionist impulse was stirring among the traditional landholding class. There simply are no data on the number of landowners engaged in rudimentary commercial operations during this period who were forming a new type of entrepreneurial elite, and the number who were traditional elites enlarging their holdings.

During the 1920's and 1930's life on the estates, into which this process of enserfment drew increasing numbers of Venezuelan peasants, was difficult for the labor force. In the commercial operations, wage work was usually seasonal. Wages, when paid in cash, were low—on the order of sixty cents a day—and were forced lower still as the market situation failed to improve.[5] More often wages were paid in coupons or special metal tokens made up on the estate, which were redeemable only at the "company store."[6] Payment in kind was also common, as when an estate owner would pay for labor with part of the crop, valuated by himself. There are reports of a particularly monstrous practice in which wage laborers were obliged to take one half of their remuneration in "Lazarus Pork," the colloquial term for hog meat infected with trichinosis. Because working hours for the peons were quite long (from 5 A.M. to 6 P.M. being the norm, and from 6 A.M. until dark the practice on the cattle ranches), meals were often served in lieu of wages. What the dietary effects of such meals were on the health and well-being of the peasant laborers can only be guessed, for there were almost no medical facilities of any kind to be found on or near the estates.[7]

The lot of the sharecroppers, tenants, and squatters living on, or dependent on, estate holdings was more complex. In much of the literature of this period, one finds renters (*arrendatarios*), sharecroppers (*aparceros*), and squatters (*ocupantes*) all lumped together as "pisatarios" because of the fluidity and complexity of the tenure arrangements. That is, the analytic distinctions drawn today between the renter, who pays a fixed fee in cash or kind, the sharecropper, who pays a fixed percentage of his production, and the squatter, who is allowed to live on estate property in return for labor obligations, fail to hold up in this period. In a common and widespread arrangement, an owner would permit a peasant to build a shack on his land and to cultivate a plot; in return, the peasant had to agree to pay the owner a stipulated amount of the crop he was growing—which resembles a rental arrangement. But in addition, the peasant had to agree to deliver a fixed percentage of any charcoal he made with the owner's trees and any fruits he picked on the property—which is a sharecropping arrangement. On top of that, the peasant had to agree to furnish a stipulated number of days of unpaid labor during the harvesting of the owner's crops, and an additional number of days (if the harvest merited additional labor) at a low wage rate established by the owner—which resembles a squatter relationship. Furthermore, if the owner were commercially inclined, the peasant had to agree to sell the balance of his own produce to the owner on demand, and at a price determined by the owner rather than by the market.[8]

This pattern of labor subjugation by the landowning class was maintained by various measures. General Gómez garrisoned a number of army units in the rural areas, particularly on his own properties, because of "peasant unrest" under such conditions.[9] In addition, it has been reported that many peasants were impressed into military service, during which they labored on "haciendas of the Despot and his bootlickers."[10] In fine, one of the ways in which the system of labor suppression was maintained was through the use of the army.

Another way in which control was assured was through the semi-formal granting of police powers to estate owners and supervisors. Evidence of this practice was furnished in the September 1934 issue of the *Bulletin* of the Chamber of Commerce of Caracas, which carried an article describing with some care a thriving coffee and sugar operation on the nearby Caribbean coast. It was pointed out that the 25,000 acres actually in production were scattered among several operating units, and that some 2,600 peasants made up the labor force. So as to manage such a complex operation in an orderly and efficient manner, the *Bulletin* noted, "each operation has an overseer who serves at the same time as the local Constable, reporting to the Chief of Police, which in this case is the owner of the hacienda."[11] There is no quantitative measurement available to indicate exactly how widespread such a practice was.

Finally, there is some indication that more subtle means were used by the latifundistas to keep their labor forces in line under conditions of severe exploitation. In 1937 it was noted that in April of that year, "before the Municipal Council of San Cristóbal, a group called 'Social Action of Táchira' denounced the practice of 'doping' peons with a fermented sugar-cane liquor. This alcoholic drink is administered to them in order to increase their output, under the effect of the excitant."[12] Since alcohol is a depressant, not an excitant, it was unlikely to have been used to "increase production," but it may well have been used, and probably was, as a means of accommodating severe mental stresses among the impoverished peons. It was, and continues to be, a widespread practice in the Peruvian Andes to give Indian farm laborers coca leaves (cocaine) to chew during frequent breaks in the workday. This practice, outside observers believe, helps to dull the Indian laborer to his severely disadvantaged lot, and is held by landlords to be a necessary cost of production in order to make the Indian work at all. Interestingly, in an experiment in Peru, it was found that the same Indian laborers who took seven or eight "coca breaks" during a workday on someone else's land took only one or two when working on their own land.[13]

Regardless of whether the estate operations that spread under Gómez were classic latifundia or rudimentary commercial operations, the resulting enserfment of increasing numbers of peasants meant that they were being drawn into an onerous relationship with a privileged class. When commercial agriculture began to fail in the 1920's, and continued to decline during the depression of the 1930's, conditions on both types of operation undoubtedly grew worse. Wages were lowered, working hours extended, housing and feeding arrangements cut to a minimum cost to the owner. Faced with dropping prices and increased carrying costs for operational credits, landowners adopted these and other manipulative extractions to keep a desperate situation from getting even worse. Thus, the landowning class attempted to pass on the impact of the failure in commercial agriculture to the rural labor force.[14] Into these troubled waters nosed the political and union organizers of Rómulo Betancourt.

THE PEASANT UNION MOVEMENT

After establishing an initial strategic network of members in the cities and towns, the Partido Democrático Nacional (PDN) cadres lost little time in moving into the countryside. Following the passage of the Labor Code of 1936, during the period of relaxation under López Contreras, and the meeting of the First Labor Congress in December of that year, the first peasant union was organized on February 2, 1937.[15] Called the Syndicate of Small Farmers of Magdalena Municipality, it was in the state of Carabobo.

Luís Morillo, the organizer and secretary-general of this first union, was a good example of a career ORVE-PDN-AD organizer. In 1928, Morillo, then an eighteen-year-old political activist, had helped to hide some of the student leaders who were seeking to avoid capture by the Gómez police after the Student Week outburst. He had been caught and for a time jailed with Betancourt in Puerto Cabello, but was not exiled. Going underground during the period when the Generation of '28 was barred from entering the country, Morillo, despite his lack of education, helped to publish a clandestine newspaper, *El Pueblo Internado* (The People Exploited).

Following the death of Gómez in December 1935, Morillo and others participated in the formal establishment of ORVE. After the First Labor Congress in 1936, which he attended as a peasant representative, Morillo returned to his small hometown, where on February 2, 1937, together with sixty-four of his rural neighbors and acquaintances, he formed the country's first peasant syndicate. Two months later, after the López Contreras crackdown, the syndicate was dissolved and he was jailed as a "Communist." Exiled from the state, which apparently was a traditional political practice in Venezuela, Luís Morillo was permitted to return later in the year, at which time he founded a larger union of laborers and workers on the sugar plantation "Tacarigua."

During the time that Morillo was secretary-general of the syndicate, the breach between the Communists and those in the PDN loyal to Betancourt occurred, and he sided with Betancourt. The following year, seeking to represent his union members directly in the political arena, he successfully ran for a seat on the Municipal Junta, but was later jailed for political activity and once again exiled from his home state. Morillo spent 1939–1941 in Caracas, helping to organize construction unions. He finally became secretary of organization of the Federal District Construction Workers' Union, remaining in that post until the October Revolution of 1945 sent him back to Carabobo to participate in further peasant-union organizing activities.

This pattern of clandestine organizational effort, with occasional forays into local electoral politics, was repeated throughout Venezuela during this time, especially in the central states, where the degree of land concentration was high and where tenancy was the land tenure status of a relatively high proportion of peasant farmers—which bears out the finding that tenancy is often related to social unrest in rural areas of the developing world. Though all local organizational leaders were influential in the microcosms of their small towns and villages, not all of them had a record of political activism so extensive as that of Morillo. And only the most capable and active leaders could match Morillo's record of success in several branches of the trade union movement and in electoral politics, ultimately leading to his election to the State Legislative Assembly in 1946 and again in 1958. But while Morillo's individual success was unusual, his practice of participating in electoral politics at the same time as organizing in the labor field was not.

When directly organizing unions themselves, PDN leaders like Luís Morillo, of whom there were an estimated two hundred, mostly concentrated on the villages and hamlets surrounding the cities and towns in which they lived. If there were particular areas of peasant unrest or exploitation, they zeroed in on them. On the scene, they recruited indigenous local peasant leaders, normally opinion leaders of one kind or another, who were often the "jefes" or tough guys with a reputation for standing up to trouble and conflict, especially with the local power elites. When Morillo was asked what promises were made to the campesinos to induce the local peasant "influentials" to become open opponents of the status quo, he replied, "To emancipate them from the landlords . . . and then to help bring them schools, infirmaries, water, roads, ownership of the land they worked . . . electric lights."[16]

A fuller indication of the appeals around which recruiting of local peasant syndicate leaders was organized is given in a set of model statutes for peasant associations approved by the First Labor Congress of December 1936. Among the organizational guidelines for forming a local syndicate appears the following passage, which shows clearly the kinds of appeals that were effectively made to peasants and their local leaders:

ON THE GOALS OF THE ASSOCIATION

The Association will have as its ultimate goal the conquest and defense of better conditions of life for its members, and for the peasantry as a whole, in the social and moral realm as well as the economic, employing toward this end every means to its furtherance. In particular, it will struggle for: the defense of the interests of its members in confronting the rapaciousness of the landlords and commercial usurers; a reduction of payments-in-kind and labor obligations; a moratorium on the debts which currently crush the members; payment for the products of share-tenants equal to the market price minus transportation costs; and the same for products delivered in payment for loans by owners and storekeepers; so that consumer goods being sold to peasants may be priced at the market level plus transportation costs; for equal rights for small-holders; for the elimination of payments in coupons and tokens to agricultural wage laborers; and the abolition of debts that are passed on by owners and commercial usurers from peasant father to son.[17]

The political-syndical organizers also offered the peasants a broad agrarian reform, which was what they wanted most. As early as 1936 the ORVE-PDN-AD cadres had used the slogan, "Land for him who works it," which was the complement of the goal stated by Morillo, "emancipating the peasantry from the landlords." It seemed obvious that, to free the peasantry from the onerous burdens imposed on it by the landed elites, the best method was to fragment the basis of power, the land resource, and distribute it among the powerless.

Thus was built the alliance between the challenging political elites from the urban areas and the awakening masses of Venezuelan peasants: slowly, and on a face-to-face, pragmatic basis.

The issues and causes of unrest in the peasant communities were unmistakable. That the peasant leaders and their followers needed political allies to accomplish their ends apparently required little belaboring. Thus, in functional terms, the urban partner performed the strategic planning and organizational tasks and whenever possible represented the peasant interest in the political arena. Peasant leaders in the rural communities, along with their ranks of followers, functioned as small units in the tactical confrontations with landlords and the political system at its most vulnerable periphery—its boundary of control in the widely dispersed backlands. These small units also stood in strategic reserve for the day when they could be mobilized on the electoral battlefield.

For most of this period, that is, from 1936 to 1945, skirmishes, not battles, were the order of the day. Wherever peasant restlessness burst out, whether organized or spontaneous, there the early leaders of ORVE and PDN were soon found in the front ranks.[18] And restlessness there was, often precipitated by local organizers. The rural situation in the 1930's has been described as involving "a certain campesino agitation for the land that has come to include the violent occupation of private properties . . . later comes the formation of the so-called agricultural syndicates, which group together the sharecroppers, renters and day laborers who fight to obtain lands; the landowners frequently complain that the discontented burn their canefields."[19]

Further evidence of the struggle of the peasantry during this time emerges from government descriptions of problems between coffee plantation owners or managers and their colono labor force. A number of disputes arose over the terms of payment for the colono parcels, and in some cases there was an outright challenge to ownership rights over property on the perimeter of the latifundia. In its annual report to Congress for 1937, the Ministry of Agriculture (MAC) complained of the amount of time and energy spent in efforts to deal with such conflicts: "The Ministry, besides the study of numerous cases in which either the owners, or the colonos, would try to encroach upon each others' respective rights, or not to recognize them, had to arrange the inspection, detailed settlement and conciliation of interests because of the lack of respect for privately owned land, or lack of consideration for the workers, which manifested itself in a breakdown in cultivation of the land, and consequently in the national economy."[20] Adding to difficulties in settling such disputes was an almost complete lack of certified cadastral surveys, as well as a tangled system of property titles, claims, and jurisprudence.

The Caracas Chamber of Commerce paid tribute to the organizational efforts of the PDN cadres in its *Bulletin* of February 1939. Calling on the López Contreras authorities to "protect" farm laborers from agitators and troublemakers, the Chamber mentioned the village of La Loma as "one example among many which are occurring in the Republic" of an almost complete breakdown of law and order in the face of such agitation.[21] Betancourt, in an article in his *Ahora* column during this period, gave a further indication of the activities of peasant union leaders, as well as of peasant unrest:

What, but demands for land, have been the serious disturbances of the campesinos of Carora and Quibas, which began early in 1936; and the fighting in the Sierra de Carabobo; and the clashes—more or less violent—that have taken place in almost every part of the country—among the large landholders and the sharecroppers and peons? What, but demands for land, are those constant petitions for a cultivator's Fund that daily arrive at the Ministry of Agriculture, and which, if they were filed, would by now fill any one of the ample offices of that ministerial building? The President of the Republic has received, on various occasions, visits from campesino delegations, which come to Miraflores in request of parcels to cultivate.[22]

But peasant unrest and occasional violence were not unmet by violence in return. Most clashes were small and relatively self-contained, leaving little historical record. On occasion, however, a large-scale uprising occurred—for example, in Lara state, where even during their exile in the early 1930's, members of the Generation of '28 had spoken of an embryonic guerrilla war.[23] In the case of the open rebellion by large numbers of peasants at Siquisique in the late 1930's, the reaction by the López regime was so savage that even the conservative Caracas daily *La Esfera* referred to it as "a massacre."[24]

In spite of such clashes, peasant union organizers continued their efforts. There are many indications of the high priority that the ORVE-PDN-AD leadership placed on the formation of the peasant alliance. First, it was repeatedly stressed during my extensive interviews that Betancourt himself was the prime mover in the effort.[25] Second, many other present-day or recent notables in AD—such as Francisco Olivo, Valmore Rodríguez, Carlos Behrens, and Ramón Quijada—were involved in the effort at the national level. In the states, many men who eventually became political figures of stature in AD, as well as in other political parties and movements, were involved during the 1930's in forming the peasant alliance. In Carabobo, Ignacio Pandares, Víctor Peñalever, Juan Vicente Ricones, Hernán Sastrón, Luís Felipe Bolívar, Isaías Torres, José del Carmen Monasterios, and Luís Morillo bore the brunt of the early organizing, joined in 1938 by Armando González, who in 1962 became president of the Venezuelan Peasant Federation (FCV).[26] In Aragua, Hermógenes Mendoza and Juan Hernández led the movement, along with Daniel Carías in Lara and Carlos Luís Barrera in Miranda. The final indication of the importance attached to the formation of the peasant alliance was the fact that the agrarian question was one of only four points on the agenda at the First National Conference of the PDN in 1939.

The basis for the peasant-urban alliance was complex. The urban elite partner to the alliance had as its ultimate goal the capture of state power in order to undertake a wide range of modernizing reforms. Several intermediate goals had to be accomplished to capture state power: the incumbent, traditional elites had to be overcome (or at least weakened) by a base of organized power, so that the electoral process could be made the determinant of who governed and how; then an electoral base of mass support had to be mobilized to consolidate and make legitimate the power of the challenging elites. The urban partner needed a mass base of support among the peasantry to accomplish these intermediate objectives.

The peasant partner to this alliance had as its ultimate goal a drastic change in the way that landed power was organized, distributed, and used—in other words, an agrarian reform. The urban partner could promise such a reform as part of the program of modernization that was its ultimate goal, but it could not "deliver" until the peasants helped in gaining its intermediate objectives. Thus, the most intensely desired objectives of both partners had to be deferred through a process of subordinating desire to a rational sequence of instrumental means. This intellectual discipline was obviously easier for the urban partner, which more thoroughly comprehended the means-ends relationships involved, than for the peasant partner, which was experiencing an increasingly unhappy way of life.

In this situation, some actions on behalf of the peasants had to be taken immediately, such as scattered land invasions, the burning of cane fields, and a variety of other confrontations with landowners and their representatives that on occasion were violent. Albert O. Hirschman, in describing remarkably parallel activities among Colombian peasants during this same period, characterizes such actions as a "direct problem-solving activity," which indeed they were.[27] During these activities, local representatives of the urban elite partner—that is, local politico-syndical organizers—performed an immediate service for the peasants whom they hoped to mobilize for their own long-term objectives. The manifest function of local representatives of ORVE-PDN-AD was tactical responsibility for leadership in face-to-face confrontations with repressive forces—whether army, police, or vigilante followers of the landlords. Even more important than their skills in organizing and leading a land invasion or a field-burning was the willingness of these local organizers to stand responsible in the front ranks when the showdown came with incumbent authorities. The leadership of such confrontations is commonly singled out by forces representing established authority. Furthermore, punishment or accountability are focused initially on such leadership. In fact, if the leaders can be identified as "outside agitators," local authority figures often absolve the mass of followers from blame for their actions.[28]

Perhaps more important in long-term consequences for the political mobilization of the Venezuelan peasantry was the latent function of the local ORVE-PDN-AD organizers when engaging in confrontation leadership. This latent function, briefly put, was the forging of a class consciousness among the peasant masses. Political leadership, although without an elaborate ideological frame of reference, helped in the transformation of the peasantry from a "class-in-itself" to a "class-for-itself." In explaining the Marxian use of these two terms, C. Wright Mills writes: "The first phase—a class-in-itself—refers to the objective fact of the class as an aggregate, defined by its position in the economy. The second—a class-for-itself—refers to the members of this class when they have become aware of their identity as a class, aware of their common situation, and of their role in changing or in preserving capitalist society. Such class consciousness is not included in the objective definition of 'class'; it is an expectation, not a definition. It is something that, according to Marx, is going to develop among the members of a class."[29]

Marx himself was somewhat skeptical of the peasantry's potential to undergo such a transformation. In his analysis of the French peasantry and its performance in the Revolution, Marx likened the peasants to potatoes in a sack—clearly a class-in-itself—with little or no potential for self-conscious action.[30] But if the peasantry in general exhibits limited potential for the kind of sustained revolutionary action envisaged by Marx, the definite possibility nevertheless exists for class-conscious, revolutionary activities directed at short-run, concrete objectives. Among other cases, this possibility has been demonstrated in the Mexican and Bolivian revolutions, and less drastically in Venezuela.[31]

Since the forging of a class-for-itself in Venezuela depended on the development of mutual confidence between local representatives of the urban partner and local peasant leaders and followers, it was a slow process. It was further slowed because altering class consciousness is an extremely complex learning process, requiring clearly structured learning experiences, which were not always easy to come by, as well as reflective guidance and teaching by reasonably aware leadership. Finally, the situation lacked the impetus of a cataclysmic upheaval on the order of the Bolivian or Mexican revolutions. Nevertheless, from 1936 through 1945 the peasant union movement continued to spread throughout central Venezuela.

The growth of a legally recognized movement was also a slow process, though for quite different reasons. The earliest syndicates were organized in the areas of greatest population pressure and concentrated landholdings, where large numbers of peasants came into conflict with the landowners over tenancy and sharecropping terms, as well as over employment conditions on the commercial operations. In the López Contreras and Medina regimes, the landowners used their influence to minimize the legal operations of the syndicates. Paradoxically, this repression was possible because of the detailed and seemingly progressive provisions of the 1936 Labor Law. Theoretically designed to prevent the exploitation of inexperienced laborers by union bosses, the Labor Law included many detailed regulations concerning the operation and activities of each local. First, a minimum number of forty members was required to form a union. Furthermore, they were required to constitute themselves into an assembly, register their names and addresses, legislate their internal statutes in conformance with the law, elect officers, and then seek registry with an inspector from the Ministry of Labor. If the inspector validated all of the foregoing procedures, the syndicate would be duly registered as a legal unit. However, the requirements of the Labor Law continued to bind the officers and members by details concerning the number of meetings to be held annually, the nature of a legal quorum, the annual election of new officers (that is, a one-year tenure of office for elected officials), the keeping of records, and so forth. The Labor Inspectorate could monitor and investigate these activities at any time to assure their conformity with the requirements of the legislation. If any deviation was noted by the inspector, the legal inscription of the syndicate could be canceled. This authority presented the government with an ideal administrative weapon to constrain the growth and activities of the peasant union movement. Each year, therefore, the government could inscribe a few new syndicates, demonstrating its tolerance of unionism, and each year it could cancel the legal status of an equal or even greater number of already operating unions, either to "prevent the exploitation of the workers by cynical union bosses," or because of political activities, which were expressly forbidden.[32] Table 2 shows the painfully slow growth of the recognized peasant union movement under such conditions.

On the other hand, Table 2 almost certainly fails to reflect the true dimensions of growth and membership in the peasant union movement, because of the cancellation of the inscriptions of many older unions each year. A further underestimate derives from the fact that the number of members registered in the ministry was the number of original, founding members. No growth or increase in the local's membership were reflected in the ministry data. In practical terms, however, AD brought with it to power in October 1945 a base of organized (de facto, not de jure) peasant support consisting of about 500 embryonic unions, with as many as 2,000 local peasant leaders in the villages and scattered hamlets, and an estimated 100,000 peasants within the orbit of influence of these local leaders. All of these local nuclei were to achieve legal status within three years under the revolutionary AD government, which reflected a distinct change in attitude toward the purposes and uses of the Labor Code.

Table 2. Legally recognized peasant syndicates and their membership, 1936–1945.

Year	Number of syndicates	Number of members
1936	3	482
1937	11	1499
1938	18	2182
1939	25	2858
1940	25	2858
1941	26	2925
1942	35	3649
1943	53	4432
1944	71	5823
1945	77	6279

Source: Ministry of Labor and Communications, *Memoria* (Caracas: Imp. Nacional, 1938–1945).

THE OVERALL LABOR MOVEMENT

At a higher level, the effort by ORVE-PDN-AD to establish a broad labor base continued, with the urban sector drawing the most public attention. In achieving legal recognition, the urban labor movement, including the petroleum unions, was much more effective than the peasant movement. Several factors contributed to the difference, such as the intense competition between Communist and non-Communist left labor leaders for the loyalties of the budding movement. In addition, the more clearly defined worker-employer-union relationship that existed in industrial and other urban unions (such as transport and construction workers), the greater internal base of union wealth generated by urban union members, and the fact that the petroleum unions, strongest in economic terms, dealt with extremely wealthy, non-Venezuelan employers, all gave the urban labor sector an edge over the peasant sector.[33]

The First Labor Congress, held in Caracas in December 1936, led to the later imprisonment and exile of some of its leaders. In April 1938 a national trade union conference was held, again in Caracas, and once again peasant union leaders participated. In the middle of the conference the governor of the Federal District banned further meetings as a threat to public safety, but convening in secret, the conference formed a National Labor Committee to further unification plans for the movement. As the movement increased in size and vigor, so did the competition for the central leadership between PDN-AD leaders and others seeking to build a similar power base.

By the time of the National Labor Convention, held in March 1944, a pronounced cleavage had developed between two groups, one dominated by AD leadership, and the other by Communist leadership (although there were some members of the opposition within each group). The AD group, having offered to split the National Labor Committee equally with the Communist group, walked out of the convention when its offer was rejected. In a fortuitous development for the AD union movement, the rump convention adopted several resolutions presented in the name of the Communist party, thereby violating provisions of the Labor Code, which prohibited political activities by trade unions. This error gave Medina the opportunity to break up the convention, bringing discredit to its managers.[34] Subsequently, the Communist and AD labor movements sought to smooth over their differences in an agreement known as the Pact of Cali, which permitted the initial formation in August 1945 of a comprehensive national trade union organization. However, after the blow to Communist leadership dealt by Medina's breakup of their rump convention in

1944, dominant influence in the overall labor movement had passed to the AD leadership, where it continued to grow.[35]

Inspection of Table 3 reveals even more clearly than the data of the campesino movement that a pattern of administrative sanction against operating unions organized by opposition political parties existed. The first large-scale cancellation of inscriptions oc-

Table 3. Legally recognized syndicates and their membership, 1936–1945.

Year	Number of syndicates	Number of members
1936	109	55,556
1937	199	64,385
1938	230	66,941
1939	246	69,139
1940	155	36,326
1941	113	—
1942	125	16,841
1943	174	22,933
1944	160	13,621
1945	194	21,323

Source: Ministry of Labor and Communications, *Memoria* (Caracas: Imp. Nacional, 1938–1945).

curred under López in 1940, when a general investigation and inspection were carried out by the labor inspectorate of the Ministry of Labor. Noting that a total of 251 trade unions with a membership of 89,564 members had been formed since 1936, the ministry announced the cancellation of 96 inscriptions, reducing the number of legally operating unions to 155, as shown in the table. Similar reductions in the ranks of legally operating unions occurred in 1941 and 1944 under Medina. Nor was cancellation the only administrative means to restrict the growth of trade unionism in Venezuela during this period. The simplest means was not to register the union applying for inscription in the first place. Thus, in 1941 the annual report to Congress of the ministry laconically noted: "the responsible Division has studied the statutes and constitutive acts of 24 labor organizations and is gratified to announce that during the year, 9 were legally inscribed."[36] Thus, the Ministry of Labor data would seem to underestimate the actual number of unions organized, and the number of members belonging to them, for three reasons: not all unions that formed were allowed inscription; already inscribed unions were periodically subjected to administrative inspection and dissolution; and membership figures kept by the ministry were the original ones, never up-dated.[37]

To sum up, by the late fall of 1945 the organizational basis for a massive electoral-mobilization vehicle had been constructed. Political organizers of ORVE, PDN, and AD had formed a nation-wide network of local leadership, which had in turn organized local party cells. But the mobilization strategy had further called for branching out into functional associations, with emphasis on the Venezuelan labor movement. By dominating the leadership of trade union associations, AD leaders came to influence many more people than were active, formal party members. Within the urban labor movement, AD had become dominant, but not without heavy competition from leadership active in the interests of other political parties and movements. On the other hand, in the peasant union branch of the labor movement, AD operated almost without challenge to its intensive organizational efforts. In a few scattered instances, when local Communist leaders were the ablest and most respected by the peasants in their communities, they were incorporated in the overall movement, apparently without rancor or discrimination. As a consequence of the organizational efforts by AD leaders, there were by 1945 about 1,000 local union nuclei under AD leadership, with about 200,000 members and potential members within their orbit of influence—one-half of this pool of leaders and members being peasants. Matters stood thus late in the fall of 1945, on the eve of the October Revolution.

THE MOBILIZING ELITE IN POWER, 1945–1948

Acción Democrática (AD) participation in the coup of October 18, 1945, was at once a major irony and a gamble. Representatives of the junior officers plotting the coup had in June been in touch with the AD leadership, because the young military men felt the need for professional, civilian, political allies who were aggressively reformist in character. However, part of the reforming thrust of the AD leaders was aimed at eliminating the ubiquitous traditional military elites' role in the governmental process. As advocates of constitutional, civilian government, the AD leaders, therefore, had to resolve a serious conflict of values before they could support a military coup. Four factors seem to have entered into the resolution of AD to give their full support: the threat of the old-line military leadership against the moderate Medina regime, which had become organized around support for ex-President López Contreras' return to power; the determination of the Patriotic Military Union (UPM) to proceed with the coup, with or without civilian political collaborators; the collapse of the Escalante candidacy, followed by Medina's refusal to set limitations upon the regime of his chosen successor, Biaggini—limitations which, if granted, might have won AD acceptance of the Biaggini candidacy; and finally, a simple desire to govern—to implement the wide range of sociopolitical reforms that had motivated the leaders and followers of AD since its founding.[1]

The AD decision to support the coup was made on the night of October 16, in a meeting between the AD leadership and the Patriotic Military Union. A tentative date was set for sometime in December, but when word of the impending event leaked out the following night, the collaborators acted immediately. By nightfall of October 18, 1945, the Medina government had been overthrown and, in a relatively bloodless coup, a Revolutionary Government Junta had been formed, with Rómulo Betancourt acting as president.[2] It is difficult now, decades later, to calculate the risks of failure that the coup faced, but it is not difficult to calculate the negative consequences for AD had it not succeeded—indeed, AD would probably have been relegated to the obscurity of an historical footnote. But by participating in a successful coup, AD strode onto the stage of Venezuelan politics in a decisive manner. In terms of political leadership, for example, two of the four AD members in the initial seven-man Junta went on to become constitutionally elected presidents: Rómulo Betancourt in 1958, and Raúl Leoni in 1963. The other two AD members, Luís Beltrán Prieto Figueroa and Gonzalo Barrios, were major candidates for the presidential election of 1968.[3]

By successfully dislodging the established elites from the seat of government, the coup of October 18, 1945, known as the October Revolution, cleared the way for a redefinition of the electoral process, and the legitimation of its central position in the political system. The first step in this direction was announced on October 30, when Rómulo Betancourt, president of the Junta, broadcast to the nation that a central objective of the new government was legislation that would permit the "unfettered participation of the citizenry" in the electoral process.[4] President Betancourt also stated that steps had already been taken to proscribe members of the governing Junta from becoming candidates for the presidency in the next elections. By the self-denying act of divorcing his personal political ambitions from the electoral reforms he sought as president of the Revolutionary Junta, Betancourt maximized the support of a wide range of reformist political groups, thereby enhancing the legitimacy of his actions.

Shortly after assuming power, the Junta dissolved the existing Electoral Council and formed a special multipartite committee to recommend new electoral provisions.[5] The results of this committee's work were incorporated into Decree Number 216 of March 14, 1946, in which the Junta stipulated the electoral norms and procedures that were to regulate the election of a Constituent Assembly, which in turn was expected to establish and legitimate a broad-based electoral process. The major change embodied in Decree Number 216 was the enfranchisement of all Venezuelans over the age of eighteen, regardless of sex, literacy, property, or tax criteria. This greatly enlarged the potential electorate.

The first exercise of the new suffrage occurred on October 27, 1946. Four political parties had actively campaigned to elect delegates to a Constituent Assembly. In addition to AD, there were the Partido Comunista de Venezuela (PCV) and two newly formed parties—COPEI, acronym for the Comité de Organización Política Electoral Independiente, sometimes called the Social Christian party today; and the Unión Republicana Democrática (URD). The initial electoral encounter among these four parties was won overwhelmingly by AD, which gained 137 of the 160 seats in the Constituent Assembly.

With AD leadership dominating the Constituent Assembly, the new electoral norms were written into the constitution promulgated on July 5, 1947. They were formalized in the constitution and legitimized by the participation of all the aspiring political elites, first in the Assembly election, which was the first mass-participation election in Venezuelan history, and then by the deliberations of the resulting Assembly. The first test of the new constitutional norms for the secret, direct election of Congress and the president came on December 14, 1947. Again, AD demonstrated its superior mass support. Rómulo Gallegos, who had been chosen as AD's presidential candidate, was elected by a massive majority; in addition, AD won thirty-eight out of forty-six seats in the Senate, and eighty-three out of one hundred and nine in the Chamber of Deputies.

Six months later, in May of 1948, AD consolidated its mandate to govern by winning the nationwide elections for municipal councils. In each of these electoral contests—for the Constituent Assembly, the Congress and presidency, and the municipal councils—a

Table 4. Electoral results, 1946–1948.

Date	Office	Result by major party (percentage of total vote)			
		AD	COPEI	URD	PCV
Oct. 1946	Constituent Assembly	78.8	13.2	3.8	3.6
Dec. 1947	Presidency	74.4	22.4	—	3.2
Dec. 1947	Congress	70.8	20.5	4.3	3.7
May 1948	Municipal Councils	70.1	21.1	3.9	3.4

Source: John D. Martz, *Acción Democrática* (Princeton: Princeton University Press, 1966), p. 75.

stable pattern of differential electoral effectiveness among the four competing parties was maintained, as shown in Table 4.

The electoral supremacy of AD during this period was rooted in its organizational efforts in the rural areas. Through the extension of the suffrage to all Venezuelans over eighteen years of age, the masses of peasants had become eligible to vote for the first time in Venezuelan history. Decree Number 216, later enshrined in the new constitution, had the effect of increasing the participating electorate from a pre-1945 level of 5 percent of the total population to a post-1945 level of 36 percent, a sevenfold increase. Well over one-half of these newly enfranchised voters cast their ballots for AD, most notably in the rural areas in which ORVE-PDN-AD organizers had labored since 1936.[6]

These elections were a clear case of authority legitimation by means of political mobilization—in this particular case, a peasant electoral mobilization. But the result in Venezuela was more far-reaching and profound than a mere legitimation of the authority of a particular political group to govern, for whether by design or accident, the electoral process was itself legitimized among the wide range of newly emerged, challenging urban elites. By emphasizing the electoral process as a link between the people and the governing authorities, the AD leadership acted to consolidate the emerging consensus on this value, which had been developing since 1928 among the various challenging elites trying to penetrate the political process in its traditional form. By actively encouraging the participation of competing electoral parties in a series of elections, the AD leadership maximized the legitimacy accorded the electoral process per se, at the same time legitimizing its derivative authoritative right to govern by winning the elections.

The mobilization system built up by the leaders of ORVE-PDN-AD also incorporated the function of interest articulation. As a political party, AD concentrated on authority legitimation, while the peasant union movement concentrated on articulating its interest in the issue of landed power and agrarian reform. With respect to these two functions, it is extremely important to emphasize that the same high-level leadership was managing both of them within a single, fused, mobilization system.

Just as Rómulo Betancourt had played a major, directing role in the strategic organization of a peasant base of political support, he played a major initiating role in readjusting the nature of landed power in the rural areas, and in promoting a program of de facto agrarian reform. The day he assumed power as president of the Revolutionary Junta, Betancourt convened a council of regional executives, including those selected for appointment as state governors and federal administrators, to set policy guidelines for the new government.[7] One of the most important of these policy guidelines concerned the land question:

1. The Revolutionary Junta will prepare a nationwide decree guaranteeing land tenants against arbitrary eviction. Until this goes into effect, the executive authorities will protect the peasant population against manifest injustices, if such be the case, by utilizing existing regulations pertaining to evictions.

2. Concerning the lands currently occupied and farmed by

peasants with opposition from those who pretend to be its rightful owners, a watchful eye will be kept on factual developments, while the Nation establishes if they are government lands or private properties.

3. Land rental regulations and other elements that form the relations among hacendados and colonos should be immediately and equitably readjusted by mediation of the state and territorial executives . . .

4. Regional governments should immediately study the possibilities of the efficient utilization by the peasantry of community and public lands, as well as those of the Agriculture and Livestock Bank (BAP) and the Restored Properties, to the end of increasing production and experiencing an agrarian reform. The results of these studies should be sent to the appropriate administrative organs of the Revolutionary Government, in order to proceed with the rational exploitation of these currently idle lands.

5. Regional governments ought to solicit the owners of haciendas that contain excess arable lands not under cultivation, but economically viable, in order to obtain their rental, totally or partially, by poor farmers: or to buy them for this purpose. This procedure on the part of the Regional Governments responds to the firm policy of the Revolutionary Junta of satisfying the requirement, for reasons of increased production and social justice, of granting land to the man who works it.[8]

Articles 1 and 2, in effect, empowered regional executives to prevent the eviction of any tenants or squatters from privately owned or privately claimed lands. In cases of conflict, governors and federal administrators were empowered to readjust the tenant relationship under Article 3, or to suspend eviction proceedings pending clarification of the land titles involved through the Cadastral Survey implied in Article 2.[9] Articles 4 and 5 contained the guidelines for the revolution that was about to unfold. In order to consolidate the "administrative organs of the Revolutionary Government" mentioned in Article 4, the Junta in December 1945 created a Land Commission in the Technical Institute for Immigration and Colonization (ITIC) responsible for recruiting and settling immigrant European farmers. This Land Commission was to become the focal point of the government's program of land distribution to the unionized peasantry.[10]

A flood of individual and syndicate petitions for land began to pour in to the Land Commission. At the outset Aragua, Carabobo, and Miranda states were the greatest pressure points for land distribution. Limitations of qualified personnel and the stipulated social policies of the Revolutionary Government dictated that the petitions of organized campesinos would be given priority over those of individuals or commercial farmers. Thus, for example, the Governing Board of a local syndicate would petition the Institute for Colonization for a specified piece of government-owned or private property.[11] Institute technicians would evaluate the property and its agricultural status and potential, then negotiate a lease with the owner of the land. Meanwhile the Governing Board of the peasant syndicate, as a party to the leasing contract, would undertake to organize the syndicate members for the cultivation of the leased property and to assist in management of the credit programs for the campesino tenants.

During the Land Commission's first four months of operations, this procedure was carried out as shown in Table 5. The initial surge of pressures for land was met by the distribution, under lease arrangements, of 12,991 hectares to thirty syndicates with a total membership of 5,700 campesinos. Thus, as was the case in Mexico and Bolivia, in the initial stages of the Venezuelan agrarian reform, the result of rapid land redistribution was to create minifundia. Recognizing the economic limitations of minifundia (the average campesino received only about 2.2 hectares), institute officials described the preliminary distribution pattern as merely a "transitory solution to critical problems." Among the reasons

71

Table 5. Initial land leases by ITIC to syndicates, January–April 1946.

| State | Hectares distributed | | Lessees | |
	Private land	Public land	Syndicates	Campesino members
Carabobo	4983	4039	17	4000
Aragua	610	2559	12	1400
Miranda	—	800	1	300

Source: Confidential interviews.

explaining this pattern of land distributions were the agitation for land throughout the countryside; the shortage of available land in the areas of greatest population density, and therefore the impracticality, if not impossibility, of distributing sufficiently large parcels to a few campesinos while leaving their neighbors without any; the lack of time, personnel and machinery to effect an adequate parcelization scheme.[12]

In an attempt at keeping the door open for a subsequent reconsolidation of farm operations on the lands that they leased to the syndicates, the Institute for Colonization contract included a reservation clause asserting the right of the Ministry of Agriculture (MAC), after one year, to reorganize the land-use pattern along more rational economic lines. In practice, however, this could clearly not be done. Under the revolutionary pressures for land distribution that had been unleashed in 1945, a potential conflict between social forces in action and the rational calculations and criteria of bureaucratic technicians quickly emerged. Peasants with little or no land or land rights prior to the October coup were perfectly content with two or three hectares of good land as an immediate benefit. Most of them were technologically incapable of utilizing much more than this amount. In the absence of a clearly perceived long-range benefit from not fragmenting the land, campesinos and their leaders naturally gravitated in that direction.

Technicians generally found themselves frustrated in trying to halt this short-run tendency.[13]

In addition to the distribution of land rights through leasing arrangements with the peasant syndicates, the government also placed credits in the hands of the peasant farmers. Decree No. 282 of May 8, 1946, created a Credit Department in the Institute for Colonization and funded it with an initial 10,000,000 bolivares specifically earmarked for administration to "associations of farmers"—that is, peasant syndicates—for their use in farming the lands leased to them by the government. The disposition of these funds considerably enhanced possibilities for increased income of campesino members of the benefiting syndicates. Again, however, the program technicians had misgivings about the rationality and discipline with which these credits were utilized. A little over a year after the creation of the Credit Department in the Institute for Colonization, the credit program functions were transferred to the Agriculture Bank, which commanded the greater experience and the personnel needed to administer the programs. By the time of the transfer, the Credit Department had expended eight millions of its ten-million-bolivar initial funding. After the transfer of the credit program to the bank, the Operational Plan under which credit was administered on the local level remained essentially the same. A Governing Board, consisting of a representative from the Institute for Colonization, a credit specialist, and a syndicate representative, administered the credits in weekly installments to the campesinos, with the syndicate representative having the responsibility of insuring that the campesino had performed the duties required of each member under the overall farm plan envisaged in the original leasing arrangement. Under such procedures, the Credit Department of the Institute for Colonization distributed almost eight million bolivares of its fund before transfer of the credit supervision function to the bank.[14]

Thus, within slightly over one year after the October Revolution, several powerful new dimensions had been added to the role of peasant union leader. Men who had originally been recruited because they were opinion leaders and strong personalities in their communities, were now invested by the government with tremendous instrumental powers, which further enhanced their influence in the peasant community. By virtue of their linkage with the revolutionary government, they now had the power to obtain land for the syndicate members, to obtain credits and supervise their distribution, and to influence the location of public works projects such as schools, roads, water and sewage systems. After October

Table 6. Summary of ITIC land and credit operations, January 1946–March 1947.

Item	Quantity
Number of hectares leased and in production	54,437
Number of syndicates participating	210
Number of peasants belonging to such syndicates	23,493
Average hectares granted per campesino	2.3
Average credits granted per campesino	Bs 332
Expected repayment rate of credits granted	70 percent
Repayment rate as of March 1947	30 percent

Source: Confidential interviews.

1945, the number of legalized peasant syndicates, and therefore the number of syndicate-leader posts to be filled, grew rapidly.[15] Table 6 summarizes several dimensions of this growing phenomenon of rural change.

POLITICAL CONSOLIDATION OF LOCAL SYNDICATE LEADERS

Granting local peasant leaders influence in the distribution of land and credits was bound to have an impact on their status in the rural areas, but there still remained an element of resistance and challenge to the dominance of the local syndicate leaders. In some regions, sufficient and suitable government lands were available, or private lands were leasable, to meet the pressures for distribution. But in other regions, especially those with high population pressures combined with relatively scarce and valuable land, sufficient government lands were not available, and some landholders either refused to come to terms with the revolutionary government for the lease or sale of their properties, or agreed to do so only at exorbitant rates. In other words, the traditional instrumental power and influence of the large landholder, while outflanked by the revolution, remained an obstacle to the growing power of the syndicate leader. This obstacle the revolutionary government set about to break.

On March 4, 1947, the AD-controlled Constituent Assembly passed a Decree of Rural Property Rentals, which was signed by the president of the Revolutionary Junta, Rómulo Betancourt, on March 6, 1947. In effect, it radically changed the locus of control over private land in rural areas and formalized the functions of the peasant syndicate leaders in the distribution of land to peasant tenants. In other words, it consolidated political power in the hands of the peasant syndicate leaders in the rural areas.[16]

The basic intent of the decree was to create a number of Agrarian Commissions in each state and territory, empowered to oversee the leasing of farm lands to peasants. Article 5 required all owners of private lands not being actively farmed to rent them to government agencies or "associations of farmers," the term used for peasant syndicates. Article 11 placed all government lands—national, state, and municipal—under the jurisdiction of the nearest Agrarian Commission for the purpose of leasing lands to the peasantry. Thus, sweeping and profound powers were granted to these commissions: powers to grant leases to the peasant syndicates directly or through the Institute for Colonization of lands that they judged as coming under the decree, and on terms that they considered just. The commissions were also granted powers to impose fines of up to

500 bolivares for noncompliance with their findings. However, landowners who disputed findings that they held unused tracts, or who disputed the fairness of the leasing terms ordered by the commission, could apply to a Board of Appeal for final and binding judgment.

The Ministry of Agriculture (of which the Institute for Colonization was a subordinate part) and the governors were empowered to establish the commissions in areas where there was campesino pressure for land. Actually, the ministry named only one member of each five-man commission, its own direct representative. The governor appointed a personal representative and one member of the appropriate Municipal Junta to the commission. To complete the commission, one representative for the local landowners was selected, and one representative for the local peasant syndicates. The procedures for the selection of these commission members were as follows: "For the election of the representatives of the owners or renters, the Principal Civil Authority for the jurisdiction will call a meeting of those interested, at which those attending, whatever might be their number, will effect the election by a majority of votes."[17]

The opportunity for procedural maneuvering and manipulation by local AD governmental authorities in the selection of the landowners' representative was immense. If the landowners nevertheless managed to elect an aggressive representative and thus to control one vote in the commission, there were other procedures through which their interests could be circumvented. Each commission met at the call of its president, who was the AD governor's representative, and though the Commission made all of its decisions by majority vote, it could function with only three of the five members present. Thus, both the landlords and the technician representing the Ministry of Agriculture could be outmaneuvered through the procedure of holding a meeting of the three representatives of the governor, the Municipal Junta, and the peasant syndicate—all of them part of the AD mobilization system.

Table 7. Estimates of agrarian reform totals, 1945–1948.

Type of estimate	Hectares distributed	Peasant recipients
Conservative[a]	90,000	55,000
Average[b]	125,000	73,000
Liberal[c]	165,000	80,000

Source: Confidential interviews. All projections are interpolations measured on curves plotted from data already cited from March 1946 and March 1947.

[a] Conservative assumption: the lowest rate of increase in the established curve holds from March 1947 through November 1948.

[b] Average assumption: the average rate of acceleration in the the established curve holds from March 1947 through November 1948.

[c] Liberal assumption: the maximum rate of acceleration in the established curve holds from March 1947 through November 1948.

The landlords could appeal from the findings of these ad hoc Agrarian Commissions to a three-man Board of Appeal, consisting of one Ministry of Agriculture representative, one representative of the governor, and one representative of the peasant union movement. In reality, therefore, the only real check on the potential powers of the Agrarian Commission system set up by the Decree of Rural Property Rentals was the self-restraint of the governor, operating within the policy limits dictated for him by the revolutionary government. Though the extent to which such powers were used, or abused, during the 1947–1948 period is unknown and probably unknowable, it is clear that their mere existence and the implied threat of their use would in many local communities be sufficient to shift local rural political power in favor of the peasant syndicate leaders. There were approximately 2,500 local leaders involved in this process by the time of the overthrow of the AD government in November 1948.

The importance of the effect of this decree on the peasant union movement was emphasized during interviews of Hermógenes Mendoza, the agrarian secretary of the Peasant Federation of Venezuela (FCV) in Aragua state, and other members of the staff. They were of the opinion that the decree had delivered more land into the hands of peasants in their area than any other single measure before or since.[18] This bounty suggests the roots of the continued power and influence among the campesino masses of Mendoza and other AD syndicate leaders. Table 7 gives estimates of the land distribution process in which these peasant union leaders participated, based on three alternative projections of the available data.

THE PEASANT FEDERATION OF VENEZUELA

As the AD de facto agrarian reform program spread, so did its institutional vehicle, the peasant union movement. During the period from 1945 to 1948, the peasant union sector grew steadily in size and importance in relation to the overall union movement, which was also showing considerable growth. Prior to October 1945, peasant unions had comprised about 40 percent of all local unions and had accounted for about 30 percent of all union members. By November 1948 peasant unions accounted for 50 percent of all locals and 32 percent of Venezuela's union members. At the same time, there was a tremendous absolute growth in the labor movement, as illustrated in Table 8.[19]

The peasant union movement achieved formal nationwide organization in November 1947, when the Peasant Federation (FCV) was incorporated in the Confederation of Venezuelan Workers (CTV), the first nationwide, solidary, trade-union organization in the country. Of the fifteen state federations of labor and the seven occupational federations that comprised the new Confedera-

Table 8. Legally operating syndicates and their membership, 1945–1948.

Date	Peasant syndicates	Peasant members	All syndicates	All members
18 Oct. 1945	53	3,959	215	24,336
31 Oct. 1945	60	—	248	48,789
31 Dec. 1946	312	19,113	763	99,525
31 Dec. 1947	433	36,193	934	109,592
24 Nov. 1948[a]	515	43,302	1,047	137,316

Source: Ministry of Labor, *Memoria* (Caracas, Imp. Nacional, 1946, 1947).
[a] Estimated.

tion, only one was dominated by non-AD labor leaders, the Communist-led Clothing and Textile Federation. The Peasant Federation was led by Ramón Quijada, the long-time PDN-AD peasant organizer from Sucre state.[20]

THE AGRARIAN REFORM LAW OF 1948

Paralleling these de facto developments was a series of legal steps designed to consolidate and institutionalize the government's program of agrarian reform. The important Decree of Rural Property Rentals was promulgated by the Constituent Assembly in March 1947. The final result of that Assembly's efforts, the new constitution promulgated on July 5, 1947, contained the legal plank on which the government intended to base its permanent program of land reform. Article 69 reads in part as follows:

> The State shall effect a planned and systematic program for the purpose of: transforming the national agrarian structure; rationalizing agricultural and livestock exploitation; organizing and distributing credit; improving the living conditions in rural areas; and the progressive economic and social emancipation of the rural population. A special Law shall determine the technical and other conditions, in accordance with the national

interest, by means of which shall be made effective the right which the Nation recognizes in *associations of rural workers* and individuals engaged in farming to be granted workable lands in sufficient quantities, and the proper means with which to make these lands productive.[21]

The peasant syndicate was thus openly conceived of by the leaders of the revolutionary government as one of the primary vehicles through which to carry out its program of agrarian reform. An additional (and permanent) departure from tradition in land policy made in the 1947 constitution was a shift from the doctrine of public domain to that of the social function of land as a basis for the expropriation of private property.[22]

Moving ahead on the basis of the mandate established in Article 69 of the constitution, the newly elected Congress proceeded to draft, debate, and adopt a new Agrarian Reform Law. Building on precedents established in the abortive 1945 Agrarian Reform Law of the Medina regime, the new law, as presented to and shaped by the AD-dominated Congress, represented a radical departure in one area: the peasant union organizations were neatly incorporated into the administrative processes of the law, which ratified the shift in local rural power to the syndicate leader.[23]

As in the law of 1945, a National Agrarian Institute (IAN) was to be created as the government agency primarily concerned with carrying out the Agrarian Reform Law. However, the preliminary version of the 1948 law differed markedly from the earlier law in its implicit recognition of the interest-group conflict involved in agrarian reform. The Board of Directors of the Agrarian Institute was to be selected from candidates submitted to Congress every two years by the Venezuelan Federation of Chambers of Commerce and the Peasant Federation, but below the highest administrative level, the peasant union movement was incorporated into the Agrarian Institute, while commercial interests were not. Thus, for each state and territory, one or more regional agrarian expediters were to be appointed for the purpose of permanently representing before the Agrarian Institute and its various offices and delegations the peasant syndicates that petitioned for land grants under the law. Salaried by the institute, these officials were to be selected in each case from a list of five names submitted by the Peasant Federation, and could be removed from office only in the case of negligence or lack of probity in the performance of their duties.[24]

While both peasant syndicates and individuals were under the law given a right to petition for a land grant, all petitions had to be signed by the regional agrarian expediter. If the Peasant Federation chose to exercise its influence to the utmost, the benefits of the Agrarian Reform Law could in practice be limited to its member peasant syndicates. Thus, not only was the functional power of the local syndicate leader institutionalized, but the national peasant syndicate organization was empowered to discriminate against local syndicates which might not be affiliated, or which might conceivably pertain to a competitive national federation. In reality, no such competitor existed, nor was one likely to be formed under the administrative conditions established in the 1948 law.

The local syndicate leader's power vis-á-vis latifundista was ratified by the law, and his power in relation to commercial farmers was established by Article 112. Thus, although large commercial-type farms were granted temporary inexpropriability (Article 108), Article 112 granted the local peasant syndicates the right to challenge such immunity if they could demonstrate that the acreage in question was the only acreage in the region suited for the purposes of agrarian reform, and if the majority of the actual occupants of the land in question were members of the syndicate.[25] The final version of the 1948 Agrarian Reform Law, in short, ratified and attempted to institutionalize the interest articulation function performed by AD's mobilization system. It was promulgated by President Gallegos on October 18, 1948, the third anniversary of the October Revolution. But that revolution, and most of its works, were to be shattered less than a month later by a reactionary military coup.

From the beginning of the Institute for Colonization land-leasing and credit program, special preference had been given to the local peasant syndicates affiliated with AD. Since these syndicates had been organized as a result of a deliberate interest-articulation mobilization of the peasantry by ORVE-PDN-AD leaders, it was natural that AD would respond to them when it achieved the power to do so. But the leverage which AD thus garnered was greatly resented by the leadership of other political parties, who ruefully observed the voting strength of the rural bloc of AD loyalists. Thus, in June of 1946, Rafael Caldera, the founder and leader of COPEI, made a savage attack on the Institute for Colonization land-and-credit distribution process, charging the AD government with gross irregularities and partisan favoritism in the selection of recipient groups.[26]

The day following the publication of the COPEI leader's attack, the pro-AD newspaper *El País* (The Country) published a reply by the director of the Land Commission, in which he acknowledged the fact that many of the groups and individuals receiving the benefits of the programs were indeed identified with AD, but denied that this was a calculated policy choice. Pointing out that several peasant unions led by Communist leaders had also received program benefits, the Institute for Colonization official concluded that since only the Communists and AD had been successful in organizing peasant groups, the Land Commission had no choice in the matter.[27]

A more serious and detailed set of charges of partisanship and favoritism in the de facto agrarian reform program was published two months later, during the height of the summer's campaigning for the Constituent Assembly. The charges were brought by the national leadership of the third major political party contending in the election, URD. Briefly describing how land and credits were being distributed among peasant unions and their members, URD stated that only peasants affiliated with or actively supporting AD in the approaching election were receiving benefits. As supporting evidence, it detailed one particularly flagrant example of partisanship, when weekly credit payments were disbursed by the credit committee in the local headquarters of AD, to which only card-carrying party members were granted access.[28] As the AD government was extremely sensitive to such charges, the week following the disclosure of this particular incident a new site was arranged for the credit disbursement.[29]

But if AD's authoritative legitimacy was diminished in the eyes of competitive elites by such actions, this seemed a necessary price for organizing and responding to the interest articulation process. After all, the entire urban-peasant alliance was an explicit quid pro quo: you help us to achieve power with your votes (authority legitimation), and we will respond with an agrarian reform through the channel of the Peasant Federation (interest articulation). The two were fused in the same mobilization system, which depended both on intermittent peasant contributions at the polls and on a flow of agrarian goods and services in return. But the more effective and prolonged the response to peasant interests, as articulated by and channeled through the AD-sponsored peasant union movement, the greater the loss of authoritative legitimacy for AD governance among competing electoral elites.

Moreover, the peasant interest was not the only organized interest that was cultivated by the AD regimes, and as a result, landed elites and competing electoral elites were not the only groups to come into conflict with governmental policies. AD's sponsorship and encouragement of the overall labor movement brought it into an antagonistic relationship with manufacturing interests, particularly with the petroleum industry and its commercial allies in the national economy.[30] AD's sponsorship of a vigorous public educational system brought it into an antagonistic relationship with the Catholic hierarchy in Venezuela, which had traditionally controlled almost the entire educational system. And AD's vigorous advocacy of integrity in public office, which took the form of legal proceedings against former high officials in the López and Medina regimes, deprived opponents of office, and often of property, for peculation and other transgressions against the public moral order, which consolidated the resentment of the traditional elites against the AD intruders. In short, vigorous reform activities, made more abrasive by the partisanship involved in responding to the interest-articulation structures subsumed within its alliance system, came in time to threaten the legitimacy that AD had achieved through the electoral process.

This loss of acceptability probably occurred first among the traditional elites that had been replaced by the October 1945 revolution—though AD had never achieved much support among these groups. The erosion of AD's legitimacy among competitive electoral elites was probably accelerated with each election won by AD. The electoral potency of AD's rural base seemed to be purchased in part at the price of a partisan de facto agrarian reform program. With the loss of support among some newly emerged elites, the opposition of the formerly privileged, traditional elites began to operate in a more effective manner. The response of the AD leadership proved unfortunate, though perhaps predictable under the circumstances. The party increased its cultivation of interest-based support groups, such as the peasant union movement, in order to strengthen its remaining base of legitimating support, whereby it succeeded in producing an ever more dependable, but ever narrower, support structure.

As is often the case in Latin America, the single most important group in terms of necessary support for any regime's legitimacy was found in the military. When AD's support waned in this institution, its days were numbered. In the immediate aftermath of the 1945 revolution, relations between AD and the military had been mutually satisfactory. The Patriotic Military Union was primarily interested in internal professional reforms of the military establishment and thus deferred to AD in the social reform field. Accordingly, the AD-dominated civil-military Junta had removed the old guard senior military officers of the Tachirense-circle variety, granted salary increases up to 30 percent to junior officers, and increased their fringe benefits. In general, AD acted to modernize the material and professional training of the armed forces.[31]

But as the constitutional elections led to greater civilian participation in the government and as the military members of the Junta were replaced by civilian ministers, a faction within the Patriotic Military Union, led by Carlos Delgado Chalbaud and Marcos Pérez Jiménez, began to express dissatisfaction with the loss of military influence in the policy process. Within the Patriotic Military Union, a nucleus was formed of political activists—military men whose interests and ambitions transcended their professional realm. During most of the three years of AD rule, this group had relatively little impact on civil-military relations, but the situation changed as opposition grew to AD rule. For example, AD's sponsorship and encouragement of militant action by the petroleum unions aroused considerable hostility among the powerful foreign petroleum interests. At about this same time in 1948, though perhaps only by coincidence, the fear began to grow within the armed forces that AD was determined to arm its militant trade union loyalists and, eventually, to reduce the power of the professional armed forces.[32]

By the time that the new Agrarian Reform Law had been pushed through Congress and signed by President Gallegos in October 1948, the loss of AD's legitimacy among competing electoral elites was almost complete. Furthermore, conflicting interest groups, which had been bypassed in the AD government's drive to favor its own interest-articulation subsystems, coalesced on seeing the landed elites' defeat over the agrarian reform. A period of several weeks of paralyzing crisis settled upon the capital. During this time, the Delgado Chalbaud-Pérez Jiménez faction within the military apparently established a mandate to act. Just as hints of the crisis were becoming public knowledge, the Gallegos government suspended constitutional guarantees on November 20 and imposed censorship of the mass media.[33]

Soon afterward, a military group presented President Gallegos with an ultimatum, which called for the appointment of military men and opposition political leaders to the Cabinet, the exile of Rómulo Betancourt, and a number of other political restraints. After several days of agonizing maneuvering, President Gallegos rejected this fundamental challenge to his constitutional authority. The confrontation was now considerably intensified by forces within both AD and the military. In an uncoordinated fashion, an attempt was made by several AD labor leaders to organize a general strike, at the same time that Pérez Jiménez, moving on his own initiative, began preparations for a coup. While the top AD leadership was dividing on whether to mobilize the unarmed labor battalions for a showdown with the military, the Patriotic Military Union—which had brought AD to power only three years earlier—closed ranks. Delgado Chalbaud, convinced that Pérez Jiménez was going ahead with the coup with or without his support, joined it in a reported attempt to keep the coup from veering too sharply to the right.[34] On November 24, 1948, amidst poorly organized and sporadic civilian resistance, President Gallegos was dislodged by the military.

IV

THE COUNTERREVOLUTION, 1948–1958

The newly entrenched Military Junta delivered its public defense of the coup on December 10, 1948. Speaking to the nation over radio, Delgado Chalbaud explained that the primary cause of military dissatisfaction was the attempt by the Acción Democrática (AD) government to build "a state within a state" through its alliance with, and encouragement of, a partisan labor movement. The "immediate cause" for the coup on October 24 was given as AD's attempt to mobilize its industrial and peasant labor syndicates in an abortive general strike. He hinted darkly at the further fear that AD might have created Red Battalions to the detriment of the legally established military authorities. As a result, the Military Junta had seen fit to dissolve and disband the AD party and its works, sending many of its principal leaders into exile.[1]

There followed for AD leaders and members what has been aptly called a Decade of Persecution. The military government's national security police (SN) devastated the AD leadership through arrests, torture, exile, or simple assassination, with the result that increasingly heavy responsibilities fell on the shoulders of second-echelon leaders within the party. The party organization's primary functional response to the initial wave of arrests and harassments was to focus on internal organization for clandestine political survival. The basic party structure, the cell-like base group, was invigorated as the primary, semiautonomous functioning unit. An elaborate communications system was designed to ensure the downward flow of instructions and information from the supreme command of the clandestine organization, the National Executive Committee (CEN). A special secretariat was established under the executive committee, and named Internal Vigilance, to function as a security apparatus. From this structural base, AD operated clandestinely within Venezuela (and openly through its exile organizations) for the ten years of the military dictatorship, during which

Pérez Jiménez soon became undisputed leader. The toll exacted on AD political leadership by the national security police was heavy. Of the clandestine secretaries-general of AD, the first, Luís Augusto Dubuc, lasted only a few weeks before capture and exile; Leonardo Ruíz Pineda, his replacement, was shot down in the streets of Caracas by the security police of Pérez Jiménez in October 1952; the next AD secretary-general, the respected Alberto Carnevali, was captured three months later and allowed to languish in prison and finally die of cancer without adequate medical attention; three months after Carnevali's capture, his replacement, Eligio Anzola, was picked up by the security police, tortured, and mercifully exiled.[2] During this period, the government moved steadily toward dismantling the AD-built labor movement and undoing its principal works in agrarian reform.

THE SUPPRESSION OF THE VENEZUELAN LABOR MOVEMENT

The Military Junta did not hesitate long before acting against organized labor. By Decree No. 56 of February 25, 1949, the Confederation of Venezuelan Workers (CTV) was dissolved and declared illegal. Stating that the "political nature" of the labor movement justified its disbanding, the Junta especially singled out the National Peasant Federation (FCN), charging that it "was directed by public officials and bureaucrats on holiday . . . there were no campesinos among the Directorate."[3] At the same time that the national superstructure of the labor movement was thus attacked, the Junta dissolved the executive committees of all 515 campesino syndicates and 532 industrial syndicates, and incumbent officials were declared ineligible for re-election. Local unions were permitted to reorganize under a complex formula established by the government, which included prior authorization of meetings, public registration of membership lists, and a legally certified quorum for the conduct of business. By the end of the year, only

19 peasant syndicates and 306 industrial syndicates were function-ing under these stringent requirements.[4]

In the meantime, the International Labor Organization (ILO), in response to the outcry created by the dissolution of the Confeder-ation of Workers, sent an investigating team, which was in Vene-zuela from July 22 to September 1, 1949. Receiving a modicum of cooperation from the government, the ILO Mission Report noted that most of the leaders whom it wished to interview were either in jail or in exile: "the Mission was able to ascertain that the trade union movement was struck at through the persons of the officials of all of its occupational federations and regional federa-tions." Critical of the administrative harassments imposed by gov-ernment on the reconstitution of the movement, the report noted:

> The evidence obtained reveals that the dissolution of the Con-federation had particularly serious repercussions on the condi-tions of employment of agricultural workers. The agricultural worker's trade union encounters special difficulties by reason of the nature of the work, the structure of the agricultural property-owning system, the scattered population, etc. Isolated agricultural unions, without any contact between them and without the support of a central federation, do not generally enjoy the necessary independence, and do not possess sufficient resources to defend the interests of their members with any hope of success.[5]

Acknowledging the government's contention that the disbanded labor movement had been dominated by a political party, AD, the ILO group accepted government testimony and evidence (ob-tained by a raid on the Ministry of Labor archives by the security police[6]), which suggested that the Ministry of Labor, under the control of AD, had discriminated against labor unions that were not affiliated with the Confederation of Workers. The following charges were made: Labor Inspectors ignored representations orig-inating with non-confederation unions; Labor Inspectors delayed indefinitely acting on matters referred to them by non-confederation unions; employment in public works projects, national and state, was conditioned on membership in a confederation trade union, or AD party membership; the repression of non-confederation unions, including the alleged jailing of rival union leaders. The ILO Mission found enough substance in these charges to accept many of them, pointing out that "naturally, because of what has already been stated, the trade unions connected with the Democratic Action Party were everywhere numerically superior." Yet it was unwilling to acknowledge as a consequence the desirability of dissolving the Confederation of Workers. For the ILO Mission also took into account the positive benefits that had been brought to industrial and farm labor by the AD-dominated confederation, noting with approval that "their influence was especially exercised in the conclusion of collective contracts, the number of which grew from 227 in 1946 to 483 in 1948."[7]

Continuing with its opinion, the mission stated that a close connection between the labor movement and the government was not necessarily an evil in itself. It also included in its analysis of the 1945–1948 situation the following comment: "This cooperation was more than a mere relationship between trade union leaders and the public authorities. It extended to prelegislative and legislative activity in the field of social policy, by reason of the fact that a number of important trade union leaders were at the same time members of the Chamber of Deputies or the Senate. Their influence was felt in the preparation and the voting of legislative measures which directly concerned the lives of the working class and the peasantry . . . on the initiative of the trade union Deputies . . . agricultural communities were set up"[8]

COUNTERREVOLUTION IN AGRARIAN REFORM

The Military Junta's first act in the field of agrarian reform was to bring the program initiated under AD to a halt, pending the formation of a new agrarian reform policy. Thus, land distribution and campesino credit programs were quickly terminated. As the next ten years were amply to demonstrate, this initial step was the forerunner of a drastic reversal in government policy from that of 1945–1948, effecting an almost complete shift of attention from campesino problems to those of commercial farmers.[9]

In replacing the Agrarian Reform Law of 1948, the Military Junta presented its own statutory basis for agrarian reform under the Agrarian Statute of June 28, 1949. Promulgated simultaneously with a decree dissolving the Technical Institute for Immigration and Colonization (ITIC), this statute passed the institute's functions over to the long-contemplated National Agrarian Institute (IAN), which was to bear prime responsibility for the new government's version of an agrarian reform for Venezuelan campesinos. The new statute differed from the earlier versions of agrarian reform legislation in two basic areas: expropriation of land for the purposes of agrarian reform was considerably restricted, and the application requirements for a land-grant were made quite demanding. Less land was available under the new statute, and it was harder to obtain. Article 76 spelled out in detail some of the administrative hazards that individual or group petitioners for land had to face:

Solicitants of land will present a common application without stamps before the appropriate Offices, Agencies, or Delegations of the Institute (IAN), on which they must indicate:

(1) If it is a group of villagers, the name, age, sex, occupation and number of persons constituting the family of each one of the members of the group, the acreage of land possessed by the applicants, if such be the case, and in addition, approximate data about the lands of the region, specifying, if possible, the type of cultivation, average production, rainfall data, water courses, communications roads, proximity of markets and other facts which will permit a better understanding of the local situation; and,

(2) When individuals undertake petitions, each should indicate his name, age, sex, occupation, number of persons constituting his family, technical capacity or experience in agricultural work which he may possess, economic resources of his own on which he may count, and if he possesses land, indicate the amount. The petition will also be accompanied by the written opinion of an authorized or expert person to the effect that the lands which the petitioner desires to develop are economically suitable.

All applications must contain the express declaration of the applicant to submit himself to the conditions, limitations and restrictions established in this Statute and its Regulations, and to the standards, statutes and regulations that the Agrarian Institute dictates.[10]

The technical report required in paragraph (1), which had formerly been prepared by the university-trained Institute for Colonization specialists, was thus made the responsibility of the peasant applicant, who was semiliterate at most. Equally difficult to meet were the requirements for detailed personal and family information, which were further complicated in the operating regulations of the statute. Apparently these administrative obstacles were effective in preventing most land petitions from reaching the stage where they needed to be considered. The annual report to Congress of the Ministry of Agriculture (MAC), in discussing the processing of land petitions several years after these regulations went into effect, noted the stringency of the legal requirements for the petitions, including: "background data, the state of health of the petitioner, his financial solvency, etc. We have received during the year 446 new petitions, but even more which lacked some of the required data."[11] Thus, the process of distributing new lands to peasants who desired them was slowed to a standstill.

Concurrent moves began the process of dislodging the peasants from the lands that they had acquired by the Revolution of 1945.

Tracts of land that had formerly come under government control began to revert to private hands after 1949. Even the Restored Properties, the former prizes of Juan Vicente Gómez, began reverting to the control of his heirs and claimants on his estate, on occasion accompanied by cruelly treacherous treatment of the peasant occupants.[12] The foreclosed farm properties that had been taken over by the Agriculture and Livestock Bank (BAP), as well as the Ministry of Agriculture properties, began to be sold off to private investors and speculators after the November coup. Marketable properties, which had been sold under a policy of a 25 to 30 percent required downpayment, began moving briskly as the military government dropped the requirement to 10 percent. Once again, it became fashionable for government officials to acquire the status of weekend hacendados. The private properties that had been leased to peasant syndicates under the Decree of Rural Property Rentals were immediately unencumbered for disposition of the owners as they saw fit.

The result of the changes in the status of these properties, many of which had been operating as agrarian reform projects, was a steady eviction of the peasantry from the lands to which they had been granted access under the AD government. While the exact figures are not available, this phenomenon of eviction from agrarian reform projects was by all reports widespread, and was occasionally accompanied by violence.[13] In 1955 the Ministry of Agriculture included a new entry in its annual report to Congress (*Memoria*), concerning its role in "Interventions in Eviction Problems as Friendly Broker." Citing data in 107 cases in fourteen states, the report stated that the 2,241 peasants involved in such cases in 1955 "have obtained payments for improvements, or been re-located on the same farm." The 24 cases reported the following year, and the 52 cases reported in 1957, were merely noted as having been settled in a manner "equitable to those parties with interests involved."[14] Though there is no precise way in which to measure the extent of the evictions that occurred prior to 1955 (witnesses

say the most active period was the first few years after 1948),
nor the equity with which the peasant interests were treated after
1955, my estimate is that by the end of the Pérez Jiménez dictatorship almost all the land that had been used for agrarian reform
under AD from 1945–1948 had come under private control, and
almost all of the peasants formerly settled thereon had been evicted.
This estimate is supported by contrasting the estimated land distribution and peasant beneficiaries as of November 1948 with the
actual number of peasants settled on government colonies and small
settlements at the time of the fall of Pérez Jiménez,[15] as in Table 9.

Table 9. Land reform estimates before and after Pérez Jiménez.

Year	Basis of data	Hectares	Peasants settled
1948	Conservative estimate	90,000	55,000
1948	Average estimate	125,000	73,000
1948	Liberal estimate	165,000	80,000
1957	Government documents	34,452	3,759

Source: 1948 data: see Table 7. 1957 data: Ministry of Agriculture, La Colonización Agrícola en Venezuela, 1830–1957 (Caracas:
MAC, 1959), p. 71.

THE SURVIVAL OF THE PEASANT
SYNDICATE MOVEMENT

The combined effect of the suppression of AD and the Venezuelan
labor movement, with the virtual liquidation of the 1945–1948
agrarian reform, had an understandably deleterious effect on the
legally recognized peasant union movement. Even after the creation
of Pérez Jiménez' own labor confederation in 1953, very few peasant
syndicates operated under the dictatorship. Although granted "all
rights within the suspension of Constitutional guarantees," Venezuelan peasant syndicate leaders faced a government that had de-

clared its policy as being: "elimination of all political influence in syndicates, which is contrary to the worker's interest; freezing of all syndicate funds in private and public institutions; and suspension of the right of syndicate meetings, although application for permission to hold such a meeting can be made, stating the place, date, and reason for the meeting."[16] Table 10 shows the results.

Table 10. Legally recognized peasant syndicates, 1948–1957.

Year	Peasant syndicates	Peasant members
1948	515	43,302
1949	19	—
1950	24	—
1951	32	—
1952	54	—
1953	64	—
1954	70	306
1955	72	918
1956	79	1,176
1957	—	—

Source: Ministry of Labor, *Memoria* (Caracas: Imp. Nacional, 1948–1958).

Deprived of its rights to function openly, the peasant union movement and its leadership were quickly incorporated into the clandestine resistance to the dictatorship led by AD. The fact that adversity not only failed to extinguish the movement but in fact may have more solidly entrenched it in the peasant culture, is suggested by the fantastic growth rate of peasant syndicates immediately following the overthrow of Pérez Jiménez in 1958 (see Table 14). There are several points that help to explain the successful survival of the peasant union movement in Venezuela from 1948 to 1958:

(1) The existence of a doctrine—Rómulo Betancourt's "Doctrina Redentora" or Doctrine for the Redemption—which,

by historically justifying the peasant's right to land, provided the ideological basis for a peasant resistance mystique.[17]

(2) The experience of reward under the 1945–1948 AD government, which strongly contrasted with other peasant experience with government.

(3) The experience of suppression, deprivation, and eviction under the Pérez Jiménez dictatorship.

(4) The existence of the AD clandestine resistance movement, in which many national and state leaders of the peasant union movement were involved, to whom most of the peasant masses had already demonstrated their political loyalties.

The arrest, torture, imprisonment, and exile of peasant movement leaders served to highlight the dedication and sacrifice with which such leaders were serving the peasantry, and perhaps thereby deepened the loyalty of that sector even more. AD peasant union leaders were captured while distributing resistance literature, while organizing clandestine peasant groups, and in at least one case, while attempting an assassination of the Military Junta (the first triumvirate).[18] Such acts of bravery and courage were used by remaining peasant leaders as examples to maintain an intense respect and devotion on the part of their followers. Listed in Table 11 are some of the more important peasant syndicate movement leaders imprisoned by the dictatorship.

Morillo, Hernández, Torres, and González, being the first arrested, were sent to the infamous Guasima Concentration Camp, which they managed to survive and were thereafter transferred to the New Prison of Bolívar City, where they were eventually joined by their colleagues. At the end of their sentences, many were individually exiled to Central America or Mexico. Morillo, Hernández, González, and Acuña managed to find each other in Costa Rica, where they had set up a poultry cooperative when word reached them that the dictator—"El Gordito" or "The Fat One" as they called him—had fallen.

Table 11. Some peasant syndicate leaders imprisoned, then exiled, 1948–1958.

Name	Positions held	Date of arrest	Sentence
Luís Morillo	Sec. Agr., Carabobo FCV (1945–48), Sec. Gen. National FCV (1966)	October 12, 1951	5 years then exile
Juan Hernández	Sec. Gen. Aragua FCV (1958–62), Sec. Gen. National FCV (1962–65)	October 13, 1951	4 years then exile
Pedro Torres	National FCV leader (1947–48), Acting President FCV (1961–62), Sec. Gen. FCV (1967—)	February 23, 1952	4 years then exile
Armando González	Sec. Gen. Carabobo FCV (1945–48), President FCV (1962—)	May 3, 1952	3 years then exile
Eustacio Guevara	Sec. Agr. AD (1965–67)	October 22, 1952	3 years then exile
Máximo Acuña	Sec. Fin. FCV (1962—)	April 12, 1953	3 years then exile
Tomás Alberti	National AD campesino leader (1945–48, 1958–62)	April 12, 1953	3 years then exile
Ramón Quijada	President FCV (1947–48, 1959–62)	April 12, 1953	3 years then exile
Víctor Peñalever	AD campesino leader (1945–48), FCV Disciplinary Tribunal (1962–67)	March 17, 1955	2 years then exile

Source: Interviews: Torres, August 1961, Caracas; Morillo, Hernández, González, Acuña, June–August 1964, Caracas; Guevara, April 1966, Caracas.

The military coup d'état of November 24, 1948, which had become a counterrevolution under the undisputed leadership of Pérez Jiménez, had principally concerned itself in its initial stages with AD and that party's principal works, the organized labor movement and the agrarian reform. However, increasingly after 1952, other political groups and societal interests began to manifest resistance to the suppression of political rights endemic to the Pérez regime and joined in the clandestine opposition to the dictatorship. Such opposition grew to a crescendo as the dictator's first five-year term as president drew to a close toward the end of 1957. The spectacle of a government-manipulated plebiscite to continue Pérez' presidency, which took the place of elections in November of 1957, aroused a deep-rooted and widespread public reaction, which was sufficient to bring the opposition into the open, and augmented it at last with important factions within the church and the armed forces. The result, at the end of a bloody and tempestuous month of manifestations, was the flight of the dictator in the early morning hours of January 23, 1958.[19]

These events relate significantly to the concepts of authority legitimation and interest articulation, as earlier manifested in the AD regime. That government had lost its legitimacy among competing electoral elites because of an emphasis on articulating and responding to the interests of its own electoral clienteles. A loss of legitimacy among the new electoral elites acted to strengthen the opposition of traditional elites, so that by the time of the 1948 Agrarian Reform Law, the AD regime retained little or no legitimacy except among its own partisans. The military coup followed shortly thereafter.

Now, the Military Junta, by forcibly dislodging an incumbent regime (which in the eyes of most political elite groups was by then illegitimate) for a time acquired a certain tacit legitimacy of its own. However, the AD regime had very early acted to establish the electoral process as the central, authority-legitimating process in the polity, so that after the military coup in 1948, and especially after Pérez Jiménez emerged as unchallenged dictator of the country, the new electoral elites, such as those belonging to COPEI and the Unión Republicana Democrática (URD), conditioned their accordance of legitimacy to the regime on re-establishment of a competitive electoral process. In contrast, traditional elites supported the Pérez Jiménez regime because it had chastised the AD power usurpers and because it re-established, in an attenuated form, the personalistic, patrimonial form of rule to which they were accustomed.

When competitive electoral procedures failed to materialize under Pérez Jiménez, the result was a loss of regime legitimacy among the electoral groups: URD in 1952, and COPEI in 1957. When these political elites moved into opposition to the regime, they were drawn inevitably into a cooperative arrangement with AD's clandestine resistance organization, which had formed the core of opposition to the regime since early 1949, and welcomed the addition of broader-based political allies. The result, over time, was a return to a situation similar to pre-1945 conditions, in which a military-dominated, personalistic rule was opposed by a wide spectrum of challenging urban political elites, anxious to secure for themselves participation in the political decision-making process, who in turn were opposed by incumbent, traditional elites that profited from the patrimonial system. Furthermore, as in the 1945 coup, the regime finally collapsed when the opposition of significant groups fostered a break in the solid support of the traditional elites. First, elements in the progressive, urban wing of the church withdrew their legitimating support for the regime; and then, key military figures moved decisively into the opposition. The result was the coup of January 23, 1958.

V

AGRARIAN REFORM, 1958–1968

In the final days of the Pérez Jiménez regime the incumbent elites were showing signs of disintegration while the opposition forces were showing signs of revival. Among the signs of revival was the formation of a Patriotic Junta, signifying consolidation of the opposition to Pérez Jiménez within Venezuela, in which university students and young resistance activists took a leading role. The primary concrete accomplishment of the Junta was to organize a National Strike Committee, which in turn precipitated a nation-wide, general strike of three days that was instrumental in the downfall of the dictator.[1]

Among the opposition political parties, especially within the exiled national leadership of Acción Democrática (AD), there were important indications that AD intended to pursue a collaborative role with the other electoral elites, in order to establish viable limits for electoral competition within the political system. The result was an interparty pact, known as the agreement of "Punto Fijo." The pact pledged the competing electoral elites to responsible and restrained pursuit of electoral goals in the anticipated campaign and promised to negotiate the inclusion of all major parties—except the Communist party (PCV)—in a new coalition government under the leadership of whichever party won the presidency.

By January 22, 1958, important elements within the polity had organized around Admiral Wolfgang Larrazábal in order to bring pressure on the dictator to terminate his reign. The removal of Pérez Jiménez, it was hoped, would help restore public confidence in the professional armed forces. The last military support for the dictator vanished when Larrazábal offered positions on the Military Junta to two key officers. Following their acceptance, Larrazábal advised Pérez Jiménez to leave the country immediately. Pérez acted with alacrity on the Admiral's advice, managing to take his accumulated fortune with him as he flew off to the Dominican Republic shortly after midnight on January 23. Upon Larrazábal's announcement of the composition of the new Junta, the National Strike Committee reacted vociferously to the inclusion of two identified Perezjimenistas, whereupon the Admiral prudently replaced them with two representatives of the business community. The crisis of transition began to ebb.

With the return of the country's political and labor-movement exiles, and the establishment by the Junta of conditions for participation in a congressional and presidential election in December

Table 12. Election results, December 1958.

Party	Percentage of presidential vote	Number of deputies	Number of senators
AD	49	73	32
URD	27	34	11
COPEI	15	19	6
PCV	5	7	2

Source: Institute for the Comparative Study of Political Systems, *Venezuela: Election Factbook* (Washington: Operations and Policy Research, Inc., 1963), p. 17.

1958, reorganization of the parties began in earnest. The major parties moved to nominate their most prominent leaders. Rómulo Betancourt and Rafael Caldera were named by AD and COPEI; the Unión Republicana Democrática (URD), after assessing the candidacy of its own leader, Villalba, nominated Admiral Larrazábal. Despite several attempts from the military right wing to overthrow it, the Junta administered the nation and conducted it through the election of December 7, 1958, with results shown in Table 12.[2]

Rómulo Betancourt, the successful AD candidate, honoring the pre-election pact, formed a coalition cabinet with URD and COPEI participation. Inaugurated in February 1959, Betancourt continued to govern in coalition with COPEI after URD had broken away in November 1960, largely over the government's unfavorable attitude toward Fidel Castro.[3] Despite several threats to his regime from military rightists early in his presidency, as well as the open, violent opposition of the Communist and near-Communist left, Rómulo Betancourt survived innumerable assassination attempts and completed his full term in office, becoming the first popularly elected president in Venezuelan history to do so. Following the dissolution, because of terrorist activities, of the Communist party and the Marxist Movimiento Izquierdista Revo-

Table 13. Election results, December 1963.

Party	Percentage of presidential vote	Number of deputies	Number of senators
AD	31	65	24
COPEI	19	39	8
URD	16	26	7
FND[a]	15	14	3

Source: American Embassy, Caracas.

a. Frente Nacional Democrática, the personal vehicle of support for the senator and economist Arturo Uslar Pietri.

lucionario (MIR) in the summer of 1963, the AD-COPEI government administered congressional and presidential elections in December 1963. In a final, desperate attempt to thwart the electoral process, the terrorist left organization Fuerzas Armadas de Liberación Nacional (FALN), publicly announced that any citizens going to the polls would be shot.[4] But the general public defied the threat and voted in record numbers, with results as shown in Table 13.

President-elect Raúl Leoni, the AD party winner, faced a difficult task in the formation of a new government. COPEI, having gained considerably since the 1958 election, raised its price for continued participation in a coalition, seeking additional portfolios and a system of consultations in decision making. Betancourt, who had been well served by his coalition partners, favored an attempt to meet COPEI's price while bargaining it down to the minimum. Reluctant to thus bind himself, Leoni took office in February 1964 with the issue still hanging fire. He formed his Cabinet of AD loyalists and independents while continuing interparty negotiations with a view to the formation of a viable coalition. By March, COPEI had been mostly bypassed and had taken a position of autonomy in its congressional relationships with the Leoni government.

During the spring and summer of 1964, President Leoni continued to negotiate on a program of government and on distribution of Cabinet positions and presidentially appointed governorships. He needed to gain the adherence of URD and a third minor party, which could bring with them sufficient votes in the Chamber and Senate to give the government a working majority. This search culminated in late August 1964 with the signing of an agreed program of government between AD, URD, and Frente Nacional Democrática (FND).[5] Details were gradually worked out, and the Leoni administration, assuming the name of Gobierno de Ancha Base or Broad-Based Government, continued in this form until March 1966, when the FND, strained by internal conflict over the nature of its governmental participation, left the coalition. URD finally left the coalition late in April 1968, leaving AD the task of holding on through the December 1968 elections.

RENAISSANCE OF THE LABOR MOVEMENT AND THE PEASANT FEDERATION OF VENEZUELA

Following the overthrow of the dictator, a multiparty National Syndical Committee served as the immediate focus for reorganizing the Venezuelan labor movement. Leaders returning from exile and those emerging from underground formed themselves into regional and state reorganization committees. Communist, Marxist, and other leaders of the radical left, who had served as valuable and loyal allies during the ten years of clandestine effort to keep the labor movement from being destroyed, were as a matter of course included, along with labor leaders from AD, URD, and COPEI.

As the peasant movement reorganization committees fanned out into the rural areas, they encountered a situation fraught with sociopolitical tensions. Among the rural masses who had been reached by the agrarian reform of 1945–1948 and then displaced under Pérez Jiménez, there was an understandable militancy to recapture their benefits. In the several hundred cases of spontaneous invasions of land that occurred in 1958 and 1959, many took place on lands formerly under the agrarian reform program. Local syndicate leaders who had remained in clandestine positions throughout the dictatorship had quite naturally kept the peasants' resentment and the promise of retribution alive in their organizations. Returning state leaders found that this situation had developed its own impetus, so that to maintain their own positions of leadership, they had to respond to the widespread agitation from the peasantry.[6] Further, as political reorganization efforts penetrated the rural areas in connection with the 1958 elections, a competitive escalation of militancy developed among the leadership. If a leader was unable or unwilling to lead a land invasion or a machete-waving demonstration of peasant unrest, he was stigmatized by competing political leaders.[7]

Among the major labor organizations, the Peasant Federation (FCV) was the first to reorganize nationally. The First Peasant Congress was held in Caracas in June 1959, in a militant and aggressive atmosphere. Re-elected president of the Peasant Federation was Ramón Quijada, and elected along with him to the thirteen-man National Executive Committee were two Communist peasant leaders and one independent Marxist. AD, being the best-established party in the rural areas, kept control of the campesino movement, but friction increasingly developed between the Communist and non-Communist leadership over the pace and direction of events. A critical question for the leadership of the Peasant

Federation concerned its response to the existing incendiary pressures among the peasantry for drastic, if not violent, action: should the leaders try to exert pressure for more controlled and orderly activities?

In November 1959, the remainder of the Venezuelan labor movement was reorganized on a national scale at the Third Congress of Venezuelan Workers, at which the Confederation of Venezuelan Workers (CTV) was officially reconstituted. The leadership situation in the Confederation of Workers was much the same as in the Peasant Federation. An AD labor leader, José González Navarro, was elected president of the Executive Committee. Serving with him were Communist and other labor leaders.

By 1961, the basic problem for the overall trade union movement leadership had emerged as achieving a balance between militancy for the rights of members and responsibility toward the reformist government of Betancourt. In the field of agrarian reform this issue emerged quite clearly. Should the leadership of the Peasant Federation, through land invasions and demonstrations, militate for a more rapid and drastic agrarian reform program, which might threaten the reformist government by strengthening the hand of its political opponents on the right, who opposed land reform? Or should the leadership use restraint in the pace of its demands and cooperate with the government in solving the administrative problems of the agrarian reform program, which might enhance the long-term probability of success and minimize political opposition to land reform, but at the same time might hazard the loyalty of the militant elements among the peasant masses? It was a replay of the tension from 1945 to 1948 between authority legitimation and interest articulation. In time, the question seemed to be decided according to the party affiliation of the various labor leaders. Most AD and COPEI leaders (as well as URD leaders until they left the coalition in November 1960) opted to increase the government's chance of political survival by pursuing a cooperative, rather than a competitive, strategy. This decision was reinforced by the movement of the leftist parties into violent opposition to the government. However, some younger, action-oriented AD leaders joined in the leftward drift toward violence, being dissatisfied with the restraint necessary to keep the AD regime's legitimacy intact.

The party leadership that gave highest priority to maintaining the legitimacy to govern eventually won out over those who gave highest priority to the pursuit of mass clientele interests. Communist and other opposition leadership was purged from the Venezuelan labor movement at the Fourth Congress of Venezuelan Workers, held in November 1961. A similar reorganization of the Peasant Federation culminated, at the Second Peasant Congress of June 1962, in the election for the first time of the moderate AD-COPEI leadership.[8]

The re-emergence of the labor movement and the organizational efforts of, and competition among, peasant union leaders were reflected in a tremendous surge in the number of legally operating unions and their membership. Not only did the overall labor movement make a strong comeback following ten years of suppression, but the rural sector made an unprecedentedly vigorous showing as other major parties moved into the field where formerly only AD and the Communists had operated. The dimensions of this growth are reflected in Table 14.[9]

THE AGRARIAN REFORM LAW OF 1960

The Agrarian Reform Law, passed and promulgated in 1960, is the legal basis of the extensive agrarian reforms undertaken since that date, and for which Venezuela is widely noted. The great political struggle involved in the passage of the 1945 and 1948 legislation was not repeated in 1958–1959. Nor, for a number of reasons, was the law's easy passage unexpected. AD by then had an established record of advocacy for extensive agrarian reform; its mass base was firmly established in the rural areas first organized by it in 1936, and its record in office from 1945–1948 had given a clear indication of its propensity to act when empowered to

Table 14. Legally operating syndicates and their membership, 1958–1965.

Year	Peasant syndicates	Members	All syndicates	Members	Peasant syndicates as percentage of all syndicates
1958	130	4,586	901	—	16
1959	782	39,090	1,484	48,329	52
1960	1,813	91,599	2,651	109,585	68
1961	2,197	109,698	3,106	131,914	71
1962	2,632	130,677	3,668	160,835	72
1963	2,936	145,111	4,083	183,204	72
1964	3,156	156,193	—	—	—
1965	3,476	171,299	—	—	—

Source: Ministry of Labor, *Memoria* (Caracas: Imp. Nacional, 1959–1966).

do so. Moreover, the consensus on the need for agrarian reform was widely shared among Venezuela's other parties and many influential interest groups. This consensus, first generated during the 1940's, was retained more or less intact during the reactionary Pérez Jiménez years. Additional factors contributed to the momentum for a sweeping reform at this time. Above all was the existence of acute agitation in the countryside, especially in the form of land invasions, caused by the evictions under Pérez Jiménez and his reversals of earlier gains made by the peasantry. Finally, there were by this time ample legal precedents for a basic agrarian reform law, including the 1945 and 1948 legislation, and even the 1949 statute decreed by Pérez himself.

While the attention of professional politicians and peasant union organizers was concentrated on party reorganization and electoral activities in preparation for the 1958 election, a group of economists, lawyers, public administrators, and ex-Cabinet members initiated a series of conversations with officials in the National Agrarian Institute (IAN) and the Ministry of Agriculture (MAC) concerning a program of agrarian reform. When the group was formally organized into four committees, its initial findings and activities were brought to the attention of the governing Junta by the minister of agriculture, one of the group's original sponsors. The Junta approved of the study, and by Decree No. 371 of September 26, 1958, the group was formally authorized and established as the Agrarian Reform Commission, charged with the responsibility of recommending agrarian reform legislation.[10] In addition to having to consider legislative precedents from the 1945 and 1948 laws, the commission also had to evaluate the experience under the 1949 Agrarian Statute. At the outset, the commission was an aggregative body comprised of representatives of all political parties and philosophies, as well as of a wide range of Venezuelan interest groups concerned with agriculture. All political factions could therefore be brought to a consensus on the final version of the commission's proceedings. At the same time the law could be progressive, since it was largely framed within the context of the antecedents established in 1945 and 1948. Reform provisions in the draft law were thus pressed for, not as a matter of partisan position, but on the basis of established legal precedent and interparty consensus.

Following the December elections, and on into the spring of 1959, the latent political considerations in the commission's work became more overt; yet because of the nature of the coalition government being formed, it remained multipartisan. Víctor Giménez Landínez, the new minister of agriculture, began attending commission sessions, presenting the COPEI position on various aspects of the agrarian reform.[11] The original president of the Legal Subcommission, Ramón J. Velásquez, was appointed secretary-general of the presidency, being replaced in his position on the Agrarian Reform Commission by Salvador de la Plaza, a respected Communist scholar from the Central University. Carlos Rojas Gómez, head of the Agro-Technical Subcommission, was appointed to the Board of Directors of the Agrarian Institute, and he was replaced on the commission by the minister of agriculture for the 1945 AD government, Eduardo Mendoza Goiticoa.

108

The Economic Subcommission was particularly distinguished in its composition, from both a professional and a political point of view. Headed by the outstanding independent economist T. E. Carrillo Batalla, the Subcommission included Raúl Leoni, the AD president of the Senate; Giménez Landínez, the COPEI minister of agriculture; Alejandro Osorio, the independent president of the Agriculture and Livestock Bank (BAP); and Pompeyo Ríos, deputy director of the bank, who had been director of the Technical Institute for Immigration and Colonization (ITIC) land distribution program under the first AD government. The nature of the commission's members favored well-thought-out recommendations for an agrarian reform law, and their multiplicity of political viewpoints augured well for the viability of their legislative recommendations.

With only minor modifications, the commission's final draft was unanimously approved in a meeting of the Coalition Cabinet on July 17, 1959. It was formally presented to the Congress in August by the minister of agriculture and passed by the Senate, in its definitive version, on February 22, 1960.[12] A political triumph of multiparty consensus, the Agrarian Reform Law was opposed on its final passage only by the Communist party.[13] In a dramatic ceremony held on the historic battlefield of Carabobo, President Rómulo Betancourt signed the law into effect on March 5, 1960. Among the proud witnesses to the ceremony were representatives of the Peasant Federation and thousands of their followers. The new law that they saw promulgated established an ambitious and complex program of agrarian reform.[14]

The basic strategic objective of the Venezuelan program was to create a new class of small family farmowners out of the mass of conuqueros and other peasants. While there were many government programs in agriculture, including vigorous support for commercial operations, the agrarian reform program was designed to mold about 300,000 subsistence farm families into a productive sector of the national economy. The attempt was made by means of an integral approach to raising the farm standard of living. Asentamientos, or settlements, were established on public or private lands, through purchase or expropriation proceedings.[15] Government services were concentrated on these settlements, which by 1968 numbered over eight hundred. The land was parcelized; and housing, medical facilities, water and sanitation systems, market roads, and extension services were funneled into the *asentados* (settlers). A specially designed campesino credit program was run by the Agriculture Bank, in addition to its existing price-support programs.

In an operational sense, only a few of the eight hundred asentamientos functioned with this full panoply of coordinated services. To start an asentamiento from scratch demanded not only careful sequential planning within each service program but a high degree of coordinated interservice planning and programing. Herein lay the most difficult aspect of such an ambitious and broad-gauge socioeconomic program: the provision of sustained, skilled, and properly supported public administrative services. In the Venezuelan case, the difficulties were compounded, as suggested in Table 15, by the fragmented and overlapping responsibilities of the many government ministries and autonomous agencies.[16]

Although this array of programs and services generally covered all rural areas, the Agrarian Institute, which bore primary responsibility for the agrarian reform program, concentrated most of its activities on asentamientos. The Agrarian Institute could therefore be considered the drive-wheel of the Venezuelan agrarian reform, with the Agriculture Bank's peasant credit program and the Ministry of Agriculture extension service comprising its major elements of support. Since 1958, the asentamiento program has directly affected the lives of as many as 100,000 peasant families, bringing them slowly into the main channels of the national economy.[17]

The large-scale land distribution that occurred in 1959 and 1960 was the result of intense peasant pressures, often in the form of land invasions. Although shortly after the passage of the Agrarian

Table 15. Structural-functional outline of the Venezuelan agrarian reform program, 1960–1968.

Function	Institution
Land acquisition, settlement planning, and financial administration	National Agrarian Institute (IAN)
Farm credit and marketing assistance	Agriculture and Livestock Bank (BAP) Venezuelan Development Corporation (CVF) National Agrarian Institute (IAN)
Extension services and technical research	Ministry of Agriculture and Livestock (MAC) Council on Rural Welfare (CBR) Ministry of Education (ME) Shell Experimental Station (SSPA) College of Agriculture (UCV)
Construction of housing and community centers	Worker's Bank (BO) Ministry of Health and Social Welfare (MSAS) National Agrarian Institute (IAN)
Construction of penetration roads, irrigation projects, water and sewage systems	Ministry of Public Works (MOP) National Institute of Sanitation Works (INOS) Venezuelan Development Corporation (CFV) Ministry of Agriculture and Livestock (MAC) National Agrarian Institute (IAN)

Source: John P. Clark and John D. Powell, "To Struggle Is My Destiny: A Three-Month Study of the Venezuelan Agrarian Reform Program," mimeographed (Johns Hopkins University School of Advanced International Studies Library, Washington, D.C., 1961), pp. 10–15.

Reform Law, the Peasant Federation disavowed the further use of land invasions as an instrument of pressure, analysts have argued that any evaluation of the program of the Venezuelan agrarian reform must recognize that many government decisions have necessarily been in the nature of after-the-fact acceptance or rejection of the actions of local agrarian syndicates.[18] Since 1961, the program has steadily shifted away from responding to local, ad hoc pressures from the syndicates toward a centrally controlled process. In the opinion of observers of the early stages of the agrarian reform, the initial responses to the most intense peasant pressures had largely relieved those pressures by the spring of 1961, allowing the government to move toward centralization of the program.

Orchestration of the various budgets and policy programs of the multiple agencies and institutions involved in agrarian reform activities has been a major problem. An Agrarian Reform Coordinating Committee was created in the 1960 law, under the chairmanship of the minister of agriculture. After several attempts at utilizing this administrative device, it fell into disuse because of basic policy conflicts among its participating members. These conflicts derived partly from internal competition within the various coalition governments of Venezuela since 1958, in that the Ministry of Agriculture has been under the control of COPEI (1959–1963) and, more recently, the FND (1964–1966); while the Agrarian Institute and the Agriculture Bank, with autonomous budgets, have remained under the control of AD. Agrarian reform program coordination, such as it is, has been carried out by the president's Coordinating and Planning Board (CORDIPLAN), which reviews and makes recommendations on each agency's item-line budget requests.

POLITICAL INTERPRETATION

The tension between the authority-legitimation and the interest-articulation functions within the AD-Peasant Federation mobilization system at this time was apparent. In general, it has been widely recognized that the performance of AD when in power from 1945–1948 was quite different from its performance when in power after 1958. While articulating the same interests and pursuing the same goals in the sixties, it went about its business in a very different manner. Depending on the criteria used, this development has been characterized as evidence of political maturation by some, and as a sell-out of principles by others. Rather, in view of the tension between the twin functions of the mobilization system, it seems that the top leadership in AD, having learned the hard way that emphasis on interest-articulation might cost them their legitimacy, subordinated that function to authority legitimation whenever, in the post-1958 period, a choice between the two seemed to be forced on them.

The first significant indication of this implicit policy was the decision of the AD leadership to govern in coalition with other electoral elites in the system. Though this was not always an easy task, AD for a decade managed to keep other parties involved with its governmental responsibilities. In addition, the various AD regimes managed to retain sufficient legitimacy among other elites, including the decisive military elites, to avoid a coup d'état during that period. This is an historic accomplishment for a nonauthoritarian regime in Venezuela.

A corollary indication of AD's changed style is shown in its contrasting approaches to agrarian reform in the earlier and later periods. In the first period, de facto reform was pursued in an aggressive and highly partisan manner, and the de jure reform contemplated in the 1948 law was almost entirely a product of the leadership and policy decisions of a single party. In contrast, the 1960 law was the product of a deliberate, extended process of consultation and consensus among other electoral elites, and even among representatives of traditional elites. The result embodied legitimacy at the price of restraint in the partisan pursuit of peasant interests. In carrying out the agrarian reform program, speed in land distribution was, after a brief period of activity, rejected in favor of an "integral" approach; and responsiveness to local syndicate pressures was ultimately rejected in favor of a centrally controlled, planned process. These procedures, it was argued, were necessary to retain the consensus of political elites, and to demonstrate and maintain the legitimacy of the Betancourt and Leoni regimes. They seem perfectly rational from the point of view of preserving a problem-solving system that has done infinitely more for the Venezuelan peasantry than any regime dominated by traditional elites.

However, the price of retaining the legitimating support of other elites in the Venezuelan polity was the periodic loss of younger AD leaders who were particularly oriented toward interest-articulation—not only for the peasant clienteles of AD, but for many others. These leaders either disagreed that the situation forced a choice between legitimacy and interest pursuit or, if they agreed that a choice was necessary, favored the latter. The result has been a cyclical splintering off of militant, interest-oriented AD leadership—in 1960, 1962, and finally a massive loss during the 1967–1968 crisis.

In the meantime, the agrarian reform program, which started during the early Betancourt administration with a tremendous burst of initial land distributions in areas of greatest peasant pressure, had by the end of the sixties slowed down to a calculated, orderly, and time-consuming process. Advocates of regime-legitimacy, as well as technical specialists, take this as evidence of maturity and responsibility in the conduct of so vital a public program. Others take it as evidence that the AD leadership has "sold out" the interests of its clienteles in order to maintain respectability among the political opposition to agrarian reform.

Part Two   *An Analysis of the Mobilization System*

VI

THE PEASANT FEDERATION AND THE RURAL PROBLEM-SOLVING SYSTEM

The peasant-urban mobilization alliance can be regarded from two perspectives. Seen from the point of view of the urban elites, the alliance with the peasantry functioned to mobilize political support; specifically, to ensure peasant votes. Since these votes were paid for in patronage or agrarian reform benefits, the alliance was in effect a patronage machine within the larger context of national politics. Seen from the point of view of the peasantry, however, their alliance with the urban elite functioned to mobilize governmental resources to resolve a host of environmental problems, specifically, to achieve an integrated agrarian reform program, which was paid for in votes. In other words, the alliance was and is a rural problem-solving machine. Mobilization viewed from the peasant perspective is rarely analyzed in the literature, though it is a necessary complement to national political perspectives. Therefore, the emphasis now shifts from political events on the national level to rural problems that affect the daily lives of the peasant masses, before returning to the more familiar territory of national politics. The central structure in the rural problem-solving system was the Peasant Federation of Venezuela (FCV), which through its leadership had a network of linkages to other components in the political system—national, state, and local.

FORMAL ORGANIZATION OF THE PEASANT FEDERATION

In 1956, the latest year of the Pérez Jiménez regime for which data are available, there were in Venezuela 79 peasant unions, with a claimed membership of 1,176. A decade later—after eight years of growth under democratically elected governments—the Peasant Federation consisted of 3,476 legally registered local unions with an estimated 550,000 peasant members.[1] Such a spectacular increase in size reflected not only differing governmental postures but an absolute increase in the size and complexity of the peasant union movement. As its name implies, the Peasant Federation is a national federation of regional and local peasant union organizations. Its formal organizational outlines have remained approximately the same as those established at the First Campesino Congress in June 1959.[2] The Campesino Congress is the supreme statutory body of the peasant union movement. While the federation has from its beginnings been dominated by Acción Democrática (AD), executive power has since 1962 been shared with COPEI peasant leaders, and since 1964 with campesino union leaders affiliated with the Unión Republicana Democrática (URD).[3]

It has become customary to convene a national congress about once every three years. At this time a general program of action is discussed and adopted, and members of the National Executive Committee are elected. The original statutes called for a yearly national convention at which the members of the Executive Committee and the National Disciplinary Tribunal were to be named, but the practice fell into disuse because of its cost and potential divisiveness.

Another organizational body is the National Directors Council, which may be called semiannually as a body of consultation (though it has met only rarely in recent years), and which supposedly has the same powers as the national convention. It is comprised of the National Executive Committee, the National Disciplinary Tribunal, and the executive committees of the various regional organizations.

The supreme body of permanent executive authority is the National Executive Committee, elected at the Campesino Congress. In recent years it has consisted of the president, vice president, secretary-general, secretary of organization, agricultural secretary, secretary for agricultural centers and cooperatives, secretary for labor affairs, secretary of finance, secretary for culture and publications, and two alternates having voting power in committee meetings in the absence of the regular officers.[4] The alternates vote in accordance with the instructions of the absent officer in meetings of the Executive Committee and also, if his absence is extended, perform the formal tasks of the officer until his return. The National Disciplinary Tribunal, whose function is to investigate and serve as "honest broker" in internal disciplinary disputes, is rarely convened, and such matters are normally handled by the members of the Executive Committee.

On the state level, the form of organization is called the Sectional. The state organizations are run by executive committees, which normally consist of a secretary-general, an agrarian secretary, a claims secretary, a finance secretary, and a secretary of culture and propaganda. These executive committees are elected during the regional conventions, which are held just prior to a Campesino Congress; thus, the tenure of office for a regional official is almost identical with that of the national officials, or approximately three years.

The more than three thousand local syndicates belonging to the Peasant Federation are organized along lines roughly parallel to those of the state and national bodies. All local unions have the same five basic offices as do the state organizations which are grouped into an executive committee commonly called the Board of Directors. As the unions vary in size from just under forty members to several thousand, very large unions may elect additional officers, such as minutes and correspondence secretaries or cooperative affairs secretaries, and some even elect alternates to the Junta.

In order to obtain more precise information on local peasant unions, their leadership, and the nature of the problems that confront them, I designed and directed a survey early in 1966. The data contained in the following tables derive from that survey and are frequently compared with comparable data on state and national leaders obtained during interviews with them.[5] As of early 1966, the average size of a local syndicate was one hundred and fifty-three members, spread evenly over the range reported. However, as shown in Table 16, the local unions affiliated with AD tended to be the largest. The size phenomena reflected in Table 16 are consistent with the estimates of national Peasant Federation officials to the effect that of the 550,000 members, about 65 percent belong to AD-dominated unions, 30 percent to COPEI-led ligas, and about 5 percent to URD syndicates.[6] In brief, this is the orga-

Table 16. Party affiliation of union leader related to estimated membership of local.

Estimated membership of local peasant union	Party affiliation of union leader (percent)			
	AD	COPEI	URD	Total
39 or less	2.9	3.8	—	6.7
40 to 99	16.2	11.4	3.8	30.4
100 to 199	20.9	5.7	—	26.6
200 or more	21.9	2.9	—	24.8
N = 118				88.5[a]

Source: My surveys and interviews cited hereafter as "FCV survey."

a. The total percentage of responses in this and other tables may be less than 100 percent owing to "don't know" responses, refusals to answer, or other factors.

nizational outline of the Peasant Federation. The reach of the federation, central element in the rural problem-solving system, stretches from Caracas, where its eighteen national officers are located, throughout about 3,000 rural communities, where its 550,000 members reside.

PEASANT LEADERSHIP LINKAGES WITH OTHER PROBLEM-SOLVING COMPONENTS

The Peasant Federation is tied into the political system by virtue of a network of linkages with political parties and governmental structures, including local, state, and national offices, both elected and appointed, and a large number of bureaucratic agencies. The federation leadership provides the mechanism through which these linkages are established, maintained, and utilized during the problem-solving process. Of all the types of linkage in the system, the political are by far the most important.

Leaders of the Peasant Federation at all levels manifest a considerable history of affiliation with the political parties of their choice. More important than the fact of party affiliation, however, is the nature of that relationship, because of its effect on the place of the federation in the overall problem-solving system. Peasant union leaders are not merely party members. They are party leaders, holding party offices at local, state, and national levels. The party roles they fill are related to their roles as peasant union leaders, being for the most part positions on the local, state, and national agrarian bureaus of their particular party, or service as the agrarian or labor secretary of various party executive committees.

Among the 118 local peasant union leaders in the sample, it was found that 25.4 percent hold, or had held, a local party office; and an additional 5.1 percent had held more than one local party office. That is to say, almost one-third of the local leaders interviewed had simultaneously played roles in union and party. On the state and national levels, dual role-holding is universal: all the state leaders interviewed, and all national Peasant Federation officers during the period from mid-1964 through mid-1966, simultaneously held positions in their particular political party. Thus it seems that the marriage between the peasant movement and political parties is symbolized in a fusion of leadership roles. This network of fused roles constitutes the most important linkage that the Peasant Federation maintains with the rest of the structural components of the rural problem-solving system.

The party linkages of peasant union leaders provide them with important channels of structural access to key decision-making bodies, especially at the national level. The precise channel and the actual decision-making body to which access is available depend on the party in question. Furthermore, whether the party happens to be a member of the governmental coalition or is a member of the opposition has an obvious and direct bearing on the nature of its access.

AD, as the major political party in Venezuela, held the presidency and was dominant in the several coalition governments in power from 1959 to 1969. Campesino movement leaders affiliated with AD, therefore, have for a decade enjoyed continuous access to important decision-making councils. Holding a fused union-party role, national peasant leaders affiliated with AD have been incorporated into party decision-making arenas where they found themselves in a position to represent campesino interests. For example, the national AD Agrarian Bureau, which plays an important advisory role in the setting of party policy on agrarian reform budget-making, is composed of sixteen members. In mid-1966 ten of these were leaders in the peasant union movement. The president of the Peasant Federation (1962—   ), Armando R. González, and the national AD agrarian secretary (1965—   ), Eustacio Guevara, were members of the elite fifteen-member Executive Committee of AD, which met regularly with President Leoni each Wednesday afternoon.

The access benefits that have accrued to campesino leaders affiliated with COPEI and URD have varied with their parties' relation to the coalition governments formed by the AD presidents since 1958. In the Venezuelan political system, the president is elected by the largest number of votes cast, and the Congress by a complex system of proportional representation.[7] The AD presidents, Betancourt (1958–1963) and Leoni (1964–1968), found it necessary to form coalition Cabinets in order to attract the congressional votes needed to pass legislation and budgetary requests. Thus, from 1958 through 1963, when COPEI was a member of the governing coalition, the minister of agriculture and livestock, Víctor Giménez

Landínez, was a member of COPEI, appointed by President Betancourt as part of the price for bringing COPEI into government ranks and keeping it there. During this period, therefore, COPEI campesino leaders enjoyed access to this and other key decision-makers by virtue of their common party linkages. From early 1964 to early 1969, when COPEI was out of the coalition, its campesino leaders were forced to shift to other channels for structural access to agrarian reform decision-making.[8]

The campesino union leaders affiliated with URD, who enjoyed access during the 1958–1960 period, when URD formed part of the first Betancourt government, were placed at a severe disadvantage when their party left the coalition and disassociated itself from the Confederation of Venezuelan Workers (CTV) as well. Links with the formal labor movement, which might have provided URD campesino leaders with alternative routes of access to important decision-making areas, were thus closed off. Since re-entering the government coalition formed by President Leoni in 1964, URD has also rejoined the Confederation of Venezuelan Workers, which has once more opened up important structural channels to the decision-making process. From 1964 to April 1968 the Ministry of Labor and the Development Ministry were in the hands of URD-affiliated Cabinet members.

Other channels of access for Peasant Federation leaders to important decision-making circles are not dependent solely on party affiliation but are based on law. Thus, under the terms of the Agrarian Reform Law, two members of the five-man Board of Directors of the National Agrarian Institute (IAN) must be named by the Peasant Federation. Since 1962, one of these members has been named by AD, and one by COPEI. In addition, since its renaissance in 1959, the Peasant Federation has held a nonvoting position on the Board of Directors of the Agriculture and Livestock Bank (BAP). At the request of the Peasant Federation, President Leoni in May 1965 gave its representative voting privileges on the bank's Board of Directors. Its representative has customarily been an AD leader. In addition to these important decision-making posts in the National Agrarian Institute and the Agriculture Bank, which are two of the principal government agencies concerned with the agrarian reform program, the Peasant Federation is also represented in the third principal reform agency, the Ministry of Agriculture (MAC), serving on a variety of agricultural product boards and advisory committees.[9] These positions are filled by leaders from all three parties. Finally, the Peasant Federation is entitled to representation on the National Agrarian Reform Coordinating Committee, established by law to effect cooperation and combined planning among the many agencies concerned with various aspects of agrarian reform.

Thus, peasant union leaders are linked, through political parties, with certain decision-making bodies in the executive branch of government; and further access to the executive branch is possible through direct channels of entry that have, by law and decree, been established for Peasant Federation officers. In addition to the political and legal access thus made available to peasant union leaders, further avenues of influence in the political system have been established through the electoral process. Among the local peasant union leaders in my sample, 15.2 percent had been elected to local governmental or law enforcement positions, which extended still further their knowledge of, and influence in, municipal and county governments. Of the state Peasant Federation officials interviewed, 39.1 percent had been elected or appointed to public offices at the local or state level of government. The twenty-four national peasant leaders interviewed included five who had been, or were at the time, elected members of their state legislative assemblies. Two national AD leaders, one COPEI, and one URD leader, were members of the national Chamber of Deputies at the time of interview. As members of Congress, these leaders sat on important committees, such as agriculture and labor, which put them in a position to shape and influence legislation and appropriations of direct concern to the campesino membership of the Peasant Federation. They were also in a position to introduce bills in the Chamber, to participate in floor debate and speech-making, and otherwise to act as representatives of the peasant masses.

In summation, peasant leaders at all levels of the Peasant Federation hierarchy—local, state, and national—have established an impressive network of linkages with the major Venezuelan political parties and with the executive and legislative branches of local, state, and national governments. By virtue of their multiple roles, Peasant Federation leaders find themselves able to move more or less freely among decision-making groups in the peasant union movement, in the multiparty system, and in government, from the most limited local forum up to the office of the president. The movement of these role-fused leaders among the decision-making arenas has woven threads of mutual influence and interdependence that bind the Peasant Federation tightly into the rural problem-solving system.

LEADERSHIP OF THE PEASANT FEDERATION

In general, the further down one proceeds through the federation hierarchy of national, state, and local leaders, the larger the pool of characteristics shared by the leader with his followers. This pattern held for every socioeconomic indicator measured in the study. The comparative level of education achieved by the various strata, for instance, is shown in Table 17. It is interesting to note that while the Peasant Federation leadership was better educated than its followers, it was also somewhat younger. The average age of the peasant respondents in the three samples was forty-one years, while local federation leaders averaged forty, state leaders thirty-seven, and national leaders thirty-eight years of age.

In addition to varying levels of education, and probably related to them, notable differences appeared in the social origins of federation leaders at the various levels. Local leaders came overwhelmingly from peasant families; state and national leaders did so to

125

Table 17. Comparative educational level of FCV leaders and members (percent).

Level of education	FCV leaders			Peasant samples		
	National	State[a]	Local	Asentados	Nonasentados	Farm laborers
No school	—	4.3	30.5	66.5	52.5	50.0
Some primary	4.5	17.4	45.7	23.6	32.1	31.3
Complete primary	68.1	52.1	18.6	1.4	3.6	4.0
Some secondary	36.3	21.7	4.2 ·	0.5	0.7	2.0
	N = (24)	(23)	(118)	(191)	(183)	(166)

Sources: FCV survey. Peasant sample data are from a survey conducted in October–November by the Massachusetts Institute of Technology and the Central University of Venezuela, cited hereafter as CONVEN.

a. State is used instead of *Seccional* because in all but two cases the units coincide.

a much lesser degree. Many state leaders were found to come from small business backgrounds, such as storekeepers and laborer families, while national leaders who came from nonpeasant families tended to emerge from laboring or professional backgrounds, as shown in Table 18.

Table 18. Father's occupation: comparison of local, state, and national leaders of the FCV (percent).

Father's occupation	Local	State	National
Campesino	83.9	56.5	45.8
Small business	5.9	21.7	8.3
Laborer	3.4	8.7	20.8
Professional	1.7	—	16.6
Large landowner	—	4.3	4.1
Other	—	4.3	4.1
N =	(118)	(23)	(24)

Source: FCV survey.

There were also differences in the branch of the labor movement with which the various strata of Peasant Federation leadership were first affiliated. Local leaders manifested little experience in labor activity other than peasant unions, whereas national, and especially state, leaders reported a great deal of experience in other branches, as indicated in Table 19.

Although local, state, and national leaders emerged from somewhat varying family backgrounds and experiences in the Venezuelan labor movement, they nevertheless seemed to be products

Table 19. Comparative labor movement background of local, state, and national leaders of the FCV (percent).

Branch of labor movement first joined	Local	State	National
Agriculture	89.8	43.4	59.0
Transportation	1.7	13.0	4.5
Construction	2.5	26.0	—
Industrial	—	13.0	22.7
Petroleum	1.7	4.2	9.0
Other	1.7	—	4.5
$N =$	(118)	(23)	(24)

Source: FCV survey.

of the same recruitment process. By comparing the period of time in which leaders were associated with their political party, with the labor movement (whatever branch), and with the Peasant Federation, a clear sequential pattern emerges as shown in Table 20. This pattern revealed that federation leaders first affiliated with their party, later became active in labor affairs, and still later became active in the peasant union movement. This sequence of associations supports the hypothesis that political parties have served as the primary recruiting instrument for labor and peasant union leaders.

Table 20. Associational sequence in the recruitment of
FCV leaders.

	Average years of affiliation		
Leadership level	Political party	Labor movement	Peasant Federation
National ($N = 24$)	17	16	14
State ($N = 23$)	16	14	8
Local ($N = 118$)	14	8	7

Source: FCV survey.

Thus, the political ties of the federation leadership are of the
utmost importance, and a number of politically significant differences within and among the various leadership strata can be demonstrated. In fact, from what is known of the historical development of the Venezuelan labor movement, particularly of the peasant
union movement, one would expect there to be important differences in the characteristics of the union leadership affiliated with
the different political parties active in this field. Among the three
parties considered here—AD, COPEI, and URD—each has evolved
its labor movement relationship in a distinct manner. AD and
its organizational forebears can truly be considered the historical
founders and stewards of the Venezuelan labor movement. AD's
activity in this field, which dates back to 1936, has consistently
been associated with the major national labor organization, the
Confederation of Venezuelan Workers, with which the Peasant Federation has been affiliated since 1947. COPEI, on the other hand,
only came into existence in 1946, and it entered the labor movement chiefly in order to combat the influence of Communist leaders,
only turning seriously to organizing peasant unions after 1958.
URD, which was founded in the same period as COPEI, managed
to attract established union leaders who were already active in
the AD-dominated labor movement, whereby it gained an experi-

enced cadre of national leaders. But URD, which has experienced an extended "identity crisis" in recent years, disassociated itself from the Confederation of Workers, the mainstream of Venezuelan labor, which it has only recently (1964) rejoined. By mid-1966, therefore, URD was in a period of rebuilding its network of state and local leaders, especially in the peasant union field. As a consequence, one political characteristic of the peasant leadership was an age difference in the leaders associated with the various parties. The AD leaders at every level were relative "old-timers" compared with the COPEI and URD leaders, as evidenced in Table 21.

Table 21. Party affiliation related to age of FCV leaders at local, state, and national levels.

Party affiliation	Average age of FCV leaders		
	Local	State	National
AD	42	44	46
COPEI	38	33	33
URD	28	25	35

Source: FCV survey.

The URD rebuilding process was reflected in the ages of its leaders at the various strata, with its most mature leaders engaged in the task of recruiting younger leaders at the state and local level.

I was also interested in the average number of years a leader had been affiliated with his political party, as well as the number of years of experience he had in the labor movement. Three conclusions emerge from the data in Table 22: the strikingly greater experience in the labor movement exhibited by AD leaders at the state level; the exception of the national URD leaders to the party-labor movement-Peasant Federation recruitment sequence; and the impact of COPEI's program of recruiting vigorous young state and

Table 22. Party affiliation related to party and labor movement longevity of FCV leaders at local, state, and national levels.

Party affiliation	Average years in party			Average years in labor movement		
	Local	State	National	Local	State	National
AD	17	22	24	10	20	24
COPEI	14	9	13	4	8	10
URD	8	8	14	—	8	16

Source: FCV survey.

national leaders. The presence of experienced union leaders at the state level in AD ranks resulted from the purge of radical leadership from the Peasant Federation in 1962 and its replacement with more moderate party loyalists from other branches of the labor movement. The URD situation was unusual in that, since it recruited labor leaders who were already active in the movement, by 1966 these leaders had been active in union affairs longer than in party affairs.

At the national and state levels, the leaders from all three parties had such a great deal of experience in labor affairs that they were clearly union professionals. At the local level, however, where 83.9 percent of the leadership sample responded "farmer" when asked what they considered their primary occupation, union leadership was a derivative, or secondary, occupational role. Among the 550,000 campesinos who belonged to the Peasant Federation, only about 20,000 of them were local leaders, so that the role of syndicate leader, while secondary in nature, was likely to be highly "visible" or noticeable in rural communities. This visibility may well have magnified differences in local leadership, probably in favor of those affiliated with AD. Local AD leaders, on the average, were active in the Peasant Federation more than twice the number

Table 23. Party affiliation of union leaders related to number of other union offices held (percent)[a]

Other union offices held	Party affiliation of union leader			
	AD	COPEI	URD	Total
None	29.0	19.0	5.0	53.0
One local office	21.0	7.0	3.0	31.0
More than one office	13.0	3.0	—	16.0
($N = 118$)				100.0

Source: FCV survey.

a. Other, that is, than the office held at the time of interview.

of years of their COPEI counterparts. In addition, AD leaders held more local offices in the peasant union movement than did other leaders, as shown in Table 23.

At the local level, therefore, the Peasant Federation leaders affiliated with AD are likely to be perceived by the rural population as especially experienced and authoritative in peasant union affairs. This also holds true at the state, and especially at the national, level of federation leadership. There it was found, as shown in Table 24, that the leaders affiliated with AD were well-established figures in the history of the peasant union movement.

Table 24. Party affiliation of state and national FCV leaders related to mean number of years in the peasant movement.

Leadership strata	Years in peasant movement		
	AD	COPEI	URD
State FCV	10	7	8
National FCV	18	9	9

Source: FCV survey.

PEASANT MEMBERSHIP IN THE FEDERATION

Membership in the federation cuts across economic and tenure strata within the peasantry. There are relatively rich peasants and there are poor peasants; there are smallholders and there are landless laborers; there are tenants and there are sharecroppers; and there are squatters with no securely defined tenure status of any kind. The common characteristic of these peasant members is that in terms of the traditional rural social stratification system, they,

Table 25. Land tenure status of local union members as estimated by their local union leaders (percent).

| Tenure status | Leaders who estimate that, for each tenure status, there are among their members— | | |
	"Many"	"Few"	"None"
Smallholders	14.4	23.7	27.1
Tenant farmers	13.6	12.7	39.8
Sharecroppers	10.2	22.0	35.6
Day laborers	33.1	27.1	11.0
Squatters	46.6	13.6	9.3
(N = 118)			

Source: FCV survey.

the tillers of the land, are at the bottom of the ladder; and in terms of levels of income among various groups in the Venezuelan national economy, they are in a similar position.

The heterogeneity of the Peasant Federation membership, in terms of tenure types, has retarded the development of functional specificity in organizational activities. That is, unless a local union is composed exclusively of smallholders, or day laborers, or sharecroppers, or tenants, local union activity must seek to meet the needs of more than one special interest. A glance at Table 25 will demonstrate the task facing local leaders in designing programs to meet the special needs of particular tenure types. Not only were all tenure types included in the peasant membership, but it was a proportionally representative cross-section of all tenure types found in rural Venezuela, with squatters and day laborers being rather more numerous than other types. This reflects the policy of the federation to recruit among all peasants in a community, and not to recruit on a specialized basis. Thus, local unions have theoretically been responsible for meeting a wide variety of special needs. Moreover, not only were tenure types mixed into the same local unions, but many peasants could not be clearly placed into different categories of tenure status. The most common type of peasant in rural Venezuela, as the data suggest, is the so-called conuquero, the slash-and-burn squatter who combines subsistence farming with part-time or seasonal work for other farmers as a day laborer. Thus, unions are faced with the task of representing a wide range of specialized interests, some of which shift according to varying crop cycles. The response of the unions has been to focus on collective, communitywide needs rather than on a variety of specific, tenure-derived problems.

First of the generalized problems is poverty. Data on poverty are found in a survey code named CONVEN, conducted in 1963 by scholars from Massachusetts Institute of Technology and the Central University of Venezuela.[10] Among its three peasant sample groups—peasants living on agrarian reform settlements (asentados), peasants living not on such settlements but in the same county (nonasentados), and peasants employed on commercial farms at the time of the survey *(jornaleros)*—the median reported income ranged from $44 to $89 per month and supported an average family of 5.6 persons. Furthermore, 38 percent of the asentado sample fell below the $44 median point, as did 33 percent of the nonasentado sample. Though such income levels may compare favorably with cash incomes in rural Africa, Asia, and other parts of Latin America, they place these peasants in the lowest decile of reported heads-of-family median income in Venezuela. Other indications of common, shared peasant problems are a high rate of affliction with gastrointestinal diseases (82 percent reported in 1961), a high rate of illiteracy for Venezuela (61.4 percent in the CONVEN samples), and squalid housing conditions.[11] For the purpose of a systematic analysis of the process by which such problems are handled, they are referred to here simply as "environmental" problems. It is recognized that some of them derive from the biological matrix of peasant life, and some from the sociocultural ma-

Figure 2.   The rural problem-solving system.

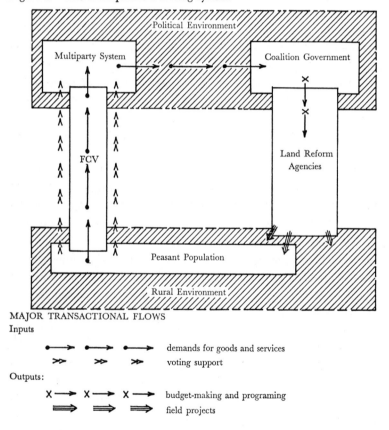

MAJOR TRANSACTIONAL FLOWS
Inputs
demands for goods and services
voting support
Outputs:
budget-making and programing
field projects

trix; but all impinge on the individual peasant and his family, and are indifferent to type of tenure or level of income.

The peasant-urban alliance was, from the peasant point of view, the principal rural problem-solving system. The complex system of transactions between peasant masses and urban political elites is diagramed in Figure 2.

Certain aspects of the rural environment posed problems for peasants. Interacting with local representatives of the federation, peasants sought to solve those problems by placing demands on the government, through the federation, and simultaneously by supporting the government through votes for particular political parties. The political party system, through coalition governments, formulated policies and programs that responded to the demands made of them by their various electoral clienteles, including the peasantry. Programs such as an integral agrarian reform, when supported over time with budgetary resources and executed through the administrative and bureaucratic arms of the government, had an impact on the rural environment. The changes wrought in the rural environment affected the peasantry, leading either to a refinement of demands for better solutions to the original problems, or to a heightened perception of problems that had previously received a lower priority. Subsequent peasant activities through the federation formed a problem-solving feedback loop and, through the electoral process, provided continuing information and support for governments committed to sustained rural problem-solving.

VII

THE GENERATION AND TRANSMISSION OF DEMANDS AND SUPPORTS

Essential to an understanding of any problem-solving process is the identification and assessment of the actual problems dealt with. Assuming that specific problems vary from community to community in both character and intensity, my survey of local Peasant Federation of Venezuela (FCV) leaders included a number of items designed to provide such information. It was further assumed that to generate problem-solving behavior, a particular situation has to be recognized and defined as a problem. Therefore, my approach to the local leadership was direct: "What do you consider the greatest problem facing the peasants in your community?" The responses appear in Table 26. The data indicate that after six years of concentrated effort at agrarian reform under Presidents Betancourt and Leoni, a basic desire for land and for an effective governmental program to obtain it still existed. In addition to land, a variety of other physical needs, such as roads and water supplies, were mentioned by local peasant union leaders as seriously confronting the members of their union. The specific problems were concentrated in the areas of health and basic living conditions, and reflected both the presence of environmental difficulties and the absence, in most rural communities, of basic public goods and services designed to overcome these difficulties.

Previous research had indicated that the range of problems mentioned in Table 26 was to be expected. In order to assess more precisely the relative gravity of each of these problems, the respondents were read a prepared list of typical rural disadvantages and asked whether, for the members of their local union, each condition was very serious, not very serious, or no problem.[1] Although local federation leaders had some differences of opinion as to which problem was the most serious in their particular neigh-

Table 26. Most serious problem in rural areas of
Venezuela according to local FCV leaders (percent).

Greatest problem	Leaders citing
Lack of sufficient land	28.0
Inefficiencies in agrarian reform	17.8
Lack of roads	11.9
Lack of potable water supply	11.0
Lack of agricultural credits	6.8
Lack of schools and teachers	5.1
Unsanitary, poor housing	5.1
Farm-related problems[a]	4.2
Lack of medical facilities	3.4
($N = 118$)	

Source: FCV survey.

a. Including lack of fertilizers and hybrid seeds,
fencing, machinery.

borhood, there was a remarkable degree of consensus on the fact
that a cluster of problem-conditions—lack of land, proper housing,
medical facilities, credit, and sanitary drinking water—were very
serious for their peasant constituents' as Table 27 demonstrates.
These problems can thus be considered the basic conditioning factors
in the process of rural problem-solving. They constitute the problematic elements in the rural environment that generate the activity
necessary to energize the problem-solving system and which provide
the basic set of goals toward which that system is working.

PEASANT PROBLEM-SOLVING BEHAVIOR

These problem conditions can be related to a wide variety of peasant behavior—some of it ineffective from the point of view of
solving the problems, but much of it instrumental in direct and
indirect ways. Perhaps the most important contribution of the peasant to the problem-solving process is his voting behavior.

In the Venezuelan peasant subculture, two periods of time are

Table 27. Gravity of problems in the rural environment according to local FCV leaders (percent).

Nature of problem	Characterization of problem			
	Grave	Minor	No problem	Gravity rank[a]
Lack of medical facilities	68.6	15.3	11.9	1.0
Lack of sufficient land	67.8	14.4	12.7	2.5
Unsanitary, poor housing	67.8	17.8	11.0	2.5
Lack of agricultural credits	64.4	11.9	16.9	4.0
Lack of roads	61.0	20.3	13.6	5.5
Lack of potable water supply	61.0	13.6	21.2	5.5
Lack of schools and teachers	39.8	22.9	33.1	7.0
Farm-related problems ($N = 118$)	35.6	23.7	32.2	8.0

Source: FCV survey.
a. Ranking percentage of "grave" responses.

regarded as unique in the sense that the national government, after centuries of neglect, addressed itself vigorously to improving the lot of the peasantry. The first such experience is identified in the peasant culture with Acción Democrática (AD) from 1945–1948, and the second with AD and with COPEI from 1958–1964. These identifications have been reflected in peasant voting behavior. For instance, massive rural voting for AD and COPEI in the 1958 and 1963 elections had two general consequences. First, peasant votes placed proagrarian reform candidates and parties securely in a framework of power, which enabled them to transform the desire for agrarian reform into effective law (by regulating and channeling government outputs to that end), and to give the reform forces an annually renewed capacity to act (by means of budgetary allocations). Second, peasant votes elected chief executives dedicated to agrarian reform, who formed coalition governments of similarly disposed political parties in order to carry out the Agrarian Reform Law, formulating and administering the host of required supporting policies and programs.

The "Party of the People," as AD styles itself, won the elections of 1947, 1958, and 1963 because of its rural support. Though its plurality declined in each successive election, this decline was not due to an absolute loss in rural votes but to an enormous expansion in urban votes, which were mostly non-AD. However, since the urban vote proved unstable, responding to a variety of left-wing parties, coalitions, and candidates that shift from election to election, the stability of AD's rural base maintained it in power as the major partner in coalition. Rural population in centers of less than one thousand correlates positively with AD and COPEI voting patterns (measuring both population and voting by state). For AD, $r = .65$ at the .001 level of significance, while COPEI is even more solidly based on rural votes ($r = .76$ at .000 level of significance).[2] The volatility of the urban vote has produced a political paradox of some note in Venezuela: the two parties that drew the largest number of popular votes in 1963—AD with 30.8 percent, and COPEI with 19.0 percent—were solidly based in the rural areas, yet the Venezuelan population was highly urbanized (almost 70 percent lived in cities of five thousand or more).

In addition to their voting behavior, which is a necessary but insufficient form of support for proagrarian reform governments, peasants have engaged in another form of closely related behavior—the public demonstration. On scattered occasions large groups of marching, machete-waving campesinos have been used to protest delays in credit payments in front of an Agriculture and Livestock Bank (BAP) branch or for other local purposes, but their major employment has been as a manifestation of support for the national government. Twice during the perilous early years of the Betancourt administration, when the government was menaced by the threat of a reactionary coup, large groups of peasants, estimated by U.S. Embassy observers at 100,000, were organized and brought by bus and truck into Caracas to demonstrate their solidarity with the regime. Of the local syndicates sampled in my survey, 41.5 percent reported having sponsored some form of public demonstrations.

Demands of a more direct nature are channeled into the system through the peasantry's participation in local union activities. Our survey data indicated that 72 percent of the peasant locals hold meetings at least once a month (bimonthly or weekly). Into these meetings come the peasant members, carrying with them their direct knowledge of problem conditions and their desire for relief. Meetings of the local unions revolve almost entirely about the discussion of community problems—ninety-five local unions (or 80.5 percent of the sample) reported that this was their most common activity. Peasant leaders report on the status of problem-solving activities already underway, and members raise new information on problems, demands for relief, or complaints about the status of unresolved problems. Thus, peasants contribute in two ways to the problem-solving process at this level: they formulate precise demands for problem-solving activity, and they provide empirical feedback on ongoing attempts at solution. The value of these contributions depends on how well the local leader functions. He must either respond directly, if the necessary resources are within his control, or must process the peasant demands and transmit them successfully to other parts of the problem-solving system.

Another form of peasant participation in directly attacking local problem situations is the land invasion. Although disavowed in 1961 as an official policy by the federation, the land invasion is still occasionally used as an instrument of local pressure. It is aimed at two targets, the landlord and the National Agrarian Institute (IAN). A land invasion can force a landlord to change local tenure arrangements and employment conditions, or to sell land to the Agrarian Institute for an agrarian reform project. An invasion also serves to bring the plight of the peasants forcefully to the government's attention. In the past such invasions resulted principally in an overgenerous settlement with the landlord whose property had been invaded. For this reason the Betancourt administration successfully sought to end federation-sponsored invasions, because it was often found that the land purchased by the National Agrarian Institute after an invasion (and payed for generously in order to squelch political resentment) was not well suited for the purposes of subdivision and settlement. Often the resulting projects were costly and ineffective. In the early days of the post-Pérez Jiménez regime, however, land invasions were frequent, and they often occurred on properties that had been utilized for agrarian reform projects during the earlier AD administration but had been returned to private hands by the dictatorship. My survey of local syndicate leaders revealed that 16.1 percent of their locals had sponsored a land invasion in the past. If these invasions, numbering approximately 550, took place largely in the 1959–1961 period, as reported, they indicate that from one-third to one-half of the unions then operating sponsored invasions—evidence of the state of rural agitation following the fall of Pérez Jiménez.

The problems with which he is confronted thus generate within the Venezuelan peasant a certain potential for behavioral mobilization. If political and union leaders can stimulate him with suggestions for ways and means of solving his problems, and guide him

Table 28. Peasant participation in syndicate and political activities (percent).

Activity	Asentados	Nonasen-tados	Farm laborers
Attended union meeting last six months	61.3	34.4	27.2
Attended party meeting last six months	35.1	26.8	14.8
Worked for party or candidate in last election	24.6	16.4	14.2
$N =$	(191)	(183)	(166)

Source: CONVEN.

into patterns of behavior related to their solution, the peasant can make valuable contributions to the functioning of the problem-solving system. In so performing, the peasant is mobilized into participation in political and union activities that directly or indirectly contribute to the solution of his problems. The national extent of his participant behavior can be inferred from Table 28, which presents data on a national sample of three peasant groups.[3]

THE ROLE OF LOCAL SYNDICATES AND LEADERS IN PROBLEM-SOLVING

Once the peasants have managed through their votes to introduce agrarian reformers into the structural elements of the problem-solving system, and once their needs have been precisely focused in the forum of local union meetings, the local peasant unions and their leaders respond in a number of ways, as shown in Table 29.

After discussing problems in meetings and doing what they can locally to solve some of the more limited problems, local leaders process peasant demands into requests for action from other parts of the problem-solving system. Local union leaders thus serve as brokers for their peasant clients in dealing with the many government agencies and programs involved in the land reform program. Although local leaders do engage in other, lesser activities (37.3 percent reported organizing educational events for union members; 36.4 percent had sponsored social activities, such as religious festivals or dances; and 24.6 percent had sponsored sports events), it is readily apparent that the major function which they perform, or attempt to perform, is bringing available government programs and services to bear on the concrete problems of their rural communities. When asked about what plans the syndicate had for initiating new activities in the coming year, the respondents indicated that 35.6 percent planned to renew pressure or resubmit petitions for unmet service requests; and another 22 percent planned to petition for a service not yet requested.

Table 29. Local peasant syndicate activities (percent).

Nature of activity	Syndicates reporting
Meetings to discuss community problems	80.5
Helping members obtain farm credits (BAP)	78.0
Petitioning Ministry of Education	69.5
Petitioning for land from IAN	66.9
Petitioning for rural housing projects	66.1
Petitioning for penetration roads	65.3
Petitioning for health and sanitary projects ($N = 118$)	65.3

Source: FCV survey.

Brokerage is not exhausted with the submission of a request. The local leader must press for action from the local representative of the agency to which he is appealing. More important, the local leader can use his linkages with the other structures in the problem-solving system to gain support for projects in his local community. This may be accomplished in a variety of ways. If the pressure is to be brought on a field representative of a government agency (assuming that the necessary resources are locally controlled), linkages with the political party, with local government officials, or with other labor union leaders in the local subsystem may be utilized. If pressure or influence on a higher level is required, the local leader may call on the Peasant Federation, contacting the state executive committee or, in some cases, the national officers directly.

For a full understanding of how the local leader functions, it is necessary to know the degree to which his brokerage contacts with representatives of government agencies are face-to-face. If the major function of a local leader consists merely of utilizing his literacy to submit a written petition to some distant government agency, he cannot be considered a potent instrument of campesino pressure. Therefore, local leaders were asked how often they had an opportunity to converse with certain types of people, with results indicated in Table 30. The fact that local syndicate leaders from rural communities interacted with regional representatives of the major government land reform agencies with considerable frequency indicated an active and aggressive pursuit of local brokerage responsibilities.

However, further inquiry was necessitated by the high proportion of respondents who indicated that they had never performed this function face-to-face. A thorough analysis of the characteristics

Table 30. Intergroup contacts of local peasant syndicate leaders (percent).

Frequency of personal contact	Leaders reporting contacts with		
	IAN officials	BAP officials	MAC extension agents
Daily or weekly	21.2	16.1	13.5
Monthly or yearly	36.5	35.5	34.8
Infrequently	6.8	8.5	10.1
Never	34.7	39.0	40.7
(N = 118)			

Source: FCV survey.

of those syndicate leaders who reported "no contact" with government agrarian reform officials revealed a number of common factors. They tended to have a lower educational level than the average leader. Usually they had joined the peasant syndicate at a later date, and were more likely to be delegates at the convention than holders of formal syndicate leadership positions. And finally, they tended to be relatively recent adherents of their political party. All these factors, while only marginal when considered individually, taken together suggest that "no contact" leaders were likely to be newcomers to their syndicate positions and never to have held

Table 31. Comparative leadership longevity of local "no contact" FCV leaders (percent).

Time in present FCV office	Leaders reporting "no contact" with			Compared with all leaders
	IAN	BAP	MAC	
Less than one year	82.1	78.8	81.8	49.3
From one to three years	17.9	18.2	15.1	18.6
More than three years	—	3.0	3.0	18.6
(N = 118)				

Source: FCV survey.

office in the local organization of their political party, a hypothesis which is supported by the data in Tables 31 and 32.

Since linkages with the local political organization appear to be an important factor in the frequency of contact with local representatives of the government's land reform agencies, it may be supposed that the affiliation of the leader with one of the three major parties is also of importance, in regard to "no contact" with officials. Since the bureaucracy in Venezuela tends to be dominated by AD appointees, because AD has been the only party in government at all times since 1958 and has controlled the execu-

Table 32. Comparative political party office-holding of local "no contact" FCV leaders (percent).

Local party offices held	Leaders reporting "no contact" with			Compared with all leaders
	IAN	BAP	MAC	
None	86.4	81.4	84.4	63.6
One	13.2	16.3	15.6	25.4
More than one	—	2.3	—	5.1

Source: FCV survey.

tive branch through the presidency, it seems that it would make a difference whether or not a local leader is an AD member. The data in Table 33 strikingly confirm this supposition.

In the absence of other data, of course, one cannot say with certainty whether the absence of contact between a local syndicate leader affiliated with one party, and a local agrarian reform agency representative likely to be affiliated with another, is related to lack of initiative on the part of the official or the syndicate leader. Nor can one know whether it is owing to the relative inexperience

Table 33. Comparative political affiliation of "no contact" leaders (percent).

| Leaders | Party affiliation of leaders | | |
	AD	COPEI	URD
Entire leader sample	60.2	25.4	4.2
Leaders reporting "no contact" with:			
IAN	37.1	57.1	5.7
BAP	47.5	45.0	7.5
MAC	43.9	48.3	7.3

Source: FCV survey.

of the "no contact" leaders, or perhaps to distrust of and distaste for government officials who are partisans of a competing party. The lack of contact is probably owing to some combination of all these factors, despite the fact that AD's political opponents charge it with out-and-out discrimination in "politically" administering agrarian reform.[4]

THE COMMUNICATIONS FUNCTIONS OF LOCAL PEASANT LEADERS

In addition to the brokerage functions of local leaders, which are performed for the direct benefit of the peasants, several communications functions are performed by local leaders, which contribute to the maintenance and effectiveness of the entire problem-solving system. In performing these communications functions, local federation leaders process information flowing into and out of the peasant community, serving as its transmission links. Included among these functions are goal setting, feedback, and goal changing.[5]

It is likely that local syndicate leaders help to structure the problem-solving goals of members. Several forms of evidence are available to support the plausibility of this hypothesis, when considered in the context of well-known communications and opinion theories. The "two-step flow" theory of information transmission is an accepted explanation of how community and group opinion leaders function to receive, interpret, and transmit out-group information to members of their in-group.[6] Local syndicate leaders might, by virtue of their role as opinion leaders, be expected to use their superior education, for example, in explaining or interpreting information flowing into their rural community from the larger, more complex "outside" world. Adding authority to their role as interpreters of the modern sectors of Venezuelan society to the peasant, is the fact that local leaders have often had first-hand experience in the urban environment. Although two-thirds of the local leaders in the sample had lived in the village where their syndicate was located for ten years or more, those same leaders reported having lived in "cities" for considerable periods earlier in their lives.[7] This probably means that they left their villages as young men to try urban life and later returned to their pastoral, presumably happier habitats: 34.5 percent of the local leader sample had lived in a city or cities for as long as ten years, and 12.7 percent for more than ten years. This period of exposure to the more modern sectors of society gave the local leaders a solid base of experience to interpret and evaluate information flowing in from the outside world for the more tradition-bound peasant. The probability of local leaders performing such an interpretive function for their constituents is further enhanced by their more frequent exposure to mass media, as shown in Table 34.[8]

147

Table 34. Comparative mass media exposure of peasant followers and leaders (percent).

Rate of exposure	Union leaders	Peasant samples		
		Asentados	Nonasentados	Laborers
Radio				
None or infrequently	11	31	19	12
Weekly	17	23	28	24
Daily	70	47	53	61
Newspaper				
None	26	65	58	44
Infrequent	26	19	13	11
Frequent[a]	44	16	29	28
N =	(118)	(191)	(183)	(166)

Sources: Data on asentados, nonasentados, and farm laborers, CONVEN; FCV survey.

a. Frequent newspaper exposure means weekly and daily.

Being in a position to interpret outside information authoritatively and receiving a larger flow of such information places the local syndicate leader in a strong position to help shape and structure the peasant's images of, and expectations from, the larger society. Conversely, the local leader also shapes and influences the goals that the peasant holds in relation to the outside world. Since the principal form of interaction between the peasantry and the larger society is through the government's agrarian reform program, it is probable that local syndicate leaders play a significant part in establishing the concrete land reform goal-orientations of the syndicate members.

When goal-seeking pressures, or inputs, have been applied in the rural problem-solving system, and the system has transformed these inputs to outputs in concrete action programs, feedback is required to assure an effective "fit." That is, there must be a flow of information back through the system reporting the relevance, efficiency, or impact of the corrective measures on the conditions that generated the demands in the first place. The peasant who lives with the problem is in the most favorable position to generate such feedback information—and it is the function of the local syndicate leader to process such information and transmit it to other, relevant parts of the problem-solving system. This operation is accomplished mainly through direct linkages within the Peasant Federation. Feedback occurs occasionally on a systematic basis, at state conventions or at the national Campesino Congress, where leaders are asked to submit detailed reports on problems, unmet needs, and the performance of the agrarian reform program in their communities. Such reports are compiled and transmitted by the national federation leadership to the top administrators of the pertinent government agencies; in 1962, copies of all reports were also sent to President Betancourt. Such systematic feedback efforts, however, are rare and are followed through haphazardly.[9] Feedback normally occurs on an ad hoc basis, depending in the majority of cases on the initiative of the local syndicate.

There seems to exist a dual-channel feedback system. Information on normal agrarian reform operations or on successful operations flows back through the bureaucratic network of the agency from its field representatives. Though government agents also transmit negative reports, to the extent that the system remains relatively unresponsive to these reports—that is, does not take them into account in subsequent behavior—they do not constitute "feedback." Critical information is also transmitted by local peasant leaders to state officials of the federation and, occasionally, directly to national leaders. Program evaluations of a negative nature that can be effectively transmitted by state federation leaders to state or regional agency representatives are handled at that level. Many situations, however, require that the negative feedback be carried up to the national officials of the Peasant Federation. These leaders, like American congressmen, spend a large amount of their time and energies servicing such "constituent requests."[10] National peasant leaders utilize their formal and informal linkages with the multiparty system, with congressional colleagues, and with top administrators in the coalition government to pass on such feedback messages and attempt favorably to influence the response. Table 35 indicates the frequency with which local leaders came into contact with the state and, directly, with the national leaders of the federation. Two-thirds of such contacts were initiated by the local syndicate, which suggests that they were not routine and were probably "negative-feedback" in nature.

Table 35. Internal contact frequency of local leaders with state and national offices of the FCV (percent).

Contact frequency[a]	With state office	With national office
Weekly	11.9	0.8
Monthly	23.7	1.7
Once or twice a year	23.7	30.5
Irregularly, when necessary	21.2	7.6
Never	6.8	44.1

Source: FCV survey.

a. The question was: "How often have you been in direct contact with the state (national) office of the Peasant Federation within the past year?"

The leadership contact pattern is largely oriented toward the state level. The contacts reported in Table 35 were mostly personal visits of the local leader to the state federation office (79.7 percent). Telephone service is not extensive in rural areas, nor is it dependable in urban areas, with the result that only 5.1 percent of the contacts reported took this form; an additional 2.5 percent were made by telegram, and 12.8 percent by mail. The routine internal communications of the federation seem to flow downward by mail; the upward-bound feedback communications are brought in person to the state offices by local leaders, and on rare occasions in person to the national headquarters.

The survey was also designed to determine whether local leaders felt that the "doors were open to them" to carry critical problems directly to state and national officials of the peasant federation. One question was: "In case you had to get in 'urgent' contact with a member of the State (National) Committee, do you think it would be: easy, not very difficult, difficult, or almost impossible?" The answers, shown in Table 36, indicate a high degree of confidence in the accessibility of the federation hierarchy. The perceived accessibility of the national leadership is especially impressive when one considers the primary reasons given for finding access "difficult" or "almost impossible." These were almost entirely related to transportation or communications obstacles, which would

Table 36. Ease of access to FCV Hierarchy according to local leaders (percent).

Contact	With state leaders	With national leaders
Easy	55.1	31.4
Not very difficult	20.3	22.9
Difficult	21.2	30.5
Almost impossible	0.8	5.9

Source: FCV survey.

prevent immediate access (one must bear in mind the dependency of local leaders on personal visits to authorities as a means of contact). Almost 80 percent of those who considered access to state leaders as difficult or nonexistent gave reasons such as distance or lack of means. Only 5.1 percent gave "lack of receptivity" on the part of the state officials. As for the national leaders, more than 90 percent of those who perceived obstacles to contacting them described the obstacles in such terms as distance or lack of knowledge in finding their way around Caracas, and only 1.7 percent felt that the national leaders would be unreceptive to their overtures.

Considered together, the data on internal Peasant Federation communications implies that feedback from rural communities via the local syndicate leader occurs on a frequent, though ad hoc, basis. Also implied is the fact that the local leader finds it relatively easy to gain access to authorities in the federation in order to transmit such feedback. The major obstacles to an effective flow of local feedback are either physical factors, which block local leaders from easily contacting federation hierarchs, or imperfections elsewhere in the system that prevent transformation of feedback demands into effective remedies.

Feedback is not a one-way street but may also function to alter initial goals. In systems that are dynamic, in which organizational learning takes place, feedback returns from output structures carrying information for input managers. Such feedback may be designed to explain an inability to respond to certain demands, or to suggest changes in demands that will make them easier to fulfill, or to suggest alternative solutions that have not been perceived. For a variety of reasons, feedback of this nature may also be initiated by top political managers in the problem-solving system. If the goal-generating structures take this feedback into account, modifying the nature of subsequent demands or changing other aspects of goal-seeking behavior, the system demonstrates a dynamism or learning capacity. The Venezuelan rural problem-solving system has demonstrated such a capacity, and there is evidence to suggest that local syndicate leaders play a vital role in bringing about such goal-changing behavior on the part of the peasantry.

For example, a major shift in goals occurred in 1961, when the federation reversed its policy of sponsoring land invasions. In that instance, President Betancourt confronted the national leadership with evidence that such invasions strengthened the political opposition to the agrarian reform program, produced little in the way of long-term peasant betterment, and, in sum, threatened the entire reform attempt. The federation leadership accepted Betancourt's recommendations, and land invasions diminished drastically. Again in 1962, President Betancourt, as one of the principal output managers, favored a change in the national leadership of the federation, with the purpose of replacing radical and extremist leaders, who demanded an acceleration of land distribution, with moderates who supported his shift of emphasis to consolidation of established settlements with infrastructures and a battery of social and economic welfare services. The formal change of leadership occurred at the Second Campesino Congress in June 1962, and the federation became more cooperative with the government's reform agencies, moderating service demands in circumstances perceived as threatening to governmental stability or fiscal capabilities. In such instances, the leadership of the federation served to transmit political feedback to the peasant members at its base. It is also probable that the leaders advocated, or at least influenced, the modification of peasant goals or changes in goal-seeking behavior. Such a function, which preserved the internal compatibility of goals held by different actors in the same system, was necessary to the survival of an integrated system. From the point of view of a system manager, such behavior appears to be a rational response to the threatened survival of a basically fruitful arrangement.[11]

Of the syndicate leaders sampled, 41.5 percent reported that their locals had "held meetings to inform the members about political problems." If the importance of goal-changing is granted, and the "political problems" discussed by the local leaders are assumed to have been similar to the problems faced by President Betancourt in 1961 and 1962, it would seem that the local leadership played an important role in the subsequent modification of peasant demands on the Betancourt regime. Furthermore, there is evidence to suggest that local syndicate leaders serve generally as a transmission link for political information flowing in to the peasantry from the larger system. The data in Table 37 indicate that peasants in general reported high rates of contact and interaction with their syndicate leaders, but much lower rates with their local political leaders; they may not even have perceived that the two were often the same. In contrast, local syndicate leaders had a rather high

153

Table 37. Comparative contact frequencies of peasant leaders and followers (percent).

Contact frequency[a]	Group reporting contact			
	Local FCV leaders	Asentados	Non-asentados	Laborers
With syndicate leaders:				
Low	12.7	25.8	35.5	45.9
Moderate	45.8	32.4	23.3	28.4
High	40.7	40.4	39.3	22.5
With political leaders:				
Low	27.9	68.3	68.5	69.5
Moderate	44.9	23.9	18.2	18.5
High	26.3	6.5	10.8	8.7
(N =	(118)	(191)	(183)	(166)

Sources: Data for asentados, nonasentados, and farm laborers, CONVEN; FCV survey.

a. Low = never, or a few times in life; Moderate = once a year or monthly; High = weekly or daily.

rate of exposure to political leaders. It would seem, therefore, that political information generated by the political system for peasant consumption would flow to local political leaders, thence to local syndicate leaders, and finally to the peasantry.

To sum up, the primary role of the local leader in the process of seeking solutions to problems faced by the peasants in his community is to function as a broker. Representing the interests of his union members before the variety of government agencies involved in agrarian reform, he seeks to bring their efforts to bear on the concrete conditions experienced by himself and his peasant neighbors. In seeking to attract and expedite the flow of goods and services from these agencies, the local leader utilizes his personal linkages with his political party, with officials in the Peasant Federation, and with other structures in the rural problem-solving system. This is manifestly a role of influence, and is highly political.

In addition, local leaders serve as important links for communications processes within the overall problem-solving system. Local leaders process and transmit information into and out of the peasant community, mainly relating to problems of agrarian reform. In so doing, they structure the problem-related goals of peasants, transmit relevant feedback information to the rest of the problem-solving system, and occasionally change the scope and nature of peasant goals, in response to the functional requirements of other factors in the system. In short, they are important influences on peasant problem-solving behavior.

NATIONAL FUNCTIONS OF THE PEASANT FEDERATION

State and national leaders act as extensions of the local leader, utilizing their more weighty linkages, political influence, and authority in response to demands transmitted from below. As leaders, they presumably help to shape these demands as well. Just as local leaders perform certain functions that have no counterpart in other levels of the hierarchy, such as directly affecting local peasant goals, so do national leaders organize and perform certain functions that have no counterpart at the state or local level. State leaders, in contrast, seem to function principally as agents for the other levels of the federation hierarchy. There do not appear to be any identifiable functions pertaining solely to state leaders. They serve faithfully as transmission links, administrative agents, and brokers for both local and national structures of the federation. They are the ubiquitous middlemen, necessary to the performance of every transactional system, yet having little or no capacity for independent or original action. They are largely "system-determined"—set in a functional trajectory by forces above and below them.[12]

The national organization, having command of a fairly broad range of resources, is in a position to perform services for its members that would be beyond the capabilities of the local or even

155

the state organizations.[13] Certain of these functions are educational in nature and are designed to equip the peasant to deal more effectively with his problems as a cultivator. Others are aimed directly at the relief of problem conditions, such as marketing obstacles and the lack of mechanized equipment or the knowledge to use it.

One of the most important of these service functions is peasant education. Beginning late in 1962, under the sponsorship and direction of the national secretary for culture and publications, Dr. Julio Manuel Montoya, the federation organized a series of Peasant Vocational Schools for its members. By 1966 the first four of a planned ten of these vocational training centers were in full operation, teaching basic farm technology, including beef and dairy cattle operations on a small scale, basic food cultivation, hog and poultry raising, use of agricultural credits, agrarian reform, and syndicate organization. Classes were organized in groups of sixty, and the courses ran for two months, six days a week, from 6 A.M. to 10 P.M., including night classes in reading and writing. The basic objective of the courses was not to produce farm technicians but to send the peasant back to his family farm with a rudimentary, but solid, basis for improving his standard of living, and to open up for him the possibility of entering the commercial market on a modest scale. Another explicit objective of the training centers was to create a sort of in-group "demonstration effect" for the other members of the syndicate. The operation of these schools, which have been successful to date, has required a minimum of investment by the Peasant Federation. The Agrarian Institute has provided the land and buildings, such as former construction camps; the Ministry of Agriculture (MAC) has provided the stock and livestock; the Agriculture Bank has provided credits to put the farm operation, in which the students provide the labor, on a self-supporting basis; and the various state governments have helped to cover operating expenses. Such cooperation is a convincing demonstration of the advantages that the federation enjoys because of its linkages with political and governmental structures.[14]

Early in 1965 the federation began to set up another series of peasant service enterprises. Given high priority by the national leadership, the first of these enterprises was Suministros Campesinos or SUCAM, a privately managed firm in which the Peasant Federation was the principal stockholder. This enterprise imported agricultural machinery for sale to syndicates and individual members. Since the federation could guarantee a large and controllable market of the 550,000 campesino members, the enterprise could contract with large manufacturers, such as Oliver or John Deere, to provide discount prices, spare parts stocking, and servicing. Such an arrangement has permitted campesino groups to purchase tractors, for instance, for as much as 25 percent below the commercial market price in their area. Closely linked to this effort was another campesino enterprise, Servicios Campesinos or SERVICAM. This organization was established under contract with the same farm machinery companies. These companies undertook to train peasants as mechanics for the repair and maintenance of farm machinery and to assist in the setting up of federation-run repair shops in the rural areas. The Peasant Federation was pressed into this area of activity because of the intransigence of local farm-machinery franchise holders, who refused to repair or service farm machinery imported by the federation's enterprise (SUCAM). By 1967, though the importation scheme had apparently become successfully and profitably established, the service program had run into serious management and logistical problems, casting doubts on its viability as an enterprise.[15]

The Peasant Federation has established another, so far successful operation called Industrias Campesinas or INDUCAM, a rice-processing factory on the huge, irrigated agricultural colony and agrarian reform settlement of Calabozo. The factory was able to enter into a contract for the sale of its high-quality rice to the nationwide Rockefeller supermarket chain, Compañía Anónima Distribuidora de Alimentaciones or CADA, which assured a solid market outlet for the rice raised by the members of the Calabozo syndicates and processed in the federation's peasant-manned rice plant.

In the field of marketing, the federation has attempted to penetrate the local networks but has run into resistance and problems. It is now seeking new ways of getting around such obstacles as boycotts of asentimiento-produced crops in favor of privately produced crops by agricultural processers. The most dramatic instance of boycott occurred in 1963, when a bumper tomato crop produced on the agrarian reform settlement of "La Julia" was lost owing to the refusal of the local tomato processers to deal with the syndicate representatives trying to sell the crop. In 1965, the national federation succeeded in obtaining an export contract with North American buyers for the output of "La Julia" and other tomato-producing agrarian reform settlements. Also underway are efforts to establish an organized net of farmer's markets, to be called Mercadeo Campesino or MERCAM. The first such markets, which provide peasant members with a direct outlet in Valencia and Caracas (eliminating the rapacious middlemen, "la rosca encapadora"), were reportedly in operation by early 1968. However, the national direct-marketing effort has run into a variety of difficulties and setbacks which seem to be partly the result of a lack of marketing experts.

The national leadership of the Peasant Federation also performs many vital functions oriented toward other structures in the problem-solving system. Among the most important of these functions are ones relating to interactions with the political parties comprising the coalition government. This is especially true in the case of AD which controlled the presidency and dominated the Agrarian Institute and the Agriculture Bank from 1959 to 1969. Perhaps the most important of these functional interactions concerns the budget-making process for agrarian reform agencies.

All of the major Venezuelan political parties have "branches" organized according to occupation or profession. In AD, the branch composed of agricultural technicians and specialists is known as

158

the Agro-Technical Branch. The primary annual responsibility of this group is to prepare technical recommendations for governmental programs and budgets in the field of agriculture and agrarian reform. These recommendations, in the form of a confidential report, are passed on to the Agrarian Bureau, the highest agricultural policy-making body in the party. In 1966, the Agrarian Bureau was composed of sixteen members, among them the national AD agrarian secretary, the president of the Sugarcane Worker's Federation, two former secretaries-general of the Peasant Federation, one of the peasant representatives on the Agrarian Institute Board of Directors, the peasant representative on the agrarian bank Board of Directors, and the federation's secretary-general for Miranda state. This elite group of peasant leaders met for three hours each Monday evening and had the responsibility of transforming technical recommendations into an action and budgetary program designed specifically for AD's peasant clientele.

Thus, in the development of the 1967 budget, the report of the Agrarian Bureau was sent in the spring of 1966, as in years past, simultaneously to the president of the republic and to the National Executive Committee of the party. The Executive Committee, which includes the agrarian secretary of the party and the president of the Peasant Federation, processed the report, using it as a target but modifying it by incorporating political considerations and policy priorities, which it is their main responsibility to monitor weekly for the president. The resulting report, issued early in the cycle of the government budget-making process, established program and budget positions as official AD party policy. The report was then furnished to the AD administrators within the government agencies concerned with agrarian reform, and it functioned as a guideline during their formal preparation of budgetary requests.

Since 1961, the individual agencies have every August submitted their preliminary budget requests to the president's Coordinating and Planning Office. The resulting overall budget has normally been ready for final Cabinet review in September, and has been submitted to Congress in October, for passage before the beginning of the budget year, which commences on January 1. The political content of the decision-making process in the budget is thus more attenuated than it is, for instance, in the United States. The main inputs of political considerations occur in the executive process of budget preparation, and national peasant leaders (at least those who are affiliated with AD) have several important access points during this decision-making period: first in the Agrarian Bureau, and then in the Executive Committee. The two members of the Executive Committee who are direct peasant representatives—the party agrarian secretary and the president of the Peasant Federation—have an opportunity to continue to monitor and perhaps influence the budget as it moves through its various stages of preparation for congressional presentation, since under normal circumstances the Executive Committee meets weekly with the president. In addition, once the budget is before the Congress, the two AD leaders who are congressmen, normally in cooperation with the federation congressmen from COPEI and the Unión Republicana Democrática (URD), have a final, if limited, opportunity to shape and influence the level of budgetary support for the following year's agrarian reform program. On occasion, the president may use his special constitutional powers to decree budgetary supplements during the budget year, and the same access to the normal decision-making process is available to the AD peasant leaders during the making of such ad hoc decisions.

The opportunity to influence the outputs of the agrarian reform program is not limited to active participation in the budget-making process. The variety of positions that the Peasant Federation has been granted on the Board of Directors of the Agrarian Institute and Agriculture Bank, as well as on a number of committees and boards in the Ministry of Agriculture and other governmental agencies, are utilized for the benefit of state and local federation leaders when they are transmitting demands or requests for influence upward, or are functioning as feedback agents. The national peasant leaders thus act as powerful and influential extensions of local syndicate leaders and their clients.

These functions are performed at a stage in the process of rural problem-solving that makes them impossible to categorize precisely as either "inputs" or "outputs," for they appear to be both simultaneously. They are not identifiable with any single structure in the system, but only with a stage in the problem-solving process. These important functions, performed by the national leaders of the Peasant Federation, might be thought of as system-management functions, being neither inputs nor outputs, but representing a transformation of inputs into outputs by directing the flow of input pressures to the proper "receptacle" in the output structures of the problem-solving system. Such a transformation requires not only a high degree of political knowledge of the communications channels in the rural problem-solving system, but the political authority to weight such messages sufficiently to make them visible to, and influential upon, the system's output managers.

VIII

THE FLOW OF GOVERNMENTAL RESPONSES

In Harold Lasswell's noted formulation, the substance of politics is defined as who gets what, when, and how.[1] In the Venezuelan case, it is now clear who places political demands on the system for agrarian reform benefits, and how. To complete Lasswell's formula, one must also understand what they get and when, or under what set of conditions. The task of determining actual gains is straightforward and fairly simple, since it may be found in the data of the government agencies concerned with the Venezuelan agrarian reform program, in terms both of budgets and of the flow of specific, concrete benefits (hectares of land distributed, peasant credit availability).

The explanation of "when" these governmental benefits flow, or under what conditions, is a much more complex task, because of the large number of variables. However, the task may be limited to testing a number of feasible hypotheses concerning the conditions governing the flow of agrarian reform benefits to the states. Thus, primary concern is to test the impact of Peasant Federation (FCV) pressure on the flow of benefits, to determine whether greater benefits flow to the states where the peasantry is more highly organized than to the other less organized states. Or is the flow of agrarian reform benefits related to the degree of political support for the government parties within the various states, as measured by votes? Or are there other variables, either ecological or intervening, which have an equal or greater impact on the flow of benefits than do union pressure or voting? These questions may be explored by means of regression analysis and other techniques.

Finally, an analysis of governmental outputs must be related back to the world of the peasant, by testing local opinions as to the impact of various government programs and agencies on the rural environment. That is, the analysis of the processes and functions of the rural problem-solving system began by asking peasant union leaders to identify their problems; it will terminate with their evaluations of the effectiveness of recent government programs in overcoming those problems.

BUDGETARY BASES AND PROGRAM OUTPUTS

Budgetary support for the three major agencies of agrarian reform—the National Agrarian Institute (IAN), the Agriculture and Livestock Bank (BAP), and the Ministry of Agriculture (MAC)—remained on a fairly stable level from 1958 through 1966. Agrarian reform budgets ranged from an aggregate high of almost $140 million ($1.00 equals Bs 4.50) in fiscal year 1961, when the Betancourt government made its strongest push for the program, to a low of about $85 million during calendar year 1963, an election year, when congressional opposition to the Betancourt government reached a peak. The figures are shown in Table 38.[2]

During the period indicated in Table 38, the composition of Agrarian Institute outputs shifted. In the early 1960's, from 50 to 70 percent of budgetary appropriations were channeled into land purchases and consolidation works. Since 1963, the ratio has shifted, so that such expenditures now account for only about one-fourth of the budgetary expenditures. The remainder of the institute budget has been absorbed in salaries, planning, research, and other overhead costs. This shift is in part a reflection of the Betancourt administration's policies in later years to slow down the rate of land distribution, consolidate and rationalize already established settlements, and increase the planning requirements for new ones. It may also be a reflection of the workings of Parkinson's Law, showing the rising costs of gradual program bureaucratization.

From 1958 through mid-1966 the Agrarian Institute budgetary outputs placed approximately 100,000 campesino families on roughly 5,000,000 acres of their own land. These families were settled on about 700 asentamientos at a cost of 7,000 bolivares per family. If overhead costs continue to increase in relation to

Table 38. Venezuelan agrarian reform budgetary support, FY 1958–
Calendar 1966 (millions of bolivares).

Budget year	IAN	BAP	MAC	Total
FY 1958	69.3	85.8	320.0	475.1
FY 1959	100.3	—	252.1	352.4
FY 1960	121.8	68.0	247.3	437.1
FY 1961	199.5	162.0	257.0	618.5
July–December 1961	159.8	79.9	209.6	449.3
1962	139.3	63.0	203.2	405.5
1963	107.8	50.0	223.5	381.3
1964	150.8	130.1	231.7	512.6
1965	150.8	150.0	278.4	579.2
1966[a]	168.7	100.0	272.3	541.2

Source: Ministry of Treasury, *Memoria Anual Correspondiente al Año 1965*
(Caracas: Imp. Nacional, 1966), p. 46.

a. Initial budget only—that is, the budget appropriated at the beginning
of calendar year 1966. Often the actual expenditures differ from this initial
estimate, because agencies ask for and get supplementary budgets, recu-
perate funds from the previous year, or wind up at the end of the year with
unexpended but available funds. With the exception of 1966, the data here
include all of these variations.

land and settlement improvement expenditures, however, the actual cost per family settled will rise sharply from this average.

The Agriculture Bank credit programs operate primarily on loan
recuperations. In addition to expanded credit capital, the annual
budgetary expenditures cover general operating costs and price
support operations, including parity purchases, storage programs,
agricultural imports when necessary to maintain price supports,
and similar marketing responsibilities. The bank's loan programs
are designed to serve both commercial and subsistence farmers.
The criterion for distinguishing one type of loan from the other
is the amount of land under cultivation. If one cultivates more
than thirty hectares, one is eligible for a commercial (*empresario*)
loan; if one cultivates less than thirty hectares, one is eligible for

Table 39. Peasant credits granted by BAP, 1959–1964.

Year	Number of loans (thousands)	Value (millions of bolivares)
1959	51.5	61.5
1960	99.6	126.6
1961	66.2	83.9
1962	70.1	107.4
1963	67.8	99.6
1964	66.0	155.5

Source: Agriculture and Livestock Bank, *Informe Anual* (Caracas: BAP, 1958–1966).

a lower-interest peasant (campesino) loan. The amount of an individual loan is pegged at so much per acre, depending on the crop to be grown and its market price situation at the time of the loan. Campesino loans are made in three installments, with each increment dependent on bank inspection and approval of the readiness of the farm operation to move into the next stage: from planting, to cultivation, to harvest. By 1966 the proportion of closely supervised loans stood at about 10 percent of total credit granted, and was growing rapidly through a number of Inter-American Development Bank and Alliance for Progress programs.

The Ministry of Agriculture has traditionally sought to increase national agricultural production. In the past this meant a concentration of effort and attention on commercial farm operations. Though the commercially oriented programs, such as increasing production in livestock, coffee, and cacao industries, have been de-emphasized by the various governments since Pérez Jiménez, they continue to function and to maintain (even increase) overall agricultural production in the midst of the land reform effort. Thus, effort within the ministry has been shifted to extension services and technical studies directed toward peasants, especially those settled on agrarian reform projects. In spite of this new emphasis on the subsistence farmer, a critical lack of trained extension agents and their assistants has limited the impact of campesino services. Although increased numbers of such personnel are in the offing because of ministry scholarships and training programs, the peasants and their leaders are keenly aware of the present lack of extension services.

THE DISTRIBUTION OF AGRARIAN REFORM BENEFITS

In order to explore the effects of various input factors on the distribution of agrarian reform benefits, I ran a regression analysis, utilizing fifteen independent variables—such as rural population, syndicate membership, Acción Democrática (AD) and COPEI votes, and the agricultural value of the land—and thirteen dependent variables—such as the amount of private and public land distributed under the program, the number of families settled, the total Agrarian Institute expenditure pattern, and campesino credits. The most practical form in which to use the data was by state, so that in effect there were twenty-two geographically based observations for the regression analysis. Although "state" was not found to be a sufficiently precise unit for an explanatory microanalysis, it yielded a general picture of which input variables accounted for differences in the distribution of output benefits. Since the analysis was exploratory in nature, various combinations of independent variables were hypothesized to account for the dependent variables and were tested in turn. Those reported in Table 40 yielded the largest coefficients of determination (r^2).

The remaining seven output variables were not meaningfully predicted by any combination of independent variables—that is, the degree of dependent variation explained well below 36 percent, the lowest score reported in Table 40. Essentially, the data in Table 40 signify that, knowing the values of certain input variables, one can predict 81 percent of the variation, by state, of the total pattern

Table 40. Maximum coefficients of determination for agrarian reform outputs yielded by best-fitting combination of inputs.

Dependent variables (outputs)	Maximum r² obtained by various combinations of independent variables (inputs)
Total IAN expenditures	.81
Campesino credits	.59
Families given private lands	.53
Acres of private land distributed	.45
Families given public lands	.41
Acres of public land distributed	.36

Source: Computations.

of Agrarian Institute expenditures, or 59 percent of the variation by state in the granting of campesino credits, and so forth. Prediction, as defined in regression analysis, involves a unidirectional relationship: in effect, the independent variables cause the dependent variables to vary as they do. The dependent variables for which one can predict more than 50 percent of the variation in their geographic distribution are the most interesting for analysis.

Table 41, for example, suggests the following explanation of variations in Agrarian Institute expenditures by state: institute outputs tend to flow to those states that make a large contribution to total national agricultural production (V-1), are densely populated (V-2), but probably small in size, since they contain a low absolute number of rural inhabitants (V-6). Squatting on land (V-3) is low in the favored states, either because most lands are privately owned (and public lands are therefore scarce), or because private lands are sufficiently available to squat on, lease, or sharecrop (V-5). The states receiving the highest Agrarian Institute outputs tend to be unionized by the Peasant Federation of Venezuela (V-4), but more likely by AD than by COPEI organizers (V-7). Finally, such states are characterized by extensive (V-8)

167

Table 41. Input variables that account for 81 percent of the variation, by state, in total IAN expenditures.

Independent variables		Beta[a]	Level of confidence
V-1	Value of agricultural production	.65	.98
V-2	Rural population density	.55	.95
V-3	Amount of public land squatting	− .55	.95
V-4	Peasant Federation membership	.34	< .95
V-5	Percentage nonowning farm operators	.20	< .95
V-6	Rural population	− .28	< .95
V-7	COPEI votes	− .39	< .95
V-8	Agricultural production per acre	− .44	< .95

Source: Computations.

a. Beta is a regression statistic: if beta is .64, for instance, it signifies that by knowing one unit of variation in the independent variable, one can predict .64 units of variation in the dependent variable.

rather than intensive commercial operations. All of these characteristics fit the group of small, densely populated, and highly important agricultural states in the central part of Venezuela, which has, as an AD stronghold, exerted intense pressure to achieve considerable agrarian reform benefits.

Campesino credits are distributed, as indicated in Table 42, in those states that are well established as agriculturally productive (V-1), where they presumably will have the most impact. These areas are also under fairly heavy peasant union pressure (V-2). Tending to be oriented toward crops and not livestock (V-3), such states again fit the pattern of the central Venezuelan states of Miranda, Carabobo, and Aragua.

Finally, Table 43 illustrates the fact that states which contain the largest number of families awarded private lands under the agrarian reform program are also the same agriculturally productive (V-1), highly unionized (V-2), but small, central states (V-3). The AD voting data utilized were number of votes, and although the central states vote proportionately high for AD, they account for only a small absolute number of AD votes.

Table 42. Input variables that account for 59 percent of the variation, by state, in the granting of peasant credits.

Independent variables		Beta	Level of confidence
V-1	Value of agricultural production	.52	.95
V-2	Peasant Federation membership	.48	.92
V-3	Livestock production per acre	− .45	.91

Source: Computations.

All three of the patterns that have been analyzed contain similar elements, in that major agrarian reform benefits flow to established agricultural areas, where organized peasant pressures have been built up. The value of the agricultural product is in every equation a major predictor of the variation in agrarian reform benefits. There are other input variables which, though they did not fit into the most explanatory equations as direct predictors of output variations, are highly correlated with the value of agricultural production and can therefore be considered as indirect contributory factors to output variation. These related factors include AD votes $(r = .72)$, COPEI votes $(r = .55)$, and combined AD and COPEI votes $(r = .78)$. This supports my general thesis that campesino votes bring agrarian reform benefits, if only indirectly since they must be transformed by the problem-solving system.

Table 43. Input variables that account for 53 percent of the variation, by state, in the number of families settled on private lands.[a]

Independent variables		Beta	Level of confidence
V-1	Value of agricultural production	.64	.99
V-2	Peasant Federation membership	.48	.97
V-3	AD votes	− .46	.96

Source: Computations.

a. About half of the lands distributed by IAN during 1958–1966 were privately owned, having been purchased with cash and bonds under the Agrarian Reform Law.

Since the intent is not to explain all causal factors involved in the distribution of agrarian reform benefits, but to explore the impact of peasant organizations on the flow of outputs, the two variables that measured union pressure—absolute number of union members, and proportion of unionized heads-of-household by state—were dropped out of the list of fifteen independent variables, and the entire process of searching for the most predictive combination of independent variables was repeated. Table 44 indicates

Table 44. Comparison of total variation explained in outputs with and without syndicate pressure inputs.

Dependent variable (outputs)	Max. r^2 with union inputs included	Max. r^2 with union inputs excluded	Differences in r^2
Total IAN expenditures	.81	.78	.03
Campesino credits	.59	.43	.16
Families given private lands	.53	.39	.14
Acres of private land distributed	.45	.21	.24
Families given public lands	.41	.12	.29
Acres of public lands distributed	.36	.07	.29
Mean	.52	.33	.19

Source: Computations.

the comparison of variations of flow in benefits with and without union pressure measurements.

Though the data in Table 44 cannot be taken to measure precisely the independent impact of syndicate pressure, since many other input variables may measure syndicate pressure effects and thus be included indirectly, the pattern of the data is consistent and clear. The existence of a peasant syndicate in an area, and the intensity of syndicate pressures, will have a positive effect on that area by bringing it benefits of agrarian reform. The data suggest that unionization has more of an effect on the distribution of certain benefits, such as public land, and the number of families settled there, than on the distribution of other benefits, such as credits, or on overall investments. This seems logical from the point of view of sound banking principles, which would operate to insulate credit criteria from such pressures as could be brought to bear by union and political forces. It is also logical to expect that the overall pattern of Agrarian Institute investments would be relatively unaffected by the presence or absence of union pressures, since such investments include large infrastructure items such as roads (which are located according to geographic factors and the existence of marketing centers or connecting transportation arteries), aqueducts, or irrigation and drainage works (which also depend for their location on natural geographic conditions).

In summary, the hypothesis that the Venezuelan problem-solving system is responsive to the inputs generated by the Peasant Federation is entirely consistent with the foregoing regression analysis. But the nature of the systematic response is limited, being conditioned by other factors, such as the potential return on agrarian reform investments in terms of agricultural productivity. The fact that the systematic response is limited by such considerations seems to be a clear indication that policy has been made in response to peasant pressures, but also that the nature of the subsequent outputs has been heavily infused with rational considerations by the government's output managers. Once again, the potential for conflict between technological and political rationality in the problem-solving process can be understood in the tension between decision-making that emphasizes political considerations, and decision-making that emphasizes technical considerations. The two criteria, of course, need not be mutually exclusive: the art of effective public policy-making seems to consist in finding ways of solving public problems that meet both criteria. In striking such a balance, the policy-maker may fail to satisfy completely the advocates of both points of view.

LOCAL PEASANT LEADERS EVALUATE THE REFORM

In the Venezuelan rural problem-solving system, the trained advisers and administrators of the government's agrarian reform agencies are the advocates of a technical emphasis in decision-making. Political advocates include those who must push for tangible rewards for their constituencies, in order to fulfill pledges of peasant benefits, and who must continually demonstrate that they are capable of influencing the distribution of such rewards. Otherwise, their leadership position will suffer from their inability to function as effective instrumental agents. If the problem-solving system withers at the base through the diminution of local leadership effectiveness, the major input energies, massive electoral support by the peasants, may also diminish. On the other hand, if technical considerations are not sufficiently taken into account to maintain effective fiscal and administrative management of agrarian reform, the flow of outputs will be endangered.

It was expected, therefore, that there would be some dissatisfaction on the part of local peasant leaders with the pace and scope of the agrarian reform program, just as there has from the beginning been a certain amount of bureaucratic criticism of the program because of the presence of political factors. In the local leadership survey, therefore, several dimensions for evaluating the agrarian reform program were probed. The questionnaire first provided a context by surveying the perceived problems with which these leaders were dealing, and by finding out how serious such problems appeared to be. Then the respondents were asked how much help specific programs seemed to give in resolving such problems.[3]

Not only were a series of problems, such as lack of land, poor housing and sanitary conditions, identified by the respondents, but most of these individual problems were ranked as "grave," rather than "minor" or "nonexistent," by from 60 to 70 percent of the sample leaders. It was necessary to check for "response set" or questionnaire-induced bias in the resulting highly critical, or negative, evaluations of problems. If leaders with certain characteristics tended to rank some problems more seriously than did leaders with differing characteristics, then the gravity measures might not be reflecting problems accurately, and the subsequent analysis of agrarian reform evaluations might also be spurious.

Therefore, those respondents who ranked problems as "grave" were analyzed for a number of possibly related characteristics that might have influenced their perceptions of the seriousness of a particular problem. Other factors being constant, age and education were tested against ranking tendencies, but yielded no perceptible difference. Next, factors connected with the respondents' labor movement experience were tested, but regardless of when the leader had joined the movement, how many offices he had held, how long he had remained in his current position, or what that office was, there was little effect on how seriously he perceived specific problems in his community. Finally, the respondents' political linkages were tested for their impact on ranking the seriousness of problem conditions: leaders affiliated with AD, COPEI, and the Unión Republicana Democrática (URD) ranked problems almost identically, with the number of party offices that the leader had held making no difference in the gravity of his problem perceptions. The only factor (of those tested) that discriminated was the date when the respondent had joined the peasant union movement. Those joining since 1958 tended to view problems much more seriously than the old-timers—which perhaps helped to explain indirectly why they had joined a political party and become active in peasant union affairs. In sum, no factor related to the background of the sample peasant leaders adequately accounted for the manner in which they ranked the gravity of the problem conditions with which they deal; it must be assumed, therefore, that the actual problems they face foster their perceptions of grim seriousness.

Cast against such a backdrop, the negative evaluations of the respondents, when asked how much help in solving problems a number of agrarian reform organizations and programs had given, strike an urgent note, as shown in Table 45.

There are two general trends in the data in Table 45 that are worth noting. First, the evaluations tend to be overwhelmingly negative, with only one of the eight entities achieving positive net scores. Second, the two highest rankings were awarded to the two institutions in which local peasant leaders enjoy the most direct

Table 45. Evaluations by local FCV leaders of agrarian reform agencies and programs with regard to solving their problems (percent).

Agency or program	Much help	Little help	No help	Net score[a]	Rank
Peasant Federation	39.8	30.5	27.1	+12.7	1
Administrative committee[b]	16.1	24.6	27.1	−11.0	2
Political party	28.0	28.0	40.7	−12.7	3
BAP credit program	22.0	38.1	38.1	−16.1	4
IAN	24.6	27.1	46.6	−22.0	5
Rural road program	14.4	26.3	55.1	−40.7	6
MAC extension service	12.7	25.4	58.5	−45.8	7
Rural housing program (N = 118)	15.3	17.8	65.3	−50.0	8

Source: FCV survey.

a. Net score equals "much help" minus "no help."

b. Administrative committees are bodies elected from among the settlers on agrarian reform projects, as provided by law.

influence—the Peasant Federation itself, and the elected administrative committees of the agrarian reform settlements, which are in almost every case synonymous with the local syndicate leadership.

These evaluations probably do not reflect a generally negative attitude toward the government or its representative agencies and agrarian reform programs. In fact, to test for such a pattern of negativism, the questionnaire included a series of probes for the emotional attitude, or affect, of the interviewee toward a series of symbolic stimuli. The list of stimuli included value-loaded words, such as "latifundia" and "dictatorship," the names of well-known political figures, and a series of terms related to the agrarian reform. The reform responses were overwhemlmingly positive: affective attitudes toward the expression "agrarian reform" were 94.1 percent positive; toward the Agrarian Institute and the Ministry of Agriculture, 89.8 percent positive; toward the Agriculture Bank, 86.4 percent positive; and toward the national government in general, 75.4 percent positive.[4] Thus, the findings show that local peasant leaders have a highly positive attitude toward agrarian reform institutions, yet evaluate negatively the performance of these institutions and programs in solving their particular problems. This strongly suggests that a valid judgement of institutional performance was tapped by the questions. The question remaining to be answered is why the performance of the agrarian reform was judged so harshly.

Analysis revealed that there were only two leadership characteristics that had a significant effect on the way in which the performance of a program or institution was evaluated: the amount of face-to-face contact the leader had experienced with representatives of the agency being judged, and the political affiliation of the respondent. A leader who had experienced no face-to-face contact and working relationship with agrarian reform representatives was more negative in his evaluation of the help provided by the agency. It was also found that while all local leaders tended to evaluate problem-solving results negatively, those affiliated with COPEI and URD manifested a disproportionate degree of negativism. These factors, reported in Tables 46 and 47, seem to be related, since the local COPEI and URD leaders reported much less face-to-face contact with agrarian reform bureaucrats than did local AD leaders.

Two qualifying observations may be made concerning the data in Tables 46 and 47. In Table 46, the most obvious point is that frequency of contact and positive evaluations are directly related. The relationship is not perfect, however, and the relationship

Table 46. Effects of contact frequency on the performance evaluation of IAN, BAP, and MAC (percent).

	Ranked as being of "no help"		
Frequency of contact[a]	IAN	BAP	MAC
High	27.2	22.2	15.9
Moderate	16.3	15.5	24.6
None	56.3	62.2	59.4
$N =$	(45)	(45)	(69)

Source: FCV survey.

a. High contact signifies daily or weekly; moderate
means monthly, yearly, or less frequently.

Table 47. Effects of political affiliation of FCV leaders on
performance evaluation of various agrarian reform entities
(percent).

	Party affiliation of leaders		
Ranked as being "little" or "no help"	AD	COPEI	URD
MAC extension agents	80.0	96.7	100.0
Rural housing program	77.1	96.7	100.0
Rural roads program	82.9	86.2	80.0
BAP credit program	72.9	86.7	100.0
IAN	60.0	96.7	100.0
Political party	60.0	86.7	60.0
Peasant Federation	45.7	86.7	60.0
Administrative committee ($N = 118$)	59.2	100.0	100.0

Source: FCV survey.

176

reversed above a certain frequency of contact. It is said that "familiarity breeds contempt." Perhaps Table 46 reflects this axiom. The data may be interpreted as follows. Leaders with no experience of face-to-face contact with agrarian reform bureaucrats are highly critical of their problem-solving performance. Limited exposure to bureaucrats brings a sobering realization of the restrictions and limitations within which government employees must function, with a diminution of performance criticism. Daily or weekly exposure, however, generates knowledge of the pettiness and irrationality of some of the restraints under which the agrarian reform administrator must work; criticism of institutional performance thus increases, although on a different basis from criticism by those with a lack of such contact. Thus, if a "no-contact" respondent was probed as to why he thought, for example, that the Agrarian Institute was of "no help," he might reply, "because they haven't given us any land yet." A "high-contact" respondent, on the other hand, might answer, "How can the institute be of any help when the top policy-makers never leave their air-conditioned offices in Caracas, and the people who are stationed in the field have to spend half of their time filling out useless reports?"

In Table 47, it appears that while political bias may operate to increase the negative evaluations of non-AD-affiliated federation leaders, the effects of the bias seem to be discriminate, and not general. COPEI leaders, therefore, are especially critical of administrative committees, the Peasant Federation, and the Agrarian Institute, all of which are dominated by AD leaders. This may be interpreted as indirect evidence of discriminatory practices by AD leaders, as political bias on the part of COPEI respondents, or as an interaction between the two.

There remains one key problem with which the survey data fail to come to grips. This is the problem of changes in the agrarian reform program over time, and changes in the composition of leadership within the peasant union movement. Though the analyses from the survey are perfectly valid, they represent a snapshot of the system and its participants at a particular point in time—specifically, during the early part of 1966.

The agrarian reform program began early in the 1958–1968 period, with a tremendous surge of land distribution and enormous budgetary inputs. The dilemma of maintaining regime legitimacy, however, convinced top party leaders that restraint in the pursuit of clientele interests was necessary. Such restraint, which could be justified by technical criteria, resulted in an "integral" agrarian reform—that is, a thoroughly planned, coordinated effort which subordinated land distribution to the distribution of a total package of reform benefits. Thus, after 1962 the rate of distributions slowed steadily, and though each peasant family received a much broader and wider range of supporting benefits, fewer families benefited.

Although the policy of restraint may have perfectly valid technological bases, it also has perfectly obvious political consequences. Those peasant union and party leaders most oriented toward the interest-articulation advantages of participation in the problem-solving system disagreed with the policy of restraint, which was advocated as necessary to retain legitimacy. The basis of system legitimacy for these particular participants was, in fact, the system's responsiveness to the demands of their clienteles. The AD government's legitimacy among competing electoral elites, and even among traditional elites, was purchased at the cost of legitimacy among some of their own lower echelon leaders and followers. The result was a series of leadership bolts, or purges, depending on one's point of view.

In any case, the survey made in early 1966 caught a sample of local leaders who had been culled in recent years of their most alienated members—which may have had an effect on the proportion of positive responses toward the government in general, the party, the agrarian reform program, and individual agencies. Such an effect would not be large, since the 1960 and 1962 splits, being mainly elite affairs, involved very small numbers of local leaders and members. However, the changes over time in the volume and nature of the flow of agrarian reform benefits cast some doubt as to the exact meaning of the data on dissatisfaction with particular governmental programs and agencies. Although the foregoing analyses would probably hold up regardless of the volume of the benefit flow, it may be that the absolute level of dissatisfaction is related to the fundamental fact that the AD government has changed the program considerably since 1962.[5] In the absence of time-series data, neither the doubts about leadership changes nor about changes in program level can be satisfactorily answered.

In summary, the outputs of the Venezuelan agrarian reform program have had a fairly stable base of budgetary support (roughly $110 million annually since 1958) for the three major reform agencies. The results, in terms of housing, credits, roads, schools, dispensaries, and the settlement of approximately 100,000 campesino families on 700 asentamientos, have spread throughout rural Venezuela. Supports such as extension services and assistance in the establishment of cooperatives have also flowed from the government.

These agrarian reform benefits, derived originally from the peasant-urban alliance that began in 1936, culminated in the 1948 and 1960 Agrarian Reform Laws, which form the basis of the present rural problem-solving system. However, the distribution of government outputs since 1958 has not perfectly conformed to the areas of peasant union or voting pressures. Although the existence or nonexistence of a peasant union in a given geographic area has had a measurably positive statistical relationship to the flow of agrarian reform benefits to that area, the relationship is imperfect. In reality, a number of other considerations have entered into the pattern of benefit distribution, in addition to that of response to union pressure. Most important among these other considerations seems to be the most rational use of the total land reform investment to achieve agricultural productivity. Thus, benefits have flowed heavily to established, successful agricultural production zones, where infrastructure investments such as roads and water control projects have benefited commercial, as well as peasant, farm operators. The rationality of this distribution policy has been borne out by the absence of a significant reaction or resistance to the agrarian reform program by commercial farm groups, and by a continued growth in overall agricultural output in spite of the transfer of about 5,000,000 acres to subsistence producers.

However, the local leaders of the Peasant Federation, who are closest in time, space, and social ties to the rural masses and the problems confronting them, are probably less appreciative of the fact that overall production has gone up than they are critical of the fact that the new well needed by the community has not yet been dug. Focusing on the concrete problems at hand, and surely aware of the imperfect response of the system to their needs, they tend to be highly critical of the helpfulness of most governmental organizations and agencies engaged in the reform effort. Yet such criticism stems not from a generally negative or hostile attitude toward the institutions involved, nor from a general sense of alienation from the entire national government. Rather, the degree of negativism in evaluating the help received from agrarian reform seems to be a true reflection of the magnitude and gravity of the problems involved in relation to governmental effectiveness in dealing with them. Lack of personal contact with agrarian reform administrators and political bias on the part of a local leader tend to increase the degree of negativism.

Local leaders clearly differentiate between the helpfulness of various organizations and programs in resolving their problems. Based on the data in Table 47, local leaders rank the organizations as follows, from the least useful to the most:

1. Rural Housing Program
2. Extension Service (MAC)
3. Rural Road Program
4. Agrarian Institute (IAN)
5. Credit Program (BAP)

6. Political Party
7. Administrative Committee
8. Peasant Federation (FCV)

This might be considered an index of perceived utility. The order of the list is extremely significant, for it almost exactly matches the relative degree of participation by local union leaders in the decision-making of those organizations.[6] Thus, the Rural Housing Program is limited by environmental, budgetary, and technological restraints from responding to the points of greatest peasant pressure, and its decisions are made in Caracas in a highly technical atmosphere. Similarly, decisions about Extension Services are essentially technical in nature, concerning the most rational allocation of extremely scarce resources.

In contrast, the Peasant Federation, the only entity to be rated positively by local peasant leaders (Table 45), is the arena in which local leaders have the greatest opportunity to participate in significant decision-making. This comes about informally through personal access to state and national leadership, and formally through the internal electoral process of the federation when choosing new local, state, and national officers and when shaping programs at the periodic Campesino Congresses. Similarly, the administrative committees, though not extremely powerful except within the agrarian reform settlements, are completely dominated by local peasant union leadership. The unions not only participate in these decisions, they all but dictate them. The performance ranking of agrarian reform entities by local peasant leaders falls into a nearly perfect pattern. Those institutions perceived as least helpful or least responsive to their concrete needs are the ones dominated by technical considerations; those institutions perceived as most helpful or responsive are the ones dominated, in the broadest sense, by political considerations.

181

IX

THE POLITICS OF AGRARIAN REFORM

Although the workings of the subsystem concerned with solving problems in agrarian reform are an important aspect of the political system, it is the inter- and intraparty pattern of competition and collaboration on the national level that is the vital stuff of agrarian reform politics in Venezuela. These patterns, manifesting themselves around general political and agrarian reform issues, interact with the rural problem-solving system in significant ways. A number of patterns of competition and collaboration have emerged

Figure 3. Patterns of competition and collaboration in the politics of agrarian reform.

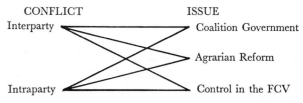

among the major political parties of Venezuela, over three issues: coalition government; agrarian reform; and control over the internal functionings of the Peasant Federation of Venezuela (FCV). The complexity of these patterns is suggested by Figure 3.

INTERPARTY COMPETITION AND COLLABORATION

After the three major political parties-in-exile—Acción Democrática (AD), COPEI, and the Unión Republicana Democrática (URD)—had collaborated for the overthrow of the Pérez Jiménez dictatorship, an interparty agreement was formulated, engaging the mutual collaboration of the three parties to the end of limiting the electoral competition in 1958 to a viable level. The parties further undertook to form a coalition government of all three signatory parties under the leadership of whichever one was victorious in the December 1958 elections. Such a coalition government was instituted under President Betancourt following his inauguration early in 1959. By November 1960, however, URD found itself at such odds with its coalition partners over the issue of how to deal with Fidel Castro that it left the government. The AD-COPEI coalition lasted until 1964, that is, throughout the remainder of President Betancourt's term of office.

In the summer of 1964, President Leoni failed to come to terms with COPEI over its continuing participation in the government, forming instead a coalition of AD, URD, and a third party, the Frente Nacional Democrática (FND). Furthermore, beginning early in 1966, internal frictions within FND began to manifest themselves publicly. The cleavage issue was whether or not to continue in the governmental coalition, and under what conditions. The head of the FND, Senator Arturo Uslar Pietri (around whom the party had been formed during the 1963 elections), let it be known that FND intended to continue its policy of coalition for the benefit of democratic institutions in Venezuela. The FND minister of justice, however, Ramón Escovar Salom, became the focal point for a dissident group of FND politicians and congressmen who favored leaving the coalition. The primary contention of this group was that the original policies of coalition, which they had adopted in joining and supporting the FND, had been gradually prostituted by the exigencies of day-to-day participation in the adminstration—participation which required compromise over issues and with political sectors that the dissidents found repugnant. Escovar began his divisionist campaign by hinting darkly that reactionary forces were threatening to gain dominance within the FND during the absence of Uslar, who was on an extended trip outside the country. It was later revealed that Escovar Salom had specifically accused the FDN minister of agriculture, Pedro Segnini la Cruz, of advocating an alliance with the Cruzada Cívica Nacionalista, (CCN) a political group formed to support the 1968 presidential candidacy of the former dictator, Pérez Jiménez.[1] Uslar was finally forced to maneuver Escovar Salom and two congressmen out of the party for their activities, which were categorized by the FND party leader as "an open conspiracy."[2] This split, which occurred late in April, was followed by a period of clashes between the Uslar and Escovar loyalists, both of whom were competing for the balance of the FND organizational cadres. The competition proved fatal to the FND as an integrated political party, and on March 19, 1966, President Leoni and Uslar formally ratified the withdrawal of the tattered remnants of FND from the government. At the same time, Jóvito Villalba, the secretary-general of URD, announced that his party had decided to continue a coalition with AD, while seeking with President Leoni to attract an independent bloc of support in Congress, in order to maintain a majority in the Chamber of Deputies. In so deciding, Villalba stated, URD had specified certain conditions for its continued collaboration with AD: elimination of discrimination against URD partisans in employment on public works projects and in hiring public school teachers, and an end to discrimination against URD-led peasants in the granting of land and credits under the agrarian reform program.[3] Thus, the general pattern of interparty collaboration from 1958 through 1966 contained muted counterthemes of interparty competition and internal discord.

The pattern of interparty relationships concerning agrarian reform showed a marked similarity. From 1958 through 1966, AD, COPEI, and URD tended to collaborate over the issue, although minor currents of competition and discord surfaced from time to time. All major Venezuelan political parties, with the exception of the Communist party, participated in the formulation and passage of the Agrarian Reform Law promulgated on March 5, 1960. Thereafter the congressional bloc of each party—regardless of whether or not it was at the time a member of the governing coalition generally gave some support to the passage of annual appropriations to continue the agrarian reform program. At the same time, however, COPEI and URD contended that in the distribution of agrarian reform benefits, the peasants who supported their parties were discriminated against in favor of peasants loyal to AD. The measure of truth contained in this charge rested partly on the fact that, in order to get maximum production for the reform investment, agrarian reform benefits flowed most heavily into the small, agriculturally productive, central states, where AD had been vigorously organizing since 1936.

URD, which from late 1960 through the spring of 1964 had pulled its peasant labor organizations out of the Peasant Federation and the Confederation of Venezuelan Workers (CTV), confined its criticisms of agrarian reform mainly to this issue of partisan discrimination.[4] Its charges were credible for the period of URD's walkout from the national government and the labor movement (1960–1964), but subsequently were difficult to assess because of the limited number of peasant groups loyal to URD and because of the relation of these charges to internal conflicts in URD. Aside from the partisan-discrimination issue, URD peasant union leaders as of 1966 pronounced themselves generally satisfied with the agrarian reform program as an instrument for the relief of the battery of problems facing the Venezuelan peasantry.[5]

COPEI party leaders have, however, indicated several shortcomings in the agrarian reform program in addition to partisan discrimination by AD government officials.[6] They have nevertheless continued to support the program because of their fundamental commitment to rural progress and because of their realization that withdrawal of their congressional support for agrarian reform could only strengthen those interested in preserving the status quo, or even in reversing the gains made since 1958. The party leaders' specific criticisms of the government's agrarian reform program have tended to be made on the basis of their distinctive doctrinal position as a Christian Democratic party. They saw, for instance, the government's agrarian reform as a "socialistic program" overly concerned with material goods and services and not sufficiently concerned with the elevation and ennoblement of the peasant sub-culture. COPEI would in general prefer less management of the agrarian reform by central government employees and more management by local participants. Such a shift in emphasis, with local cultural and moral leaders running programs of improvement of the peasantry, the human capital of agrarian reform, would fit in nicely with COPEI's own program of developing rural leadership.[7]

These interparty patterns of competition and collaboration have had both manifest and latent effects on the internal functionings of the Peasant Federation. Under the impetus of the interparty collaboration leading up to and immediately following the overthrow of the dictator, labor leaders in the workers confederation and the peasant union movement formed multiparty reorganization committees on a national and state level. Operating within the framework established by these collaborative committees, local syndicates affiliated with every political tendency organized openly in great numbers. This reorganization process culminated in the First Campesino Congress of June 1959, at which the Peasant Federation was re-established and a multiparty National Executive Committee elected to guide the movement in its drive for "the social and economic emancipation of the peasantry."

However, the Communist and other Marxist elements within the federation caused increasing problems for the AD-COPEI coalition government of President Betancourt in its efforts to carry out a viable reform. These problems grew especially troublesome in 1960 and 1961. In anticipation of the Second Campesino Congress, which was to be held in June 1962 for the purpose of electing a new Executive Committee for the peasant union movement, the top leadership of AD and COPEI reached an agreement to purge Communist and all other radical leadership from the peasant union movement. Following the successful purge, which occurred in November 1961, AD and COPEI agreed to sponsor a joint slate of candidates at the Second Campesino Congress:

the president, secretary-general, agrarian secretary, finance secretary, and secretary for culture and publications were AD leaders; the vice-president, secretary for organization, and secretary for labor affairs were COPEI leaders; and each party named one alternate to the Executive Committee. By the time of the congress, similar divisions of control in the state executive committees, based on the number of local unions and members affiliated with each party, had been worked out in the series of state conventions leading up to the national election. This was the basis for the AD-COPEI collaboration that set the trajectory for internal Peasant Federation functioning from June 1962 through August 1964, by which time a new pattern of interparty relationships had been established.

National coalition politics brought about the new pattern, which lasted from mid-1964 until the Third Campesino Congress, held in Februrary 1967. COPEI, which had been left out of the new coalition government formed by President Leoni in 1964, continued to take part in the Peasant Federation but began at the same time to lay the foundations for its own parallel peasant organization. URD, rejoining the coalition government in the summer of 1964 after almost four years of uncertain opposition, was at the same time re-incorporated into the Confederation of Venezuelan Workers and the Peasant Federation, being allotted two votes without portfolio on the Executive Committee of the federation.

The principal manifestation within the federation of the diminished collaboration between AD and COPEI and of the re-entry of URD as a participant in the peasant movement was a competitive fervor in the organization of new local unions. This competition had as its object the establishment of a new ratio of influence and control at the Third Campesino Congress of February 1967. In such a congress, each legally registered and affiliated local peasant syndicate exercises one vote in the election of a new Executive Committee and in the framing of a program and agenda for action by the Executive Committee until the convocation of the next congress. Thus, AD, COPEI, and URD each tried to increase the number of local syndicates led by its own loyal peasant leaders. Within the peasant movement this competition had two major manifestations: establishment of "parallel unions" by one party in neighborhoods where a local union of another party was already in operation, and challenges to the legal status of locals affiliated with a party competitor. The challenge could be issued on one of two grounds. An older local could be found to be in a "state of dispersion," that is, no longer retaining its legal forty-member minimum membership or meeting regularly. Or, in the case of a new local, it could be found to have been formed by persons who were not native to the community at all—a so-called "phantom league." COPEI and URD charged that many AD-affiliated locals were actually in a state of dispersion, while AD countered that URD, and especially COPEI, were in the business of establishing phantom leagues. The three leadership factions sensibly compromised in an effort to encompass the competition within reasonable limits. They agreed not to establish new syndicates within two kilometers of the site of an already functioning local, so as to control parallelism, and they established Mixed Commissions of three members—one from each party—for each state, to decide on challenges to the legitimacy of any local syndicate affiliated with the federation or seeking affiliation.[8]

The work of these Mixed Commissions was to have led up to the convening of the Third Campesino Congress, originally set for June 1965, but delayed until February 1967 by internal maneuverings. As the commissions liquidated the controversies on their agendas, the states began to report to the National Executive Committee, requesting authorization to hold state conventions. The first of these was held in August 1965, followed by a heavy roster of state conventions convened in February and March 1966.

INTRAPARTY COMPETITION AND COLLABORATION

Competition between parties is a general and persistent condition. Yet it may be accompanied by significant underlying patterns of collaboration between the contestants. Collaboration within an individual party is an equally normal condition, which may be accompanied occasionally by sharp factional competition. Among the major political parties, only COPEI has failed to manifest internal discords that have had significant effects on the three issues of coalition government, agrarian reform, and control of the Peasant Federation. COPEI has managed to preserve internal cohesion and consensus on these issues primarily owing to the fact that no serious competition has developed within the party to challenge its leader, Rafael Caldera, nor have any serious doctrinal cleavages occurred. Caldera managed to retain internal cohesion while withdrawing from the coalition government early in 1964 and assuming a position of responsible opposition to the Leoni administration. Rather than fragmenting COPEI, Caldera's anticoalition policy engendered a feeling of confidence in an electoral triumph for COPEI in the 1968 presidential elections, with the twice-defeated (1958 and 1963) Caldera as the party candidate. COPEI has maintained a consistent policy of discriminating support for the agrarian reform program and has manifested no noticeable internal dissatisfaction with this posture. In its functions within the Peasant Federation, COPEI's young peasant union leaders have maintained a correct, if somewhat detached, attitude toward their fellow leaders affiliated with other parties. They have sought to reap whatever positive benefits accrue to their followers from federation affiliation, while at the same time organizing a national peasant organization of their own in the wings, the Social Christian Agrarian Movement (MASC), founded on June 16, 1964, by decree of the COPEI National Committee.[9] By the end of 1965, the organization of this shadow peasant movement had borne sufficient fruit to justify calling the First National Campesino Assembly from February 25 to 27, 1966, in Caracas. This assemblage of leaders was in the nature of a caucus, since it was composed mainly of leadership cadres rather than of the rank and file.[10] Seemingly, COPEI had no set intentions of splitting from the existing Peasant Federation. Rather, the

189

establishment of its own organization was envisaged as a prudent measure in anticipation of unknown future developments, especially those that might follow the 1968 elections. Directly involved in such unknown future developments were politically important peasant leaders in the URD party.

URD has never succeeded in establishing a well-defined political personality.[11] Though something of a personal vehicle for the "maestro," Jóvito Villalba, the party has over the years built up a considerable institutional machinery and has included several political and peasant leaders of great stature in its ranks, as well as many capable and talented leaders of a more ordinary sort. Among the notable leaders has been Jorge Pacheco, a congressman and, until mid-1966, the national campesino director of URD.[12]

Following the re-entry of URD into the Peasant Federation in August 1964, the national URD Campesino Directorate began a campaign of recruitment and syndicate formation. The First National Campesino Meeting of URD was held from July 4 to 11, 1965, under the leadership of Pacheco. By early 1966, URD could claim 672 peasant unions, either in being or in the process of formation.[13] It was at this point, however, that Pacheco, a peasant leader since 1936 and a founding member of URD, became deeply involved in a profound internal party crisis.

The conflict that rent URD in the spring of 1966 was so serious that the party may never recover from its effects. At stake were presidential ambitions for 1968, but the issue over which the conflict emerged was participation in the government coalition. Jóvito Villalba, the acknowledged father of the party, had one fatal shortcoming in the eyes of many politicians—he could not win an election. Villalba had tried for the presidency in 1947, in 1952, and again in 1963. In the opinion of many party professionals, for the 1968 election URD needed a fresh, young personality, such as Alirio Ugarte Pelayo, the party's "number two" man and its astute leader in Congress. In a move to forestall the possibility of a challenge to his candidacy, Jóvito announced his own candidacy in December 1965. This precipitated the train of events that culminated in the crisis of May 1966.

Resentment at the maestro's premature play for the party's presidential nomination crystallized a realization by important segments of URD professionals of the party's institutional weakness. The careers and future ambitions of all URD political figures seemed inextricably entangled with Jóvito's ceaseless quest for the presidency, and his record as a three-time loser was less than inspiring in this context. A reformist movement thus began to develop around the figure of Ugarte Pelayo. This movement sought two related adjustments in internal party life: first, a more autonomous and critical role within the coalition government than Jóvito was playing, in order to project a more distinct electoral identity; and second, an active search for issues and programs that might form the basis for the URD electoral equation for 1968—a search that included the choice of the party's most attractive candidate. The question was therefore a variation on the dilemmas faced by all minority parties in a coalition government: how to strike a balance between responsibility to the government and responsibility to the party's electoral future.

One of the first public evidences of this growing internal ferment was reported on March 19, 1966, following FND's retirement, when Jóvito announced that URD intended to remain in the coalition. URD's decision was based on a vote of the National Directorate, in which twenty-two had voted with Jóvito to remain in coalition, and six had voted with Ugarte Pelayo to leave. Among the six was Jorge Pacheco.[14] By the end of March, denials of internal crisis were frequently carried in the newspapers of Caracas and the interior. They were originated by central party figures as well as by provincial chiefs, which indicated the geographically broad basis on which the controversy was developing.

Internal party ferment was apparently met by Villalba with increasing rigidity; and the dissident faction, having exhausted avenues for redress within the party framework, began to increase the pressure for change by contacting political leaders outside the party. Specifically, by mid-April rumors were circulating of a pending alliance between the amorphously organized but popular Fuerza Democrática Popular (FDP), and the dissident faction of URD. The basis for the alliance was said to be the delivery of Ugarte Pelayo's organizational cadres to the FDP in return for uniting that party's fervent following behind his presidential candidacy. The situation reached crisis proportions on April 23, when news stories reported that later in the week Ugarte, Wolfgang Larrazábal, and Jorge Dager of the FDP would meet to discuss electoral coalitions for 1968.[15]

Faced with this grave evidence of discord, which Ugarte would neither confirm nor deny, Villalba called a meeting of the National Directorate to suspend Ugarte Pelayo from all party positions and activities, and to present his case to the party's Disciplinary Tribunal. On April 26, 1966, after nine hours of agonizing debate on the issue, Ugarte Pelayo was suspended from party activities by a vote of sixteen to twelve. Voting against the suspension were such important and able members of the directorate as the national labor director, the national campesino director (Pacheco), the national woman's director, and the URD boss in the federal district.[16] It soon became evident that if Ugarte left the party over his suspension, he would take with him the twelve members of the National Directorate who had backed him against Villalba, eight congressmen, and at least ten state organizations.[17]

Three days after Ugarte's suspension, Arturo Infante, Jorge Pacheco's assistant, and a group of other peasant leaders called for Jóvito Villalba's suspension and the submission of his case to the Disciplinary Tribunal.[18] Faced with this dramatic evidence of the depth of the split within his party's ranks, Jóvito became even more rigid. Party resignations, individual and group, began to be announced. On May 5, 1966, the entire National Campesino Directorate announced that it was bolting the party over the suspension of Ugarte. At the same time, Pacheco announced that he and his peasant leader colleagues had formed the First of May Peasant's Movement, an indication that Pacheco would carry most of the organizational cadre of the URD's peasant movement with him.[19]

Since the effective functioning of peasant leaders in Venezuela depends on their influence in an established political party, the URD peasant union leaders who left the party with Pacheco could no longer function within the Peasant Federation as an independent leadership structure. Following the bolt from URD of Pacheco's group, it continued for a time to function formally as an organization representing the local peasant unions affiliated with the party. Gradually, however, the dissident leaders were replaced by Villalba at the national, state, and in some cases local levels; that is, new leaders stepped into the roles occupied by the dissidents, who still claimed to represent all of the URD-organized peasants.

A major clash between the Pacheco-led dissidents and the URD loyalists over control of the Pacheco-organized peasant movement failed to develop. Following the tragic death of Ugarte Pelayo on July 1, 1966, the effort to form a new party with its own peasant movement seems to have disintegrated.[20] By the time of the Third Campesino Congress, held in February 1967, most URD peasant leaders who had bolted the party in May 1966 had sought readmission, which had been granted under certain punitive conditions. Thus, the URD members of the Executive Committee elected at the Third Congress could still claim the allegiance of most of the peasant union locals organized by URD since 1964.

AD has experienced two periods of internal competition which bear on the politics of agrarian reform. One period provoked the crisis that led to the purging of radical leadership from the FCV in 1962; the other led to the 1967–1968 crisis, which cost AD the presidency in the 1968 elections. The first controversy concerned the pace and scope of the Betancourt administration's agrarian reform program. Involved in this dispute were political forces outside of AD, in particular the Communists and other neo-Marxist movements. In part because of their close working relationship with leftist underground groups during the ten-year period of suppression under the dictatorship, many younger AD leaders had themselves adopted a posture of intransigent militancy for radical socioeconomic reform. Though no youngster, Ramón Quijada, the AD president of the Peasant Federation elected in 1947 and again in 1959, was also such a leader. By April 1960 one group of these leaders had broken away from AD. Generally dissatisfied with the restrained pace of the government's reforms, they formed the Movimiento de la Izquierda Revolucionaria (MIR). This was the first external evidence of the growing interest-versus-legitimacy dilemma.[21]

Throughout the remainder of 1960 and into the summer of 1961, a controversy developed within AD, specifically over agrarian reform. Aligned on one side was Ramón Quijada, with the support of radical AD, Communist, and other leftist leadership elements within the Peasant Federation. On the other side were the AD moderates: President Betancourt himself; Ildegar Pérez Segnini, the president of the board of National Agrarian Institute (IAN) and Armando González, secretary-general of the important Carabobo state Peasant Federation.

The dispute was carried on principally by Pérez Segnini and Quijada, who also held a position on the Agrarian Institute board as one of the two peasant representatives. The issue was whether to foster a radical reform, by immediately distributing land and credits to all campesinos who applied for them, or an integral reform, by coordinating the distribution of land with supporting services, roads, housing, and marketing arrangements. Quijada advocated accomplishing the reform within two years. Pérez Segnini and the moderates warned that the reform would require from four to ten years to work out. Quijada and the other interest-articulation leaders claimed that AD would alienate its peasant power base if it did not respond radically to the militant rural mood. But technicians and pragmatic politicians felt that only a rationally integrated program would succeed in altering the conditions which were the basis of the peasant discontent and that an AD government had to stay in power in order to see such a program through. President Betancourt temporarily shelved this dispute by replacing both Pérez Segnini and Quijada on the board of the Agrarian Institute with AD middle-of-the-roaders.

The problem continued to manifest itself, however, and by mid-1961 it was a recognizable factor in a larger labor-government problem. The Venezuelan labor movement was in general being asked by the Betancourt government to restrain its demands on governmental resources during this period of trial, during which Venezuela was simultaneously recovering from a panic recession and attempting to maintain political stability in the face of cross-cutting threats from the left and the right. Communist, neo-Marxist, and radical AD labor leaders such as Quijada were reluctant to accept the pleas of President Betancourt, perceiving a sellout to the forces of reaction. A decision was therefore made in the highest councils of AD to purge the labor movement of its far leftist leadership, within and without the party.

The Fourth Congress of the Confederation of Venezuelan Workers, held in November 1961, was chosen as the vehicle for the purge. Increasingly alienated from his own party, Quijada announced that the Peasant Federation woud not attend the congress. With the help of COPEI, the AD moderates at the congress isolated and undermined the radical leadership, including Quijada, within the labor movement. Thus, in plenary session of the labor congress the Quijada-led federation was declared to be "intervened," and Armando González was elected agrarian secretary of the Confederation of Workers, replacing Quijada. González was also named chairman of a reorganization committee, empowered to undertake the internal rehabilitation of the Peasant Federation. Quijada, however, refused to accept the findings of the Confederation of Workers or to recognize its authority. The rump Peasant Federation continued to occupy its Caracas headquarters and to prepare for the

Second Campesino Congress, which was to be held in June 1962. The Armando González group opened up a new Peasant Federation office and also began to prepare for the Second Congress. Since the Betancourt government no longer recognized the legality of the Quijada-federation, the subsidy from the Ministry of Labor went to the González-federation. These two organizations then fought it out, state by state, in a series of conventions that led up to the Second Campesino Congress. President Betancourt himself took to the hustings during the spring of 1962, backing the replacement of interest-oriented leaders with leaders for whom regime-legitimacy and survival were most important. The exciting series of state conventions culminated on June 1 with the opening of not one but two Second Campesino Congresses. Ramón Quijada opened his congress in the Caracas Sports Palace; Armando González and President Betancourt opened theirs at the government-built labor resort of Los Caracas, on the Caribbean. One state organization and the representatives of about 100 local unions attended the Quijada congress. Nineteen state organizations and the representatives of about 2300 local unions attended the Second Campesino Congress at Los Caracas, which signaled the end of the conflict over agrarian reform policy and the establishment of a new, more moderate AD-COPEI leadership for the Venezuelan peasant movement. The old Peasant Federation, like the proverbial old soldier, gradually faded away.[22]

In political parties that are institutionalized and which no longer depend for their impetus on individual leaders, competition for important party nominations is a normal aspect of party life. AD is such a party. Its second relevant experience of internal competition, therefore, centered on ambitions for the presidential nomination in the 1968 election year. The first conflict, which had been initiated by disagreement over an issue, agrarian reform, had gradually transformed itself into a struggle for factional supremacy within the party. In contrast, the more recent contest started out as part of the leadership competition normal to political life but came in time to involve agrarian reform as one of its many issues. The conflict was carried into the internal functionings of the Peasant Federation and finally resulted in the most farreaching split so far experienced by AD.

The antecedents of the contest reached back to the AD convention held prior to the presidental election in 1963. It was appropriate on such occasions to nominate the party candidate for the approaching election and thus to open the campaign. President Betancourt, however, favored a departure from tradition. He advocated that the convention nominate five party leaders capable of carrying the party banners in the presidential race. On the basis of negotiations with other political parties, such as their coalition partner, COPEI, the Executive Committee would select the actual candidate at an appropriate time. Thus, the lame-duck president hoped to maintain the close cooperation and participation of COPEI, which had been indispensable to the survival of his government, for the benefit of the succeeding administration. Specifically, President Betancourt felt that the leading contender for the AD nomination, Senator Raúl Leoni, had been identified for too long as an AD militant who had little affection for, or rapport with, the COPEI forces. Betancourt hoped, by the panel nomination maneuver, to include other men, not so identified, among the political nominees.

The convention thwarted President Betancourt in his desire to keep the nomination decision fluid and solidly endorsed the candidacy of Raúl Leoni. A key organizational figure in Senator Leoni's successful drive for the nomination was Jesús Angel Paz Galarraga, who was elected at the convention to the powerful and influential position of party secretary general. Like Leoni, Paz was not known as an ardent fan of the COPEI party. President Betancourt tried to prevail upon president-elect Leoni to find a basis for continuing the coalition with COPEI, but the price they demanded was unacceptable to Leoni, and he found another equation for the successful formation of a government in the summer of

1964. In the meantime, after traveling through the United States, ex-President Betancourt prudently chose to retire to Europe, far enough from the daily hazards of Venezuelan politics to ensure a degree of personal tranquility and safety (as president he had been the object of innumerable assassination attempts by the left and right alike), yet close enough to maintain an interested vigilance over political developments in his homeland. Within the party he left behind there was still a considerable minority faction that deferred to his leadership, tending to consider him, as the party founder, the soundest and wisest counselor for the party. Among this group of men was Armando González, president of the Peasant Federation. There was no question, however, of Betancourt trying to compete with President Leoni for influence within the party, which would have been not only fruitless but repugnant to both men, who were old and steadfast friends as well as mutually respected political allies.

The question emerged again, however, as it had in 1963, of whether the presidential nominee for the 1968 election should be selected by the top party leaders, on the basis of their judgment of the political situation, or by free and open internal competition for the candidacy. President Bentacourt was a believer in the former method of selection; President Leoni, a product of the competitive method, nevertheless advocated neither, but typically let events themselves determine the nature of the selection.

The party secretary-general, Paz Galarraga, apparently habored ambitions for the nomination himself, for he set about vigorously utilizing his key role to build up support in the state party organizations. His basic position was roughly that AD, which had been in the government since 1958, had allowed the balance between governmental and electoral responsibility to be tipped too much in favor of governmental responsibility. The recognition of AD's basic responsibility in the conduct of the government (legitimation) had not won it any votes, while the restraint it had exercised in the pursuit of its reformist goals (interest-articulation) had threatened to lose it electoral support in the 1968 campaign. Therefore, the argument continued, what was needed was a reinvigoration in the pursuit of such reforms—not governmental irresponsibility, but a shift in emphasis back toward electoral responsibility. Paz steadily built up support within the party among the elements that concurred generally with this analysis. In looking forward to his own possible nomination for the presidency in 1968, Paz spoke concretely of a needed "opening to the left" in the Venezuelan coalition system, likening such a development to Italy's postwar political evolution. Implied in the Paz analysis was the hypothesis that the self-restraint with which the Venezuelan labor movement, including the Peasant Federation, had been conducting itself since the 1962 leadership purge was no longer so necessary or desirable.

Within AD, two competing leadership groups thus emerged. One was deferential to the leadership and pragmatism of Rómulo Betancourt, favoring a continuation of moderate, responsible reform policies in order to continue the viability of coalition. In the matter of selecting the party's next presidential candidate, this faction favored letting the party elders, especially Betancourt and Leoni, make the selection, with full consideration of the requirements for continued coalition government. For the sake of convenience, this will be called the Betancourt faction. The other group believed in the benefits of competition. Regarding internal party competition, it advocated free competition in the selection of the most capable party leader for the presidential nomination. Externally, it favored competition for the voting support of the growing urban sector, and a refurbishing of its traditional bases of labor and peasant support by reinvigorating AD's reformist policies, which had been the basis of its initial formation as a party and were presumably responsible for its electoral successes in 1958 and 1963. For convenience, this will be referred to as the Paz faction.

Competition between these groups first appeared in the internal politics of the peasant movement during September 1965, at the party's annual convention. At that time, the Betancourt faction, led by congressional majority leader Carlos Andros Pérez, lost a close fight to block the re-election of Paz Galarraga as secretary-general, contending that a candidate for the presidential nomination should not hold the party's top organizational position. In winning his re-election, Paz carried with him a new agrarian secretary, Eustacio Guevara, who succeeded Armando González. González, the president of the Peasant Federation, continued as a political secretary on the National Executive Committee.

Paz Galarraga and Eustacio Guevara, working through the various state party organizations, began quietly to recruit leadership support from within the party sectors, including the Peasant Federation, on the basis of the reform reinvigoration thesis. The consequences of this campaign were to become manifest in the state conventions leading up to the Third Campesino Congress.

STATE CONVENTIONS OF THE PEASANT FEDERATION

All of these patterns of competition and collaboration materialized in the 1966 series of Peasant Federation state conventions. Six such conventions, chosen at random, are here described—those convened in Miranda, Barinas, Trujillo, Aragua, Mérida, and Carabobo. All Peasant Federation conventions were held on weekends, the majority being scheduled for two days, but often concluding in one. The state executive committee was responsible for organizing and conducting the convention, which was to accomplish three things: receive the reports of incumbent state officials on their conduct of office since the last convention; debate and recommend, on the basis of these reports, the programs, policies, and requests for action to be carried to the Campesino Congress (which is convoked only at the conclusion of the series of state conventions); and finally, elect a slate of leaders to the state executive committee, to serve until the next convention. Delegates to the conventions were elected by local unions, each being allotted up to seven seats, according to the number of members in the local. The conventions were held in appropriate and available locations, such as union halls, government auditoriums, or theaters rented for the occasion. They commonly opened about 10 A.M. on the scheduled Saturday mornings.

On the morning of the six conventions under discussion, the local union delegations began to arrive by rented transportation if necessary, by private transportation if available, or by government vehicle if possible. Upon arrival at the city or town where the convention was being held, the individual delegations proceeded, not to the convention site, but typically to the headquarters of the party with which they were affiliated. There they held a Pleno Agrario or Agrarian Caucus, to decide on a common posture vis-à-vis the delegations affiliated with the other parties and on the issues and candidates with which the convention would deal.

During the Agrarian Caucus, the state federation leaders representing each of the three parties (AD, COPEI, and URD), and at least one national leader from each party, also met in the proverbial "smoke-filled room" to find a compromise basis for electing new state officers. At issue in these meetings were the following points: how many local affiliates each party controlled; the size of the locals controlled by each party; the old division of state offices among AD and COPEI, still in effect from the 1962 conventions; and an appropriate new division, or a continuation of the old, based on all of these factors. These bargaining sessions, conducted by political negotiators, normally resulted in a compromise completely satisfactory to no one, but acceptable to all. If no compromise was reached, a party (COPEI, URD, never AD) might decide to boycott the convention, loudly decrying all of the "politics" involved in the activities. In most cases, however, at the conclusion of the interparty bargaining session, telephone calls were made to various party headquarters, and the delegates were sent to the convention hall.

From this point on, during the public sessions, interparty collaboration was at a maximum. State and national leaders sat together on the platform and gave speeches, reports, and problem-analyses as representatives of the peasant masses, not as representatives of their party. Partisan affiliation was not a taboo subject on such occasions, but it was gracefully subordinated to more general identifications. Thus, it was normal, during the nomination proceedings for the new slate of state leaders, to accept open nominations from the floor, then in some cases to present the outgoing leadership's compromise slate of candidates, balanced among leaders representing all parties—"in the interests of representing *all* campesinos." If strict majority rule procedures had been followed, AD would have elected its leaders to all of the state federation positions, except in Trujillo, Mérida, and Táchira, where COPEI would have elected its own one-party slate. The compromise system, based on tough, tight bargaining, managed to represent the peasants of all party affiliations in a ratio roughly proportional to their numbers. Even if a particular party was not a member of the government coalition, and therefore had no direct access opportunities for its local union leaders, local officials representing significant numbers of peasants could normally achieve indirect structural access through means of the state convention bargaining-and-election process.

The major political pattern encountered in the six sample state conventions—interparty competition and intraparty cohesion—was characterized by interplay with a minor pattern, which was its dialectical counterpart. The minor pattern—interparty cohesion and intraparty competition—burst forth in one of the state conventions that I attended, and became the dominant pattern of politics, as illustrated in the following miniature case study.[23] The actual situation in the state prior to the convention was such that all four of the state officers elected in 1962 were affiliated with AD, but two of them were substitutes for radical leaders who had been purged, having been recruited by Armando González from other party positions outside of the peasant movement. The third officer was a powerful, old-time peasant leader (his career began in 1936) who felt that the two moderate party loyalists recruited by González were not vigorous enough in their representation of the peasant interests in the state. The fourth, a dependable, mild-mannered party loyalist, was essentially uninvolved in any factionalist considerations and maintained a posture of neutrality. The old-timer was supported, in his conflict with the two substitute leaders, by the state secretary-general of AD. This powerful ally had been sent to the state by Paz Galarraga to reinvigorate the party machine. The old-timer's ally had formerly been a Peasant Federation leader in the state and was later made national secretary-general of the federation. Prior to the interparty maneuverings involved in the conventions, therefore, there had been a considerable amount of competition in the state between the Betancourt and Paz factions of AD.

The opening steps were taken by the two leaders, one of whom was the titular head of the state Peasant Federation, identified with the Betancourt faction and the AD-COPEI national alliance headed by Armando González, president of the federation. They named an organizing committee for the convention, on which the truculent old-timer held only a minor, virtually powerless position. Their own men were named to the finance, transportation, and food committees—positions from which they could presumably influence the delegates to the convention. Then the secretary-general officially declared that the organization committee was meeting in permanent session, during which time the normal business of the state executive committee was suspended. The state headquarters were closed until after the convention. By this series of maneuvers, the two officials cut off the administrative base of the old-timer, effectively bypassing him in the accreditation of delegates by correspondence and other convention prearrangements critical to the internal control of the convention.

But the old-timer's base of support was not dependent on administrative advantages. It consisted of a solidly woven network of interpersonal relationships with local leaders, built up over the years of his work as a peasant leader, which was on this occasion reinforced by his alliance with the state party boss, the ex-federation secretary-general. These two took to the road, personally contacting the local leaders affiliated with AD and gathering support for the showdown with the convention leaders.

The day of the convention arrived and, with it, the occasion for negotiation. Only in this case the bargaining and competition were to be intraparty instead of interparty. Each party headquarters became the scene of the individual Agrarian Caucuses. Within an hour or two the URD and COPEI representatives had concluded their sessions and come out to the convention site to await the arrival of the AD delegates. As far as interparty affairs stood, the AD leaders of the Paz faction (old-timer and party boss) were expected to win in the internal struggle, and they had made it understood that they were ready to create a fifth state leadership post, albeit a relatively minor one, which they would allow to be filled by URD. In spite of the fact that URD controlled fewer local unions in the state than COPEI did, the AD leadership found the COPEI leadership abrasive and were going to exclude them in favor of URD. Nevertheless, the COPEI delegates and a talented young national leader were on hand, pending the final outcome of the AD caucus.

What actually transpired at the AD meeting may never be clearly revealed, but it is significant that before it was ended, both the president of the Peasant Federation (Betancourt faction) and the party's national agrarian secretary (Paz faction) had hurried in from Caracas for a face-to-face confrontation. Out of the encounter came an extraordinarily balanced compromise: the old timer (Paz faction) was elevated to state secretary-general; the two controversial officers were removed but replaced by two other officers recruited from the Betancourt faction; and the neutralist was moved to a slightly more powerful position, vacating his post as secretary for culture and publications to URD's choice for state official. The AD delegates finally straggled into the convention at 5 P.M., after their strenuous, nine-hour caucus, confidently expecting to control the interparty competition, now that they had successfully surmounted their own.

But the COPEI and the URD leaders had a surprise in store for the AD delegates. Sitting around in the sun all day, waiting for the AD conventioneers to arrive, had given them time to plan. After a while the two national peasant leaders from each party had gone out together for a cold beer. When they returned, they brought with them the basis for a clever and mutually beneficial convention alliance. URD would support the claim of COPEI to representation in the state executive committee. In return, COPEI would nominate and support the URD candidate, not for the post that AD intended to grant them, but for a more powerful one. Thereby URD could get an influential post, and COPEI would not be excluded, but would for the first time in the state get representation on the state executive committee, if only in the lowest post.

This alliance was carried to a successful conclusion through a series of skillfully executed "cross-roughing" floor maneuvers by the URD and COPEI national leaders.[24] The AD leaders, exhausted by their own struggles, gracefully accepted the adroit moves of the URD-COPEI alliance. The confluence of the many interacting patterns of political competition and collaboration in the convention thus produced an outcome in which no particular faction or party was completely dominant, but in which each shared power in a fairly equitable ratio. In a speech following the election of the tripartite executive committee, the AD state party boss astonishingly asserted that the composition of the new committee, representing as it did the interests of "all campesinos, regardless of their political affiliations," was an indication of the "nonpartisan" nature of the peasant movement in the state. In the sense that multipartisan, and not exclusively AD, interests had been met in the convention process, he was ironically correct.

THE 1967–1968 CRISIS OF AD

The internal struggle within AD, manifested in the series of state conventions of the Peasant Federation, was carried out in all forums of the party and affiliated interest organizations in a similar manner. The organization men behind the struggle—Secretary-General Paz Galarraga and ex-President Rómulo Betancourt—concentrated on recruiting supporting leadership at all levels. The struggle seemed to be kept within viable bounds, however, and appeared to most observers in 1966 to be just another family fight, if a fairly brutal one.

In September of 1966 the national convention of AD provided additional evidence of the internal maneuverings of the party. Dr. Luís Beltrán Prieto Figueroa, one of AD's historic leaders and president of the Senate since 1962, was elected president of the party. Named as first vice-president was Paz Galarraga. Gonzalo Barrios, another historic leader of the party and minister of the interior in the Leoni regime, was elected secretary-general to replace Paz. Most observers viewed Barrios as a probable candidate for the presidential nomination by the Betancourt faction. Prieto resigned as president of the Senate in October, and Barrios as minister of the interior in November—both resignations being viewed as freeing Prieto and Barrios from constitutional responsibilities and allowing them greater room to maneuver in the political arena.

Early in 1967 both men began to act like candidates for their party's nomination, making speaking tours and engaging in much the same behavior as is associated with candidates in the United States. The nomination was expected to be decided at the annual party convention in September 1967, since the presidential election was scheduled for December 1968, and quite elaborate campaign organizing is required. Party practice had been to hold a series of district conventions, to which the delegates had been selected by the local party committees. The district conventions elected delegates to the state conventions, and so forth, leading up to the climactic national convention. During the spring of 1967, however, for reasons that are not clear, the National Executive Committee decided to allow a series of party primaries, in which the delegates to the district conventions would be elected by the mass membership instead of being named by the municipal party committees. This was a decision that many of the leaders of AD were sure to regret.

During the summer of 1967 it became clear that Paz Galarraga was solidly behind the Prieto candidacy and that Betancourt was similarly committed to Barrios. There were definite indications, similar to those which surfaced at the series of Peasant Federation conventions, that many of the most activist, militant, and interest-oriented leaders, having the closest ties to the membership base, were moving with Paz behind the Prieto candidacy. Consequently, there was confidence in the ability of Prieto to carry the day in the party primaries. However, it was impossible to foresee accurately how many of the party rank and file these subleaders could actually take with them into the Prieto movement. As a result, within the Barrios camp was an equal degree of confidence in their ability to win the primaries, since Barrios, as secretary-general of the party, had the greatest formal control over the internal party administrative and organizational machinery, as well as the backing of a large number of party loyalists to whom continued regime legitimacy was a primary value.

The first rounds of the primary, in which the rank and file elected delegates to the district conventions, went heavily for Prieto—reportedly between 65 and 75 percent.[25] The Paz faction was jubilant, expecting to control the district conventions with a majority of delegates. The Betancourt faction, however, apparently felt confident that the district conventions still offered an opportunity for internal control of the convention proceedings, as had always been the case in the past, through control of internal party mechanisms. That is, in many of these district conventions a situation similar to the peasant convention in the case study was shaping up: a group of activist leaders with a strong following among the rank and file was opposed by another group in control of the traditional party mechanisms. During the course of these district primaries, the first public disturbances broke out, and the National Executive Committee, in which Barrios' followers had a majority, suspended the first Prieto followers for their part in the outbreaks of violence.

Early in October the Barrios forces selectively convened those district conventions in which the rank and file had, according to their calculations, elected a majority of pro-Barrios delegates. When these district conventions also came out strongly for Prieto—indicating the kind of undercover organizing that can be conducted by skilled activists outside traditional party channels—the Barrios people convened a special meeting of the party's National Executive Committee, which, with all of the Prieto loyalists boycotting it, suspended all further district convention proceedings. Prieto, as president of the party, ordered the district conventions to proceed. The die was cast. The two factions were moving in opposite directions, and in various districts throughout the country the struggle broke out into the open. In the districts controlled by the Gonzalistas, the conventions were called off; in those controlled by the Prietistas, they were held, with overwhelmingly pro-Prieto slates named as delegates to the state conventions; and in districts where neither faction had the upper hand, a vicious struggle for control took place.

In response to the widening breach in party discipline and integrity, the National Executive Committee, with a Barrios majority, convened a seldom-used but superior body known as the National Director's Committee, which consisted of the National Executive Committee plus the executive committee of each state and federal territory (unincorporated states). The close division in the Director's Committee emphasized the depth and seriousness of the breach: reportedly, Barrios controlled seventy-four votes, and Prieto sixty-six, out of the one hundred and forty member total. As the vote shaped up for a formal action, the Prieto members boycotted the meeting, and only the party president himself attended for a brief defense of his actions, coupled with criticism of the violation of internal party democratic procedures. The committee suspended Prieto—the party president—and Paz Galarraga—the party vice-president—for defying the order of the executive committee to call off the district conventions, which were still being carried on in many places and going heavily for Prieto. Both Paz and Prieto refused to recognize the suspensions, as did the executive committees of twelve of the twenty-three state organizations.

There followed a turbulent period as each faction tried to purge the followers of the other from party positions at the national, state, and local levels. The Director's Committee met again and formally removed the party president and first vice-president from office, although according to internal party statutes, only the National Disciplinary Tribunal had the power to do so.[26] In addition, many other national backers of Prieto were purged from party positions, including many key figures in the rural problem-solving system, such as Eustacio Guevara, the party agrarian secretary; José González Navarro, president of the Confederation of Workers; Carlos Behrens, president of the Sugarcane Workers' Federation; Pedro Torres, secretary-general of the Peasant Federation; and Máximo Acuña, finance secretary of the Peasant Federation.

During the closing months of 1967, the struggle for internal control of the party by both factions continued. The Prieto followers utilized the courts—specifically, the Supreme Electoral Tribunal—to try to contest their suspension and removal from party offices and responsibilities. The court ruled the suspension legal, although actual removal from office was held the sole responsibility of the Disciplinary Tribunal, and denied the request of the Prieto people for exclusive use of the party name and ballot in future elections. An appeal to the Supreme Court likewise failed. The Prieto people had lost control of internal party power, and the party was no longer a remotely unified force. Behind the Prieto surge were apparently the schoolteacher's unions, journalists, most professional groups, more than half of the state peasant movement organizations, and the most militant AD unions, including the petroleum workers, transport workers, and dock workers. In addition, the radical youth branches were solidly behind Prieto. On the other hand, the party clienteles behind Barrios included the party and administration bureaucrats, some youth wings, and a number of state peasant federations. It seems reasonably clear from this line-up that party leaders and members oriented toward vigorous low-status interest group responses were ranged on one side of the breach, and a number of interests that had been created by, and were dependent upon, the party's incumbency in government were ranged on the other. The primary value of one faction was interest articulation. The primary value of the other was continued legitimacy in government.

Moving ahead with their series of district and state conventions, the Prieto forces convened a national convention in Caracas, nominating Prieto for the presidency early in December. At this point, the Prietistas were still claiming to represent the AD party. Following their failures in the courts later that month, however, the struggle for internal party control gradually subsided, and an exodus began. Although frequent attempts were made to negotiate a compromise candidate and hold the warring factions together within the party, they all failed. By the spring of 1968, a new and significant electoral organization had emerged, called the Movimiento Electoral del Pueblo or People's Electoral Movement (MEP).

The seriousness of the breakdown in the unity of AD is beyond dispute. In carrying with it almost one-half of the prominent AD leaders and many rank-and-file members, the MEP faction, while building a creditable electoral machine of its own by the time of the 1968 elections, came in only fourth in the balloting for the presidency. At the same time, AD lost its first freely contested presidential race in four attempts to the COPEI candidate, Rafael Caldera. The loss of this presidential election clearly signaled the end of a decade of AD hegemony in Venezuelan government. The party remained, of course, a significant factor in congressional, state, and local politics, but it no longer controlled the national agencies and programs that it had as the senior partner in the coalition governments from 1958 through 1968. Although one cannot consider this the beginning of the end of the kind of democratic government characterizing the AD era, one can certainly consider it the end of the beginning.

X

CONCLUDING PERSPECTIVES

Tracing the history of peasant mobilization and agrarian reform in Venezuela is a difficult task, but to adequately explain these phenomena is a yet more complex problem, for they are only two elements—albeit critical ones—in the massive socioeconomic transformations occurring in Venezuela during the forty-odd years of my case study. The overall transformation may be broken down into three elements: commercialization in agriculture, urbanization, and the politicization of the masses. A few general remarks may help to foster perspective on these three phenomena, which are significant processes in the politics of most of the developing nations of Africa, Asia, and Latin America.

The attempt by landed elites to commercialize agriculture, suggested Barrington Moore, Jr., is likely to have enormous political consequences, whether it succeeds or fails.[1] The failure of such an attempt will probably have more drastic consequences than its success, since the attempt may succeed in breaking the social bonds that hold the traditional rural society together, but fail to replace them with ties to some new kind of socioeconomic order. Particularly prone to failure will be an attempt to capitalize on the sort of peasant obligations that underlay traditional landlord-peasant relationships. Hans Bobek characterizes this kind of commercialization of agriculture as "rent capitalism," pointing out that it differs significantly from modern capitalism, in which two areas of decision-making, production and distribution, are highly developed.[2] In rent capitalism, traditional landlords focus only on distribution decisions, that is, on how to make a profit from the distribution of the surplus which, in some form of "rent," they extract from the peasantry. Since little thought is applied to production decisions, however, the development of this form of agricultural capitalism suffers serious limitations. In the case of Venezuela, such a form of commercialization of agriculture was apparently attempted in the early part of this century, only to founder on the shoals of domestic credit and international marketing. The primary consequence of this unsettling attempt was to create conditions favorable to a mobilization of the peasantry.

The early stages of urban growth and commercial development in Venezuela were intimately related to the mobilization of the peasantry. Urban-commercial development necessarily creates role specialization and complicates status differentiation. The petit bourgeois, skilled artisan, trader, and financier become new statuses that must be accommodated in the old status hierarchy. It seems to be the general case that the accommodation involves a struggle for upward mobility—a striving for traditional elite, or near-elite, status and rewards—and ultimately, a political conflict between aspiring and entrenched elites. This struggle provides incentives for the upwardly mobile elites, whose aspirations have been blocked by the entrenched political elites, to seek control of the state. Their attempts often take the form of seeking a mass base of support. In the Venezuelan case, this base of popular support was available among the discontented peasantry.

The politicization of the masses may or may not precipitate a prolonged period of political instability. As Samuel Huntington argues, it depends on the rapidity of the process and, even more important, on whether institutions exist, or can be created, to channel mass participation into stable patterns of interaction.[3] Elite interests—both traditional and newly formed—are differentiated, requiring a complex pattern of accommodation. Similarly, mass interests are differentiated, and they become more so as urbanization proceeds, whether or not it is accompanied by industrialization. The politicization of upwardly mobile elites and the masses, if it is not institutionalized into some form of political order, produces an open-ended political struggle, or instability. The same processes of politicization, if channeled into institutionalized patterns of interaction among conflicting interests, lead to political struggle bound within a coherent system, or stability. In the Venezuelan case, the mobilization of the peasantry took place within an institutional framework—the peasant union movement—and the struggle for the interests of the peasant masses took place within a newly created context of political struggle, the multiparty system and the electoral process.

The early stages of urbanization, which precipitate new, upwardly mobile urban elites, are a necessary context for political development, and may prove beneficial if the challenging elites manage to institutionalize the mass mobilizations that they tend to attempt. The middle and later stages of urbanization, however, provide quite a different context in which to politicize the masses. That is, it makes a great deal of difference which comes first—a high degree of politicization of the masses, or a high degree of urbanization. Of the three variables—agricultural commercialization, politicization, and urbanization—the urbanization variable seems to have the greatest consequences for the timing and impact in variations of the other two.

If the degree of urbanization is low—say 30 percent of the population or thereabouts—the impact of politicization of the masses and commercialization in agriculture will have major consequences for political development. Holding the urbanization variable at a constant level, one can speculate about the consequences of variations in the other two processes. If politicization of the masses has not yet occurred, the attempt to commercialize agriculture will have little if any impact in the event that it succeeds. It may have long-range indirect importance if it feeds a rural-to-urban migration and if politicization of the masses occurs at a later stage of urbanization. Great Britain may be a good example of this alternative. If politicization of the masses is low and the attempt to commercialize agriculture fails, the impact will again be relatively indirect. As in the case of Venezuela, an aspiring urban elite group may capitalize on the unrest of the peasant masses resulting from the failure of the commercialization attempt, and may mobilize, or politicize, them in a struggle against the entrenched elites.

If politicization of the masses—that is, the peasantry—has already occurred, still with a low degree of urbanization, and if commercialization of agriculture is attempted and fails, the conditions will be appropriate for an agrarian revolution. Even if the commercialization attempt succeeds, providing new forms of socioeconomic mobility for the peasantry, there is likely to be a great deal of political change as new relationships are worked out among the traditional elites, the new agrarian commercial elites, and the peasant masses. If this fluid struggle is channeled into a coherent pattern of interaction, there may be rapid socioeconomic development, marked by strong farm labor unionization, a variety of agrarian reforms and cooperative programs, and a vigorous, broadspectrum agricultural development. If the struggle is not channeled into an institutionalized pattern of interaction, there may be an agrarian revolution in spite of the successful transition from traditional to commercial agriculture. There is, of course, no reason to assume that success or failure will occur simultaneously in all parts of the rural society, or that the result will be uniform. There may be pockets of failure in regions of commercial success, leading to the kind of peasant revolution, or counterrevolution, that Charles Tilly describes for France.[4] Summing up, in a situation of low urbanization, the attempt to commercialize agriculture will have a major and immediate impact in the event that the peasant masses have been politicized prior to the attempt. If the peasantry has not been politicized prior to the attempt, the consequences are much more problematic and, while they may be important, will emerge indirectly and over a longer period of time.

On the other hand, it is logical to suppose that if urbanization is high—on the order of at least 70 percent of the population—there will be little or no impact from the attempt to commercialize agriculture, whether the masses are politicized or not, and whether the attempt to commercialize succeeds or not. In a situation of low politicization of the masses, with a constantly high urbanization, a failure to commercialize agriculture may have no immediate and direct effects. In such a hypothetical situation the urban population is presumably fed by means of outside supplies of foodstuffs, since traditional agriculture, by definition, can not provide, organize, and sustain sufficient production. The incentives for commercialization will in all likelihood come from the central government; and if the attempt fails, its impact, if any, will probably be budgetary in nature. As long as outside suppliers continue to produce and trade, or produce and give, the necessary foodstuffs to keep the urban population alive, there will be no drastic impact from either failure or success in the commercialization attempt.

If urbanization is high and politicization has already occurred, there is more probability of an impact, but not a drastic one. In such a case, the attempt to commercialize is again likely to be sponsored by the government, entailing a diversion of budgetry resources from other alternative expenditures, which may be more in the immediate interests of the urban population. If commercialization then fails, there may be a reaction against the judgment and capabilities of the incumbent government; but such a government could take relatively painless steps to redress the discontent, either by shifting budgetary priorities or by appealing for external assistance in one form or another. Though India is not highly urbanized, it certainly seems to exhibit some of this behavior in coping with the problems of feeding the population of some of its urban agglomerations.

In summary, the outcome will vary according to the sequence in which agricultural commercialization, urbanization, and politicization occur. If commercialization of agriculture and politicization of the masses both occur at low levels of urbanization, the probability of producing a drastic, destabilizing change in the political order is high. If commercialization of agriculture and politicization of the masses both occur at high levels of urbanization, the probability of producing a drastic, destabilizing change in the political order is low. If either commercialization of agriculture or politicization of the masses occurs at a low level of urbanization, and the other occurs later at a high level of urbanization, the probability of producing a drastic, destabilizing change in the political order is indeterminate.

The possible variety of these sequences, in descending order of their probability to produce drastic change in the political order, is as follows:

First	Second	Third	Possible outcomes
politicization	commercialization	urbanization	agrarian revolution
commercialization	politicization	urbanization	agrarian reform
politicization	urbanization	commercialization	uncertain
commercialization	urbanization	politicization	uncertain
urbanization	politicization	commercialization	little effect
urbanization	commercialization	politicization	no effect

Such an arrangement of propositions, while only speculative, is useful for several reasons. First, the propositions as to sequence and outcome can be empirically tested and verified, refined, or rejected. This might be done with aggregate statistical indicators of various kinds, providing the very difficult problems of precisely defining measurable variables could be overcome. Such testing could also be done with case study materials. In fact, these propositions were inductively generated from the Venezuelan case study, which followed the commercialization-politicization-urbanization sequence, and they led to the exploration of other possible combinations. Second, the set of sequence propositions may give important insights into the logic of leadership strategies that might be available in many of today's underdeveloped nations with large peasant populations.

Three possible leadership strategies are here considered, from the points of view of three different elites: an entrenched, traditional elite; a reformist elite newly arrived in power; and a challenging elite that seeks power. From the list of sequence propositions, it can be seen that urbanization is the only variable which falls into a definite pattern. Though too much weight should not be placed on this fact, it suggests that alternative strategies may revolve around the encouragement or discouragement of urbanization and the attempt to control the timing of commercialization in agriculture and politicization of the masses. Thus, an entrenched, traditional elite will logically do everything in its power to promote urbanization in a controlled manner, while simultaneously seeking to insulate the peasant population from politicization by any other group in society, and deferring, or discouraging, the commercialization of agriculture. An alliance with the traditional rural elites will be both natural and necessary in order to maintain control over the peasantry in the rural areas, while at the same time promoting a deliberate and controlled transfer of population into a carefully prepared, highly structured urban context. Thus, an entrenched traditional elite, if it wishes to remain in power, must successfully control the timing and auspices of all three processes—urbanization, politicization, and commercialization of agriculture—which is a highly unlikely prospect.

A reformist elite, newly arrived to power in such a situation, faces an extremely difficult task in similarly encouraging a deliberate, orderly program of urbanization while at the same time fostering either politicization of the peasantry or commercialization in agriculture. Politicization of the peasantry may help in the development of a controlled transfer of population to the urban areas, if all circumstances are favorable. The major problems will be administrative capability and securing an outside supply of foodstuffs for a growing urban populace. On the other hand, commercialization of agriculture will help to anticipate the foodstuffs problem and aid in the selection of the population to be transferred to the cities, though some sort of political adjustment process must be functioning in the urban centers. In this case the bottlenecks are technical, financial, and organizational inputs for agriculture, and political-administrative skills for the urban adjustment program. The timing and logistics of attempting to control, or at least influence, these three consequential processes simultaneously are delicate matters indeed.

The task of the challenging elites seems to be the easiest of the three, at least until power is assumed. At that point, an authoritarian, revolutionary elite will embark on a strategy much like the one suggested above for an established elite that wishes to perpetuate its power. There will be one major difference, however: the newly arrived revolutionary elite is more likely to succeed than the traditional elite, since it is more likely to have the necessarily high degree of social engineering skills to control all three variables simultaneously.

Prior to the seizure of power, a challenging elite, whether of an authoritarian-revolutionary or a reformist nature, will follow a similar strategy. Unlike the other two elite groups, challenging elites do not have to try to foster and control urbanization. In fact, their problem is to strike before urbanization reaches a certain level. A challenging elite's primary task will be to politicize the peasantry, and anything that promotes this process, such as an abortive attempt to commercialize agriculture or any other means of disrupting the traditional rural socioeconomic order, will tend to free peasants for mobilization into new patterns of politically relevant behavior. If, however, the traditional rural order is functioning in a classical feudal manner—that is, with the landlords providing security, leadership, and paternalistic favors to their peasants—the bonds between landlord and peasant will be extremely difficult to break.[5] It is precisely the attempt of traditional landlords to commercialize, thereby reducing their contributions to the maintenance of a reciprocal landlord-peasant relationship, which makes the peasantry ready for mobilization by others who show promise of replacing, or improving on, the former provider. Carrying this point one step further, one might logically develop a patron-client theory of guerrilla warfare, based on the proposition that the objective conditions of peasant life foster a high level of need or dependency on others. This "need-succorance" is logically directed at others with the power to provide relief from life's problems, or the power to magnify them—very often, that is, a landlord.[6] Since the provision of help by traditional landlords forms the bonds of the traditional community, the severing of that supportive relationship during the course of commercializing agriculture disrupts those bonds, freeing the peasantry for mobilization by others. These others, however, be they reformers or guerrilla revolutionaries, must meet the same high level of need among the peasantry in order to form a dependable clientele. In other words, a guerrilla movement must offer something to the peasantry and be able to deliver the goods—whether security against a predatory, exploitative central government, assistance in meeting family needs, or subsistence farming inputs, such as land, seeds, tools, credit, and marketing aid of a rudimentary sort. When guerrilla movements can provide some or all of these needed elements—as did the Viet Cong in southern Vietnam—they are strong and well-grounded.[7] When guerrilla movements cannot provide such needed elements—as was apparently the case in Ché Guevara's Bolivian attempt—they are weak and vulnerable. Seen in this light, ideology has little or no effect on the outcome.

The processes of commercialization in agriculture, politicization, and urbanization occurred in Venezuela in an ideal sequence for the successful development of competitive, mass-based democratic politics. The unsuccessful attempt to commercialize agriculture broke the peasantry loose from its traditional moorings, favoring its mobilization by some other benefactor. Urbanization had proceeded to a point where upwardly mobile elites were generated but were not yet accommodated by the traditional ruling elites. Yet urbanization had not proceeded to the point of mass urbanization; the peasantry still formed the bulk of the national masses. Therefore, the kind of stabilizing urban elite-rural mass alliance that Huntington considers critical on one pathway to political development was made possible and successfully consummated. Huntington's argument is that such an urban-peasant mass alliance may prove essential to coping with the destabilizing effects of urban growth. The Venezuelan case demonstrates clearly that because of a tendency toward fragmentation in the urban electorate, a peasant electoral base can maintain governmental stability even after the proportion of rural population has declined below 50 percent.[8] As urbanization further proceeds, the size of the rural electorate eventually becomes inadequate to this task. In addition, urban political interests become more capable of exerting pressure on the government, so that the utility of the urban-peasant mass alliance evaporates. Huntington expresses it thus: "As urbanization proceeds, the city comes to play a more effective role in the politics of the country, and the city itself becomes more conservative. The political system and the government come to depend more upon the support of the city than upon that of the countryside."[9]

There seem to be four distinct phases to the possibility of effecting an urban-peasant alliance. Phase I, in which the urban population is under 25 percent, is unlikely to precipitate sufficient challenging urban elites to initiate such an alliance—unless additional variables intervene, such as war, military intervention, or ideologically directed revolutionary elites. Phase II, when the proportion of urban population is in the 25–50 percent range, provides maximum opportunity for the formation of a viable and effective urban-peasant alliance. It is also the period of maximum effectiveness of such an alliance in compensating for the instability of the city. Phase III, in which the proportion of urban population is in the 50–75 percent range, offers a decreased likelihood both for the formation of such an alliance and for its effectiveness as a stabilizing factor in the political system. However, as in the case of Venezuela, if such an alliance has been formed in the second phase, it can still be effective far into the third. In Phase IV, when the proportion of urban population is over 75 percent, there are too few peasants to make the formation of such an alliance attractive to urban elites, or to make it effective in the event that it was formed earlier. These four general phases are illustrated in Figure 4, using population data from the case study.

When the commercialization of agriculture and politicization

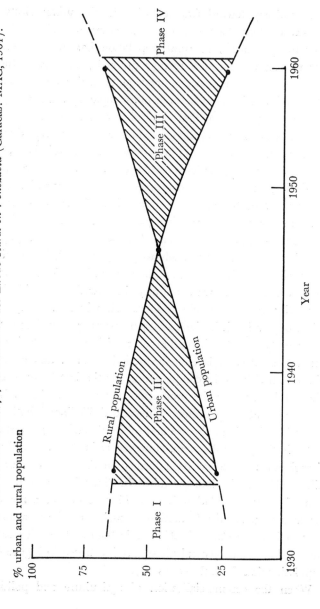

Figure 4. Venezuelan urbanization and the formation of an urban-peasant mass alliance. Based on data from Pola C. Ortíz and Yoland D. Shaya, *El Problema del Exodo Rural en Venezuela* (Caracas: MAC, 1964).

variables are reintroduced into this opportunity matrix, the circumstances in Venezuela for peasant mobilization and agrarian reform appear fortuitous indeed. Commercialization of agriculture was attempted in Phase I, and the impact of its failure reached a peak in the early 1930's, giving the peasantry a high mobilization potential. An alert sector among the challenging urban elites perceived and grasped this opportunity in the initial part of Phase II, and proceeded to politicize or mobilize the peasantry. During most of Phase II, the institutional base of support among the peasantry, the peasant union movement, was being clandestinely organized. The urban elite partner in this peasant alliance gained access to power toward the end of Phase II and proceeded to mobilize its peasant base of support in what Huntington refers to as a "ruralizing election."[10] The first (1945–1948) regime of Acción Democrática (AD) also set in motion basic organizational changes in the political system, such as universal suffrage, direct and secret elections of the president and Congress, which reformed the electoral process and elevated it to a central position in the determination of those who governed. At the outset of Phase III, however, the government directing the urban-peasant alliance was ousted by a reactionary military coup, which ushered in a ten-year period of governmental stability, based not on mass peasant support but on police and military power. This form of support proved inadequate, however, and on the overthrow of the Pérez Jiménez regime in early 1958, elected governmental power eventually returned to the hands of AD—fairly far along into Phase III. The electoral base of peasant support, while clearly declining in relative terms, again proved decisive in the 1963 elections. Though I have no analytic data on the 1968 election, the fact that AD was finally voted out of office is consistent with this sequential analysis, since Venezuela's urban-rural population balance was then in the initial portion of Phase IV. After a ten-year period of governmental stability based on a series of rurally dominated elections, Venezuela seemed firmly established in a period of urban domination of politics.

As shown by this brief recapitulation of the Venezuelan process of development during the period covered by the case study, roughly from the mid-1920's through the mid-1960's, understanding the consequences of variations in the processes of commercialization of agriculture, urbanization, and politicization of the masses can generate important insights and suggest significant avenues of research. The opportunity matrix also helps to sharpen awareness of the interrelatedness between the possibility for a peasant mobilization and the degree of urbanization existing in any particular case. But these propositions are not intended to comprise a predictive or even explanatory model in a formal sense. As clearly revealed in the case of Venezuela, additional variables intervene, which affect the outcome of various combinations of agricultural commercialization, urbanization, and politicization. These other variables—such as prices in the international agricultural market, which may affect the success or failure, or even the undertaking, of commercialization in agriculture; or military intervention in the political process, which may affect the nature and auspices of both mobilization and politicization of the masses—are essentially impossible to predict at this stage with any probability of success.[11] A general perspective needs to be developed on the interaction of these and other variables that affect the particular timing and rhythm of development in one country or another. My task has been limited to the achievement of such a perspective on three broad, socially transforming processes that are closely related to the general prospects for peasant mobilization and agrarian reform.

Agrarian reform fits into this perspective as the instrument used by an urban elite to cement its alliance with the peasantry. Naturally, there is no inevitability about the formation of such an alliance; indeed, it requires great effort and skill to achieve. Furthermore, an agrarian reform program can serve the purposes of many different types of political elites: an entrenched traditional elite can use it to forestall challenges from aspiring elites (as in Iran); a revolutionary elite, newly arrived in power, can use it to consolidate and expand its base of political support (as in Egypt); or a challenging elite can use its promise to organize a mass base of support to assist in its ascent to power (as in Venezuela). In all of these situations, an agrarian reform program implemented by government is essentially a program of organized patronage, whose purpose is to build or maintain a base of legitimizing political support. Agrarian reform, therefore, does not comprise an independent variable for analysis; it is dependent on the perceptions, abilities, and initiatives of an urban-based elite of some kind. Peasant readiness for mobilization and elite readiness for leadership of "the Green Uprising" are interdependent, but unequal in weight. Peasants cannot achieve their objectives without such an alliance; urban elites can, and often do, achieve theirs without one.

When the agrarian reform program of Venezuela, as carried out through the workings of the peasant-urban alliance, is analyzed from the bottom up—that is, from the peasant-welfare point of view—what appears is a rural problem-solving system in action, functioning to ameliorate or resolve certain pressing problems in the peasant life situation. The peasantry paid for this assistance with votes. Viewed from the top down, a system of organized patronage emerges, designed to secure votes that legitimate and maintain a series of coalition governments in office. Of these alternative ways of viewing the same system, the latter is more useful for general political analysis. Agrarian-reform-as-patronage fits in nicely with the facts of peasant existence—a high level of need, derived from a threatening environment; a low level of material and technological resources with which to meet these needs; and thus a high degree of dependency on others for assistance. In traditional systems of rural society, this situation was partially alleviated by patron-client ties. In more modern circumstances, the government, through an agrarian reform program, may partially alleviate, or respond to, this high level of "need-succorance." Moore's theses apply to Venezuela in the sense that it was the attempt of rural elites to commercialize their agricultural activities which led to

225

the erosion of their contributions to the patron-client system and thereby freed the peasantry for mobilization by others, who were more sensitive and responsive to their needs. When mobilized and organized by an urban elite and tied into a program of government patronage—called agrarian reform—the peasantry was established as a mass clientele. Almost all of the features of the classical patron-client relationship—such as inequality in status, bargaining power, and initiative, as well as great stability—existed in this more "modern" form of clientelism. Case studies of other national agrarian reform programs, as in Italy, Bolivia, and Mexico, clearly establish an identical pattern of peasant clientelism and government patronage.[12]

The hegemony of AD in Venezuelan politics was intimately linked with the mobilization of rural political resources and maintained by an organized program of benefits to rural voters. The 1968 elections, however, marked the end of the control of governmental patronage by AD, as they also marked the end of the viability of an electoral base that depended so heavily on an ever-shrinking proportion of the electorate. It remains to explore the probable consequences for the urban-peasant alliance when the elite partner is turned out of governmental control. Simply put, the question is: once mobilized, what happens when the peasantry is demobilized? If Tarrow's study of the Italian case offers guidelines for Venezuela, it seems likely that in time the party which controls the patronage will control the mobilization machinery.[13] This would be consistent with the high level of peasant need and the agrarian-reform-as-patronage interpretation. The obstacle to such a shift of identifications, on the part of local leaders of the peasant union movement and their followers, will be the intensity and duration of existing identifications with AD. Such was not the case in Italy, where loyalties to the Communist party, which developed among the southern Italian peasantry, were fostered less than a decade before the use of agrarian reform patronage became an important instrument of Christian Democratic influence, attracting the membership of local peasant unions, both leaders and rank-and-file, away from the Communist peasant union movement. Identification with, and loyalty to, AD is of more than thirty years' standing among the Venezuelan peasantry.

However, as indicated by the local peasant union leader's evaluations of the reform program, there has been a great deal of dissatisfaction and criticism about the way the program met the particular needs of individual peasant communities. One possibility consistent with all of these factors is that, if COPEI can organize and offer a more effective system of patronage than AD did in its last years in office, many local leaders and members of the peasant union movement will come in time to be identified with the new source of patronage. It is highly probable, moreover, that once the leaders of COPEI are in control of the agrarian reform program, they will be in an ideal position greatly to increase their program of recruitment and local party-building in the remaining, unorganized rural areas of Venezuela. Whether or not this occurs will simply be a matter of costs and benefits. It seems more probable, however, that COPEI will invest in urban patronage systems than in expanding their rural clienteles.

Finally, the experience of participation in the urban-peasant alliance fostered by AD seems likely to have produced irreversible, long-term benefits in terms of the political competence of peasant leaders and followers. Not only has this experience made the participants in the system more effective as consumers of governmental goods and services, but it has made them more effective and knowledgeable as petitioners. Despite the fact that they participated in a patronage system, a rudimentary form of civic culture has resulted. And perhaps because of the fact that they participated in an effective patronage system, peasant leaders and followers have been politically socialized into a roughly democratic polity, in much the same way that European immigrants to the United States were socialized into the "democratic process" early in this century through city machines. The important point seems to be that such patronage systems have significant contributions to make to the stability of the polity, as well as to the welfare of the clienteles. Only time will tell whether the Venezuelan rural problem-solving system has made sufficient contributions in both of these areas to produce a healthy, functioning, democratically oriented political system capable of meeting the needs of all of its constituents.

Notes   Index

NOTES

INTRODUCTION

1. "The World of 'La Miseria,'" *Community Development Review,* no. 10 (1958), p. 26.

2. For a bibliographic essay and analysis of varying definitions of the term, see Joel Halpern and John Brode, "Studies in Peasant Society," in *Biennial Review of Anthropology* (Stanford: Stanford University Press, 1967), pp. 46–139.

3. See Robert Redfield, *The Little Community* (Chicago: University of Chicago Press, 1955); I. Chiva, *Rural Communities: Problems, Methods and Types of Research* (Paris: UNESCO, 1958). For an indication of Max Weber's far-reaching studies, see Paul Honigsheim, "Max Weber as Historian of Agriculture and Rural Life," *Agricultural History,* 23 (July 1949), 179–213, and "Max Weber as Rural Sociologist," *Rural Sociology,* 11:3 (September 1946), 207–218.

4. Gordon Wright, *Rural Revolution in France* (Stanford: Stanford University Press, 1964); Sidney Tarrow, *Peasant Communism in Southern Italy* (New Haven: Yale University Press, 1967); Chalmers Johnson, *Peasant Nationalism and Communist Power* (Stanford: Stanford University Press, 1962); George Jackson, *Comintern and Peasant in Eastern Europe, 1919–1930* (New York: Columbia University Press, 1966); David Mitrany, *Marx Against the Peasant* (Chapel Hill: University of North Carolina Press, 1951); Carl Gil Alroy, *The Involvement of Peasants in Internal Wars* (Princeton: Center for International Studies, 1966), Research Monograph No. 24.

5. Mehmet Bequiraj, *Peasantry in Revolution* (Ithaca: Cornell University Center for International Studies, 1966); Barrington Moore, Jr., *Social Origins of Dictatorship and Democracy: Lord and Peasant in the Making of the Modern World* (Boston: Beacon Press, 1966); Henry A. Landsberger, ed., *Peasant Movements in Latin America* (Ithaca: Cornell University Press, 1969).

6. Samuel P. Huntington, *Political Order in Changing Societies* (New Haven: Yale University Press, 1968).

7. Elias H. Tuma, *Twenty-Six Centuries of Agrarian Reform* (Berkeley: University of California Press, 1965).

8. Hung-Chao Tai, "Land Reform in Developing Countries," paper presented at Annual Meeting of the American Political Science Association, Chicago, September 1967.

9. J. P. Nettl, *Political Mobilization* (New York: Basic Books, 1967).

10. See esp. Tuma, *Twenty-Six Centuries of Agrarian Reform;* Moore, *Social Origins.*

11. Landsberger, *Peasant Movements,* p. 2.

12. Andrew Pearse, "Agrarian Change Trends in Latin America," *Latin American Research Review,* 1:3 (1966), 49–50.

13. Adapted from data taken from the Inter-American Agricultural Development Committee's studies, cited in Pearse, "Agrarian Change," p. 62.

14. See Seymour M. Lipset and Aldo Solari, eds., *Elites in Latin America* (New York: Oxford University Press, 1967).

15. Richard N. Adams, "Rural Labor," in *Continuity and Change in Latin America,* ed. John Johnson (Stanford: Stanford University Press, 1964), pp. 49–78.

16. Considerable information and insight into peasant conditions vis-à-vis large landowners appear in a series of articles in *América Latina:* Benno Galjart, "Class and 'Following' in Rural Brazil," 7 (1964), 3–24; Gerrit Huizer, "Some Notes on Community Development and Rural Social Research," and Galjart, "A Further Note on 'Followings': Reply to Huizer," 8:3 (1965), 128–152.

17. Huizer, "Some Notes," p. 134.

I. THE STRUGGLE FOR POWER, 1928–1945

1. Federico Brito Figueroa, *Historia Económica y Social de Venezuela* (Caracas: Universidad Central de Venezuela, 1966), I, 72.

2. For an apology of the Gómez system, which illuminates much of the social history, see Laureano Vallenilla Lanz, *Cesarismo Democrático,* 4th ed. (Caracas: Tip. Garrido, 1961). See also Robert Gilmore, *Caudillismo and Militarism in Venezuela* (Athens: Ohio University Press, 1964).

3. George W. Hill et al., "Social Welfare and Tenure Problems in the Agrarian Reform Program of Venezuela," in *Land Tenure,* ed. K. H. Parsons, R. J. Penn, and P. M. Raup (Madison: University of Wisconsin Press, 1956), pp. 293–304.

4. Brito Figueroa, *Historia,* I, 297.

5. For a synthesis of the historical materials on these developments, see John R. Mathiason, "Political Organization and Attitudes among Venezuelan Campesinos," mimeographed (Political Science Department of MIT, September, 1967).

6. Edwin Lieuwin, *Venezuela,* 2nd ed. (London: Oxford University Press, 1965), pp. 42–43.

7. On the advent of the Andean dictators, see Domingo Alberto Rangel, *Los Andinos en el Poder* (Mérida: Universidad de los Andes, 1964). Rangel, a member of the radical left opposition in Venezuela, refers to the Gómez tenure as the "siesta Gomecista" (p. 174).

8. Lieuwin, *Venezuela,* pp. 48–49.

9. Gómez was the kind of colorful figure who excites much attention and comment, most of it unflattering. See, e.g., John Lavin, *A Halo for Gómez* (New York: Pageant Press, 1954); Thomas Rouke, *Gómez, Tyrant of the Andes* (New York: W. Morrow and Co., 1936).

10. Harry Bernstein, *Venezuela and Colombia* (Englewood Cliffs: Prentice-Hall, 1964), p. 51.

11. Lieuwin, *Venezuela,* p. 49.

12. Guenther Roth, "Personal Rulership, Patrimonialism, and Empire-Building in the New States," *World Politics,* 20:2 (1968), 203, 196.

13. The properties of Gómez were so substantial and had in a number of cases been acquired in so high-handed a manner that upon his death they reverted to the state as the "Bienes Resituídos" (Restored Properties), and a special commission was established to oversee their use and disposition. Estimates of Gómez' personal holdings vary widely. One source claimed almost thirty million acres. José Silva Michelena, "Factores que Dificultan y Han Impedido la Reforma Agraria en Venezuela," in *Resistencias a Mudança* (Rio de Janeiro: CLAPCS, 1960), p. 136. Most accept 126 million bolivares, the figure initially estimated by the commission of Restored Properties as the value of his farm properties, although how this valuation was established is unclear.

14. Brito Figueroa, *Historia,* II, 379–386.

15. Interview with Luis Fermín Pérez, secretary for culture and publications of the Aragua section of the Venezuelan Peasant Federation, Maracay, Aragua, July 2, 1964.

16. José Fabbiani Ruíz, *Latifundio* (Caracas: Ed. Elite, 1937), p. 48. *Latifundio* is a relatively little-used singular form of the generic term *latifundia.*

17. Fabbiani, *Latifundio,* p. 48. Fabbiani presents data from the 1932 survey.

18. For the use of such data in a pro-Acción Democrática history, see Luís Troconis Guerrero, *La Cuestión Agraria en la Historia Nacional* (Caracas: Ed. Arte, 1962).

19. For further data on government programs during this era, see John

D. Powell, "The Politics of Agrarian Reform in Venezuela: History, System and Process," Ph.D. diss., University of Wisconsin, 1966, Ch. II.

20. For an analysis of these developments, see Ramón Fernández y Fernández, *Reforma Agraria en Venezuela* (Caracas: Tip. Vargas, 1948).

21. John Friedmann, *Venezuela: From Doctrine to Dialogue* (Syracuse: Syracuse University Press, 1965), p. 5.

22. For a history of the many other opposition forces at that time, now mostly forgotten, see José Rafael Pocaterra, *Memorias de un Venezolano de la Decadencia* (Caracas: EDIME, 1966), 4 vols., including a documentary appendix complete with photographs of political prisoners in the Gómez era.

23. Lieuwin, *Venezuela,* p. 50.

24. For the impact of the rise of petroleum on the demise of agriculture, see Gustavo Pinto, *Agricultura y Desarrollo: El Caso Venezolano* (Maracaibo: Sociedad Venezolana de Ingenieros Agrónomos, 1966). For a contemporary statement of the anti-imperialist (i.e., petroleum-penetration) argument, see Fabbiani, *Latifundio.* For a retrospective analysis of the entire petroleum-development nexus, see Rómulo Betancourt, *Venezuela: Política y Petróleo* (México: Fondo de Cultura Económica, 1956).

25. Interview with Betancourt in Luís Enrique Osorio, *Democracia en Venezuela,* (Bogatá: Ed. Lit. Colombia, 1943), p. 157, cited in John D. Martz, *Acción Democrática: Evolution of a Modern Political Party in Venezuela* (Princeton: Princeton University Press, 1966), pp. 24–25.

26. Luís Enrique Osorio, "Rómulo Betancourt: Historia de un Político Popular," in Joaquín Gabaldón Márquez et al., *Rómulo Betancourt: Interpretación de su Doctrina Popular y Democrática* (Caracas: Ed. SUMA, 1955), p. 29.

27. For a memoir-based description of the plot and its results, see Francisco Betancourt Sosa, *Relato Histórico de la Sublevación Militar del 7 de Abril de 1928* (Caracas: Ed. Garrido, 1959).

28. Powell, "Politics of Agrarian Reform, Ch. IV.

29. See Betancourt's own story of his days as a Marxist, during which he referred to the romanticism of the Generation of '28 as follows: "We began to dream of a bolshevik revolution, with the 'czar of Maracay' shot at dawn. Nevertheless, none of those who later would found Acción Democrática became members, during this first exile, of political groups subordinated to the Third International." Betancourt, *Venezuela,* pp. 69–70, quoted in Martz, *Acción Democrática,* p. 123. On the question of Marxism and communism in the political opposition, see Martz, *Acción Democrática,* Ch. IV.

30. There is a minor discrepancy among writers as to exactly what "ORVE" stood for: Movimiento de Organización Venezolana, or Organización Revolucionaria Venezolana. Martz, *Acción Democrática,* p. 27, employs the former usage. Robert Alexander, *The Venezuelan Democratic Revolution* (New Brunswick: Rutgers University Press, 1964), p. 20, uses the latter. Probably both forms were used—the revolutionary version during the early underground stage, and the other version when ORVE was formally organized following Gómez' death.

31. Martz, *Acción Democrática,* pp. 39–40.

32. For documentary and photographic data, see Rodolfo Luzardo, *Notas Histórico-Económicas, 1928–1963* (Caracas: Ed. Sucre, 1963).

33. Martz, *Acción Democrática,* p. 39.

34. Martz, *Acción Democrática,* pp. 127–129.

35. Martz, *Acción Democrática,* p. 43.

36. The *Ahora* columns were collected and published by Betancourt while in exile in Chile. See Rómulo Betancourt, *Problemas Venezolanos* (Santiago de Chile: Ed. Futuro, 1940).

37. For a theoretical analysis of Latin American political systems, in which power capabilities (political resources) and power contenders (political elites) are analyzed in similar terms, see Charles W. Anderson, *Politics and Economic Change in Latin America* (Princeton: Van Nostrand, 1967).

38. Martz, *Acción Democrática,* p. 52.

39. Martz, *Accion Democrática,* pp. 58–59.

40. Luís Lander, a prominent AD participant in these events, stated that, whereas an agreement had been reached with Escalante promising to transform the electoral system and enable AD to gain control of the Congress and possibly of the presidency through the electoral process, the attempt by Medina to impose Biaggini "was simply a continuation of all the traditional forces in Venezuelan politics." As a result, AD opposed this development. Interview, Caracas, February 14, 1966.

41. Martz, *Acción Democrática,* pp. 58–60.

42. For a first-hand account, see Ana Mercedes Pérez, *La Verdad Inédita* (Caracas: Ed. Artes Gráficas, 1947).

II. BUILDING THE MOBILIZATION BASE, 1936–1945

1. According to census data, 65.3 percent of the total population in 1936 lived in localities with less than 1,000 persons, despite the fact that a massive rural-urban migration had begun in the late 1920's. See Pola

C. Ortíz and Yolanda D. Shaya, *El Problema del Exodo Rural en Venezuela* (Caracas: Ministerio de Agricultura y Cría, 1964).

2. Fabbiani, *Latifundio*, p. 69. For examples of contracts used during this period, see pp. 73–76.

3. Fernández y Fernández, *Reforma Agraria*, p. 26.

4. Fabbiani, *Latifundio*, p. 76.

5. Fabbiani, *Latifundio*, p. 170. Wage data are given on p. 66.

6. This practice has been common throughout Latin America. In Venezuela I was shown a collection of such tokens, which bore the name of the hacienda or latifundia plus a numerical value—for which reason they were named "vales" by Armando González, president of the Peasant Federation of Venezuela (FCV).

7. Fabbiani, *Latifundio*, pp. 64–65.

8. Fabbiani, *Latifundio*, pp. 64–76. See also Ramón Quijada, *Reforma Agraria en Venzuela* (Caracas: Ed. Arte, 1963).

9. Interviews with local peasant union leaders on "La Linda," one of Gómez' favorite properties, located at Güigüe, Aragua, January 1966.

10. Fabbiani, *Latifundio*, p. 7.

11. Cited in Fabbiani, *Latifundio*, p. 65.

12. Fabbiani, *Latifundio*, p. 65.

13. The communal norms were explicitly positive toward many breaks while working for the landlord, and negative while working for one's own benefit. See Paul L. Doughty, "The Interrelationship of Power, Respect, Affection and Rectitude in Vicos," *American Behavioral Scientist*, 8:7 (March 1965), 14.

14. There is much evidence of the anguish of commercially oriented landowners during this period. See John D. Powell, "Politics of Agrarian Reform," Chs. I and II.

15. All of the data in this section were taken from interviews with the late Luís Morillo, Secretary for agricultural centers and cooperatives of the Peasant Federation. Caracas, July–August 1964.

16. Interview with Morillo, July 28, 1964.

17. Fabbiani, *Latifundio*, pp. 232–233.

18. Morillo interviews, July–August 1964.

19. Fernández y Fernández, *Reforma Agraria*, p. 78.

20. Cited in Fernández y Fernández, *Reforma Agraria*, p. 78.

21. Cited in Rodolfo Luzardo, *Notas Históricas-Económicas, 1928–1963* (Caracas: Ed. Sucre, 1963), p. 71.

22. Reprinted in Rómulo Betancourt, *Problemas Venezolanos*, p. 237.

23. Osorio, Márquez, et al., *Rómulo Betancourt*, p. 22.

24. Cited in Joaquín Gabaldón Márquez, *Archivos de Una Inquietud Venezolana* (Caracas: EDIME, 1955), p. 267.

25. For a list of persons interviewed, see Powell, "Politics of Agrarian Reform."

26. The González pattern is not uncommon. He started his union career in a furniture factory in Valencia, then became an "adviser" to peasant unions in the nearby rural areas, and finally became a full-time activist in the peasant union branch of the labor movement. González interviews, Caracas, June–August, 1964.

27. Albert O. Hirschman, *Journeys Toward Progress* (New York: Twentieth Century Fund, 1963), p. 259. On pp. 101–106 Hirschman details these activities, whose results, much the same as in Venezuela, he characterizes later on p. 150 as "a revolution by stealth."

28. There may even be occasions when the followers take advantage of outside leadership in such a way as to minimize the risks to themselves. Mancur Olson, Jr., in his *The Logic of Collective Action* (Cambridge: Harvard University Press, 1965), p. 29, develops propositions about the conditions under which, in similar contexts, "there is a systematic tendency for 'exploitation' of the great by the small."

29. C. Wright Mills, *The Marxists*, cited by Gerrit Huizer, "Some Notes on Community Development and Rural Social Research," *América Latina*, 8:3 (July–September 1965), 131.

30. Karl Marx, *The Eighteenth Brumaire of Louis Bonaparte* (New York: International Publishers, 1963), pp. 123–124.

31. See John Duncan Powell, "Agrarian Reform or Agrarian Revolution in Venezuela?" in *Reform and Revolution: Readings in Latin American Politics*, ed. Arpad von Lazar and Robert Kaufman (Boston: Allyn & Bacon, 1969).

32. The first peasant syndicates were organized in Carabobo, Aragua, Lara, and Miranda, where the number of cancellations of inscriptions was high. These states were the same in which the Agricultural Census of 1937 registered large numbers of tenant farmers and colonos. Kathryn Wylie, "Venezuela's Agricultural Problem," *Foreign Agriculture*, 6 (June 1942), 236. All of this suggests a high potential for landlord-peasant conflict.

33. See John D. Martz, III, "The Growth and Democratization of the Venezuelan Labor Movement," *Inter-American Economic Affairs*, 17:2 (Autumn 1963), 3–18.

34. The minister of labor stated that the convention, which began on March 20, was dissolved by the governor of the federal district on March

24 (after AD's walkout), "because the Convention passed a resolution framed in the name of a known political party; which circumstance changed the nature of said Convention; so for the sake of Public Order and Safety, it was disbanded." See Ministry of Labor and Communications, *Memoria* (Caracas: Imp. Nacional, 1944), p. 123.

35. International Labor Office, "Freedom of Association and Conditions of Work in Venezuela," *Studies and Reports* n.s., no. 21 (1950), p. 42.

36. See *Memoria,* 1940, pp. 55, 10.

37. Though the specific degree of underestimation of the ministry data cannot be determined, there is empirical evidence on the other two points. Within a year from the time of the October coup, the number of legalized unions had grown to 763, of which 312 were campesino unions. Just before the end of the AD regime the number was 1,047 unions, of which 515 were campesino unions. The total number of founding members was then registered at 137,316. From this, I estimated 1,000 unions with 200,000 members. The initial AD vote in 1946 for the Constituent Assembly was close to 1,000,000. This seems consistent with the estimate of 200,000 active supporters, if each party militant is assumed to have influenced five votes in a given election. The syndicate data come from the *Memorias* of 1946 and 1947; the 1948 data are interpolated, since no *Memoria* for that year were published because of the military coup of November 1948. For detailed voting data, see Armando Veloz M., *Manual Electoral* (Caracas, 1963); Institute for the Comparative Study of Political Systems, *Venezuela* (Washington: Operations and Policy Research, Inc., 1963).

III. THE MOBILIZING ELITE IN POWER, 1945–1948

1. For the details of how AD decided to support the coup, see Martz, *Acción Democrática,* pp. 60–62, 301–305. Betancourt wrote that, "Like all politically organized collectivities with a vocation for power, Acción Democrática wanted to govern. Its men and women were not inconoclasts with anarchic inclinations. . . . They wanted to contribute, with hands and hearts, to the building of a new order, based on effective democracy, with economic nationalism and social justice. In such circumstances, the proposition of the Unión Patriótica Militar was particularly tempting." Rómulo Betancourt, *Trayectoria Democrática de una Revolución* (Caracas: Imp. Nacional, 1948), p. 324.

2. For a documentary analysis and early record of the Junta's tenure, see *El Gobierno Revolucionario de Venezuela ante su Pueblo* (Caracas: Imp. Nacional, 1946).

3. Prieto and Barrios were the symbolic candidates of the two factions within AD which rent the party during the winter of 1967–1968.

4. Martz, *Acción Democrática,* p. 64.

5. Martz, *Acción Democrática,* pp. 64–65.

6. Martz, *Acción Democrática,* p. 122. On the electoral influence of the peasantry in Venezuela, see S. J. Serxner, *Acción Democrática de Venezuela* (Gainesville: University of Florida Press, 1959), ch. II; Peter P. Lord, "The Peasantry as an Emerging Political Factor in Mexico, Bolivia, and Venezuela" LTC Research Report No. 35, mimeographed (Land Tenure Center, University of Wisconsin, 1965), esp. pp. 83–86.

7. The meeting lasted for four days and established a number of significant policy benchmarks. Under the Venezuelan federal system, incidentally, state governors and territorial administrators are presidential appointees—a practice that continues to this day. For background analysis, see Leo B. Lott, "Venezuelan Federalism: A Case Study in Frustration," Ph.D. diss., University of Wisconsin, 1954.

8. Cited in Betancourt, *Trayectoria Democrática,* p. 175. See also pp. 194–195 for similar conclusions reached at the Second Convention of Regional Executives, held May 10, 1947, at Miraflores.

9. The Ministry of Agriculture (MAC) eventually carried out such cadastral surveys in Trujillo, Zulia, Falcón, and Yaracuy states, covering about 76,000 hectares of property.

10. The rest of this chapter contains a great deal of information, both official and private, from privileged sources. Some of the official information exists in other forms, including such publications as the annual reports to Congress of the Institute for Colonization (ITIC), but the ITIC internal files and archives have been destroyed or otherwise lost for research purposes. Some of these files were confiscated by the security police of the dictatorship succeeding the AD government, in circumstances similar to the confiscatory raids on the Ministry of Labor archives. But most of them were lost through an incredible act of neglect, when in 1949 the Agrarian Institute (IAN) was finally established and took over ITIC's administrative responsibilities. IAN was set up at first outside of Caracas, on a large hacienda belonging to MAC, to which the ITIC archives were transferred. But they were never properly stored or protected against the elements, and when IAN moved back to Caracas, they were abandoned. Jorge F. Schuster, a MAC researcher, reports that when he tried to utilize the ITIC archives for research in 1958, they were unusable owing to damage and neglect.

I interviewed a number of former officials of ITIC, some of whom granted me access to their private files from their tenure in office. Included in these sources were official records, unofficial notes and diaries, and some internal party documents. I have cited information from other sources when possible. When this was not possible or feasible, I have cited information gathered in these interviews and papers as "ITIC File."

11. Decree No. 183 of February 11, 1946, authorized the parceling of certain government farmlands.

12. Radio Broadcast on Radio Nacional, May 31, 1946.

13. ITIC File.

14. ITIC File. This credit fund is mentioned in Rómulo Betancourt, *Venzuela: Política y Petróleo,* p. 356.

15. The ITIC File includes an allegation that opposition political leaders encouraged AD-affiliated campesinos who had received ITIC credits to default on the payments, telling them that the credit was a payment for voting the AD ticket. While ostensibly this might have discredited the ITIC program because of a high default rate, it would seem to have been an inept maneuver for a political opponent to credit AD with such attractive capabilities!

16. Decree by the Constituent Assembly, "Arrendamiento de Predios Rústicos," *Gaceta Oficial* (Caracas: March 13, 1947), Nos. 22, 261. The decree was regulated and detailed by the Revolutionary Junta as Decree No. 557, published in the *Gaceta Oficial* (Caracas: June 4, 1947), Nos. 22, 327.

17. Constituent Assembly, "Decreto de Arrendamiento de Predios Rústicos," *Compilación Legislativa de Venezuela, Anuario 1947* (Caracas: Ed. Andrés Bello, 1948), p. 898.

18. Interviews, Maracay, July 1964.

19. The trend of growth in the peasant branch of the labor movement accelerated rapidly after 1958. By 1960, peasants formed the majority of unionized Venezuelans.

20. See John D. Powell, "Preliminary Report on the Federación Campesina de Venezuela," LTC Research Report No. 9, mimeographed (Land Tenure Center, University of Wisconsin, 1964), pp. 4–5.

21. *Gaceta Oficial* (Caracas: July 30, 1947), Special Edition No. 194.

22. For commentary on this shift in legal basis, see Fernández y Fernández, *Reforma Agraria,* p. 76. See also Kenneth Karst, "Latin American Land Reform: The Uses of Confiscation," *Michigan Law Review,* 63 (December 1964), 346–368.

23. For a more detailed discussion of Medina's Agrarian Reform Law, see Powell, "Politics of Agrarian Reform."

24. Cámara de Diputados, *Proyecto de Ley Agraria* (Caracas: Imp. Nacional, 1948), Third Discussion, Article 14. I have used the preliminary version of the law, rather than the final, somewhat modified version, because it so clearly shows the intentions of the AD policy-makers. Revisions of these political intentions were made for reasons of legal precedent and procedure, not for lack of desire for a radical departure. The Chamber of Deputies' version captures the thrust of these desired departures. The final version of the Agrarian Reform Law of 1948 appears in *Leyes Agrarias de Venezuela* (Caracas: Ministerio de Agricultura y Cría, 1958).

25. The right to challenge immunity strikes one as a tempting invitation to syndicate leaders to organize land invasions. Whether used as a weapon or not, the implied threat of such invasions could be an important bargaining instrument.

26. *El Heraldo* (Caracas), June 21, 1946.

27. Pompeyo Ríos, quoted in *El País* (Caracas), June 22, 1946.

28. *El Universal* (Caracas), August 12, 1946, p. 13.

29. ITIC File, where this particular incident was described as a simple administrative convenience.

30. See esp. Edwin Lieuwin, *Petroleum in Venezuela: A History* (Berkeley: University of California Press, 1954), Betancourt, *Venezuela: Política y Petróleo.*

31. On the breakdown of harmonious relations between the military and AD, see Martz, *Acción Democrática,* pp. 301–309.

32. Martz, *Acción Democrática,* pp. 306–307.

33. Martz, *Acción Democrática,* pp. 307–308.

34. Alexander, *The Venezuelan Democratic Revolution,* p. 36.

IV. THE COUNTERREVOLUTION, 1948–1958

1. Republic of Venezuela, *Documentos Oficiales Relativos al Movimiento Militar del 24 de Noviembre de 1948* (Caracas: Oficina Nacional de Información y Publicaciones, 1949), pp. 17–23, 37, 81–85.

2. Martz, *Acción Democrática,* pp. 161–188. The suppression became much more marked following the mysterious assassination of Delgado Chalbaud and the emergence of Pérez Jiménez as dictator. Martz covers the clandestine reorganization of AD and the party's important political activities during the 1952 elections. It was after the 1952 elections that URD was dissolved and its leaders sent into exile. The last of the major parties, COPEI, was disbanded during the final phase of the Pérez Jiménez dictatorship, when he openly clashed with the church over his

repressive political tactics. Martz estimated that by the end of the Pérez Jiménez regime nearly 10,000 persons were in political exile. For a grisly record of the National Security Police (SN) and its methods of operation, including documentary evidence from its archives, see José Vicente Abreu, *Se Llamaba SN* (Caracas: Ed. Catalá, 1964). Abreu, a Communist, wrote from first-hand experience.

3. Venezuela, *Documentos Oficiales*, p. 85.

4. Powell, "Preliminary Report," p. 6.

5. International Labor Office, "Feedom of Association and Conditions of Work in Venezuela, *Studies and Reports* (Geneva) n.s., no. 21 (1950), pp. 80, 122.

6. Interview with Luís Manuel Pérez, assistant to the chief of the Division of Syndicates, Contracts, and Conflicts, Ministry of Labor, July 15, 1964.

7. ILO, "Freedom," pp. 42–43.

8. ILO, "Freedom," p. 45. The agricultural communities mentioned in the ILO report were the so-called Agrarian Communities, a hybrid cooperative-collective farm operation, of which fourteen were established by the AD government under the Venezuelan Development Corporation (CVF), created in 1947. These communities, comprising some 33,000 hectares, had been liquidated by 1951, under Pérez Jiménez. See Ministry of Agriculture, *La Colonización Agraria en Venezuela, 1830–1957* (Caracas: MAC, 1959), p. 50.

9. International Bank for Reconstruction and Development (IBRD), *Economic Development of Venezuela* (Baltimore: Johns Hopkins University Press, 1961), pp. 97–98. This is not to say that the 1945–1948 policy was of no benefit to commercial farmers. Rather there was a radical increase of programs directed toward the peasantry.

10. United States of Venezuela, *Estatuto Agrario* (Caracas: Imp. Nacional, 1949). Article 1 is practically identical with the statements of purpose found in the 1945 and 1948 Agrarian Reform Laws. The favored treatment of large landowners included grants of "temporary concessions of inexpropriability" for thirty years under a great variety of circumstances. See Articles 68–71.

11. Ministry of Agriculture, *Memoria* (Caracas: MAC, 1956), p. 140.

12. Jorge Schuster, in a 1965 case study of six agrarian reform asentamientos or settlements, included a property history. One of the asentamientos, "La Linda," near Güigüe in Carabobo state, had an especially informative background. The hacienda, given to Gómez in return for a favor for one of Venezuela's most famous latifundistas, Pimental, became part of the dictator's land empire. In the 1920's he built a barracks

there to garrison troops because of peasant unrest in the area. Following Gómez' death, "La Linda" became part of the Restored Properties and, as a fairly valuable farm operation, was managed by the Agriculture Bank (BAP), coming under Institute for Colonization (ITIC) control during the 1945–1948 period. Following the 1948 coup, the settlement was allowed to languish and die out, although the approximately 200 peasant tenants continued to farm the property. In 1951 two of Gómez' sons appeared, claiming ownership rights to the land, which were granted them by Pérez Jiménez's government. The Gómez boys then promised the peasants that if they would move off the cleared areas, they could move into and farm any acreage that they cleared elsewhere on the farm. Shortly after the peasants had moved from the cleared areas and begun deforestation, they were evicted from the property altogether. Jorge F. Schuster, *La Estructura Económica en Seis Asentamientos Campesinos* (Caracas: MAC, 1965).

13. Interviews with national, state, and local officials of the Peasant Federation of Venezuela (FCV), summer 1964, sponsored by the University of Wisconsin's Land Tenure Center.

14. The actual phrase is "Amigable Componedor," literally, the "Friendly Fixer." Ministry of Agriculture, *Memoria* (Caracas: 1956), I, 139. The evictions were concentrated in states that had experienced the most land reform—Miranda, Aragua, Carabobo—which were both populous and central.

15. The 1948–1958 land reform activities of the government were actually limited to several large, high-cost, "showplace" colonization projects, designed for commercial-type farming. See IBRD, *Economic Development of Venezuela*, pp. 139–193. Although the Ministry of Agriculture (MAC) and Agrarian Institute (IAN) budgets leveled off at about Bs 120 million and Bs 33 million respectively, the reduced scope of their clientele was reflected in a steady attrition of the personnel that had been built up under the AD government. This also occurred in the BAP with the termination of the campesino credit program. The drop is shown in the following figures for personnel levels for the years 1953–1957:

Institution	1953	1954	1955	1956	1957
BAP	1674	1174	980	916	865
MAC	3589	2024	—	—	—
IAN	—	—	—	583	—

BAP, *Memoria* (Caracas: 1958), p. 113; MAC *Memoria* (Caracas: 1955), p. 25; IAN, *Memoria* (Caracas: 1956).

16. Ministry of Labor, *Memoria,* 1948–1952 (Caracas: Imp. Nacional, 1953), p. 80.

17. The Doctrine for the Redemption was first developed by Bentacourt in his *Ahora* columns during 1937–1939. The doctrine stressed the role of the campesino foot soldiers in the War of Independence and the Civil Wars of Venezuela, their services having been rendered on the basis of semiformal, occasionally written, promises of land grants by the victors. The doctrine held that the nation must redeem these promises, which had never been honored. See Hill et al., "Social Welfare" pp. 297–299.

18. Juan Hernández was caught by the security police on October 13, 1951, in connection with a futile attempt to assassinate the military Junta with bombs at a public ceremony. This attempt, verified in a follow-up interview with Hernández in Maracay on March 24, 1966, was planned by the AD underground for execution by Hernández and others. These facts temper Martz's judgement (*Acción Democrática,* p. 169) that the October 1951 terrorist accusations by the government were merely a politically inspired attempt to discredit AD.

19. For a collection of petitions and manifestos from this period, see *Los Manifiestos de la Liberación* (Caracas: Pensamiento Vivo, 1958). For photographs, documents, and news reports of events leading to the downfall of Pérez Jiménez, see José Umaná Bernal, ed., *Testimonio de la Revolución en Venezuela* (Caracas: Tip. Vargas, 1959). See also Philip B. Taylor, Jr., *The Venezuelan Golpe de Estado of 1958: The Fall of Marcos Pérez Jiménez* (Washington: Operations and Policy Research, Inc., 1968).

V. AGRARIAN REFORM, 1958–1968

1. Armando R. González, *Presencia del Proletariado de Venezuela en al Acontecer Político Contemporáneo* (Caracas: Acción Democrática, 1963), p. 18.

2. For a more complete coverage of these post-1957 events, see Lieuwin, *Venezuela;* Alexander, *The Venezuelan Democratic Revolution;* Martz, *Acción Democrática;* and the forthcoming detailed analysis by Philip B. Taylor, Jr., tentatively entitled "Democracy and Authority in Venezuela: The Dynamics of Politics and Culture."

3. For a more detailed account of these events, see John D. Powell, "A Brief Political History of Agrarian Reform in Venezuela," MS thesis, University of Wisconsin, 1964, pp. 82–104.

4. The threat to shoot voters was credible, since they had slain scores of police and National Guardsmen since going into violent opposition in 1961.

5. See "Tripartite Program for Broad-Based Government," mimeographed translation of interparty pact (Caracas, n.d.).

6. Interviews, especially with Hermógenes Mendoza (secretary of organization, later secretary-general for Aragua state) of the Peasant Federation of Venezuela (FCV), Maracay, July 1964; Juan Hernández (secretary-general of the Aragua FCV 1959–1962, national FCV secretary-general 1962–1965, and later national assistant agrarian secretary of AD and the party's secretary-general for Aragua state), Maracay, March 1966.

7. At the Inter-American Development Bank's Seminar on Land Reform and Economic Development of December 1, 1965, Víctor Giménez Landínez, the COPEI minister of agriculture (1959–1964), recalled that during those hectic days Communist peasant union leaders would prearrange a land invasion with maximum public fanfare, such as posters, radio announcements, and newspaper advertisements. To undercut the Communist leadership, the other parties would arrange their own invasions of the selected property, executing it a day or two before the Communist-announced D-Day. Approximately 500 land invasions occurred; that is, roughly one-half of the local unions sponsored invasions between 1958 and 1962.

8. For this reorganization see Powell, "Preliminary Report," pp. 28–31. For an international, conservative view of the early phase of post-dictatorship labor reorganization, see Inter-American Regional Organization of Workers, *El Movimiento Sindical Libre del Continente y la Reforma Agraria* (México, D. F.: ORIT, 1961), pp. 42–47.

9. For an inside view, see Armando González, *Presencia del Proletariado,* and his speech "La Reforma Agraria y el Movimiento Campesino," delivered to the Thirteenth Inter-American Conference on the Caribbean, December 8, 1962, at the University of Florida. González replaced Quijada as president of the FCV in June 1962 and was re-elected in 1967.

10. Agrarian Reform Commission, *Reforma Agraria* (Caracas: MAC, 1959), II, 15–17. This four-volume work records the sessions of the four Subcommissions—legal, economic, agro-technical, and social—with their recommendations.

11. Agrarian Reform Commission, *Reforma Agraria,* I, 341–344. In an appendix to this volume, Giménez Landínez included "La Doctrina Social-Católica y los Problemas Agraria," which describes the sources of Catholic

doctrine toward social change and social justice. According to Giménez, the primary source included "Rerum Novarum" and "Quadragesino Anno," encyclicals of Leo XIII and Pius XI. Presumably one could add John XXIII's "Mater et Magistra" and "Pacem in Terris" to today's list of guides to the social philosophy of the Christian Democrats.

12. For a record of congressional debates on the bill, see National Congress, *La Ley de Reforma Agraria en las Cámaras Legislativas* (Caracas: Imp. Nacional, 1960), I and II.

13. As late as July 1959, Pompeyo Márquez, Communist party senator, was still backing the draft version of the Agrarian Reform Law, citing the need to "stay united in the face of reactionary forces." When said reactionary forces failed to emasculate the measure and the Communists failed to radicalize it, they opposed its passage. See Pompeyo Márquez, *Hacia Dónde Va el 23 de Enero?* (Caracas: Pensamiento Vivo, 1959), pp. 62–153. For the transition of the Communist party position on the government's agrarian reform, see the documents published by the Agrarian Commission of the Communist Party of Venezula *Sobre la Cuestión Agraria en Venezuela* (Caracas: Ed. Cantaclaro, 1960). By August 1961, three months prior to being purged from the Confederation of Venezuelan Workers (CTV) the Communists were openly opposed to the Betancourt government's social and agrarian reforms. See El Velazco (pseud.), "Venezuela: New Conditions Call for New Tactics," *World Marxist Review,* 4 (August 1961), 60–62.

14. For a simplified explanation of the law, see Phanor J. Eder, "Agrarian Reform in Venezuela," *Journal of Comparative Law,* 9 (Autumn 1960), 667–670. For a translation of many of the most important provisions of the law, Powell, "Brief Political History," Appendix I.

15. For the complicated legal expropriation process, see *National Agrarian Institute, Adjudicaciones de Tierras al Campesinado Venezolano* (Caracas: IAN, 1962), pp. 5–15. In addition to developing settlements, the government had a plan to legalize the rights of squatters on public lands. See *National Agrarian Institute, Plan de Regularización de Tenencia a los Ocupantes de Tierras Baldías o Ejidos* (Caracas: IAN, 1962).

16. For a consultant's report on the complexities of the autonomous agencies, which "have the common characteristic of assignment to, and dependency from, one Ministry or another," see Public Administrative Service, *Autonomous Administrative Entities* (Chicago: PAS, 1960), p. 73.

17. Preliminary findings based on field work by the Inter-American

Committee on Agricultural Development (CIDA), however, indicate that the asentimiento program raised only the material standard of living of the beneficiaries, not their farm-derived income. See John R. Mathiason and Eric B. Shearer, *Caicara de Maturín (Case Study of an Agrarian Reform Settlement in Venezuela)*, Research Papers on Land Tenure and Agrarian Reform, No. 1 (Washington, D.C.: Inter-American Committee for Agricultural Development, 1967).

18. Interviews in Washington, D.C., February 27–30, 1964, with officials in the Library of Congress, Department of State, and Venezuelan Embassy.

VI. THE PEASANT FEDERATION AND THE RURAL PROBLEM-SOLVING SYSTEM

1. The national leaders of the Peasant Federation (FCV) often claimed a membership of "about one million," but the figure used here is a more reliable estimate, based on two sets of consistent data: an extrapolation from an internal FCV audit, and the projection of my survey results.

2. Peasant Federation of Venezuela, "Estatutos de la Federación Campesina de Venezuela," mimeographed (Caracas: FCV, 1959).

3. For the nature of the power sharing and individual sketches of men elected to national FCV offices in 1962, see Powell, "Preliminary Report," pp. 28–40.

4. At the Third Campesino Congress, held in February 1967 at Los Caracas labor resort, the National Executive Committee was expanded as a means of officially incorporating the Unión Republicana Democrática (URD) peasant leadership. A second vice-president, a secretary for Indian affairs, and a secretary for international affairs were thus added to the committee, and the secretary for culture and propaganda's functions were redefined in two new posts—a secretary for education and a secretary for press and publications. A third URD alternate to the committee and a URD member on the Disciplinary Tribunal were also added.

5. Numerous interviews and a survey were conducted in Venezuela in 1961, 1964, and 1965–1966. The resulting data are presented in tables in this and subsequent chapters. Sample sizes and characteristics for the interviews differed according to strata. The twenty-four national leaders of the FCV interviewed included all leaders in office from 1964 through 1966 and is thus a statistical population. The twenty-three state leaders of the FCV interviewed included approximately 15 percent of all such

leaders in office from 1964 through 1966, but is, statistically, an accidental sample. The one hundred eighteen local leaders of the FCV interviewed represented a 10 percent random sample of union leaders attending randomly selected state FCV conventions conducted early in 1966. Though six states had been selected for the interviews, only five could be covered owing to time and lack of resources, so that it is impossible to assign a precise sample error. The data presented, therefore, are technically applicable only to local leaders attending the conventions in the five states indicated. The national and state leaders were questioned by means of a directed interview, the local leaders through a verbally administered questionnaire consisting of sixty-two items, each lasting approximately forty-five minutes. Interviewers and support for the survey were furnished by the Inter-American Committee on Agricultural Development from their field staff.

6. AD and URD local chapters of the FCV are almost invariably called *sindicatos* or unions. COPEI peasant leaders prefer to name their locals *ligas* or leagues, in the belief that this term encompasses more meaningfully their social philosophy.

7. For a detailed explanation of the proportional representation system, see Institute for the Comparative Study of Political Systems, *Venezuela: Election Factbook* (Washington: Operations and Policy Research, Inc., 1963).

8. COPEI left the government when President Leoni took office in 1964. In the December 1968 elections, Rafael Caldera, the COPEI candidate, was elected president, taking office early in 1969.

9. FCV representatives sit on the National Planning Board of the Ministry of Agriculture (MAC), National Agricultural Extension Service Board (MAC), Rural Housing Board of Consultants (Vivienda Rural), Directorate of the National Institute for Culture and Education, National Coffee and Cacao Board (MAC), National Cotton Board (MAC), National Copra Board (MAC), National Rice Board (MAC), National Pork Board (MAC), National Beef Board (MAC), National Milk Board (MAC), National Tobacco Board (MAC), National Sisal Board (MAC), National Agricultural Machinery Board (BAP), National Supervised Credit Board (BAP), National Agricultural Credit Board (BAP), and National Board for Conversion of Coffee and Cacao Debts (BAP).

10. The CONVEN study, which surveyed about forty distinct societal groups, such as peasants, student leaders, politicians, and businessmen, was called "A Study of Conflict and Consensus," from which the acronym CONVEN derives. For the theoretical bases of CONVEN, see Jorge

Ahumada, "Hypothesis for the Diagnosis of a Situation of Social Change: The Case of Venezuela," *International Social Science Journal,* 16:2 (1964), 192–202. For preliminary results, see Frank Bonilla and José Silva, eds., *Studying the Venezuelan Polity* (Cambridge: MIT Press, 1968).

11. For health statistics, see U.S. Army Medical Service, *Health and Sanitary Data for Venezuela* (Washington, D.C.: Medical Information and Intelligence Agency, 1961).

VII. THE GENERATION AND TRANSMISSION OF DEMANDS AND SUPPORTS

1. For earlier research, carried out in the Peasant Federation (FCV) archives in 1964, see Powell, "Preliminary Report," Ch. II. Special characteristics of the local FCV leaders in the sample should establish their credentials to speak on problems facing peasants. First, they were "live-in" rather than "absentee" leaders—79.9 percent gave as the address of their personal residence the same community or village in which their syndicate was located, and another 13.6 percent lived in an adjoining neighborhood. The local FCV leaders, moreover, were not newcomers in their place of residence—29.7 percent were born there, an additional 12.7 percent had lived there for twenty years or more, and another 21.2 percent for ten to twenty years. Finally, they came overwhelmingly from peasant backgrounds (83.9 percent), considered farming their primary occupation (86.4 percent), and, in a cross-check question, reported that their primary source of income was derived from "farming" (84.7 percent). In short, the sample local FCV leaders were themselves peasants.

2. From a multiple-correlation (Pearson product-moment) program run with a variety of statistical data on Venezuela. For the rural population data, see Ministry of Development, *IX Censo Nacional de Población: Resultas Preliminares* (Caracas: Imp. Nacional, 1962), p. 9. Voting data appear in *El Nacional,* December 13, 1963. Thus, the population data had a 1961 base, and the electoral data a 1963 base.

3. The CONVEN samples contained both union and nonunion members, party and nonparty members, in about the same proportion as they actually exist in the peasant population (since they were selected on a random basis). The level of reported participation in political and union activities is thus amazingly high.

4. Charles B. Erasmus, a perceptive cultural anthropologist who spent about four months in rural Venezuela in 1964, charged that some local

syndicate leaders, especially state FCV leaders who worked in the Agrarian Institute (IAN) and Agriculture Bank (BAP), were "extremely partisan." Erasmus, "Agrarian Reform: A Comparative Study of Venezuela, Bolivia and Mexico," mimeographed (Land Tenure Center, University of Wisconsin, 1964).

5. For an introduction to these communications functions, see Karl Deutsch, *The Nerves of Government* (New York: The Free Press of Glencoe, 1963), Ch. V.

6. See Elihu Katz, "The Two-Step Flow of Communication: An Up-to-Date Report on an Hypothesis," *Public Opinion Quarterly,* 21 (Spring 1957), 61–67.

7. The term "cities" was chosen, after agonizing debate, as a deliberately vague and nonreferential term. Interviewers were instructed that if the respondent asked what was meant by the term (the question was: "How much of your life has been spent living in cities?"), he was to answer, "Cities like Caracas, or [capitol of the state where the interview occurred]." In most cases, respondents were not puzzled by the term, and often gave the name of each city in which they had lived, as well as the duration of their stay. These amplified responses, marginally noted, were found to be centers of population of over 5,000 (by 1961 Census data). Charles Wagley characterizes such peasant leaders as "cultural brokers" in "The Peasant," in *Continuity and Change in Latin America,* ed. John Johnson (Stanford: Stanford University Press, 1964), esp. pp. 45–48.

8. Comparative media exposure is the primary source of evidence used by those who employ the two-step flow hypothesis. See Katz, "Two-Step Flow of Communication," pp. 63–64.

9. The follow-through efforts are characterized as "haphazard" on the basis of my 1964 field work, which was spent mostly in the national headquarters of the FCV.

10. See Charles L. Clapp, *The Congressman: His Work as He Sees It* (New York: Doubleday and Co., Inc., Anchor Books, 1964), pp. 56–62.

11. That is, the response is rational if survival of the system is accepted as the ultimate goal. For many participants in the system, the goal appears somewhat differently. The issue once again is the tension between authority legitimation (and its retention by the regime) and interest articulation (and its pursuit by the subleaders closest to the peasant members at the base of the system).

12. The emphasis on the national organization does not mean that the state leaders are unimportant in the overall leadership structure. All of

the national FCV leaders elected in 1962, for instance, were state officials at the time of their elevation.

13. The annual operating budget of the FCV is close to Bs 1 million, most of which (Bs 55,000 monthly) is received in the form of a subsidy from the Ministry of Labor. Fifty percent of this budget is used for national functions, 25 percent is distributed equally among the various state offices, and 25 percent is dedicated to the direct support of local union activities. Interview with Máximo Acuña, finance secretary of the FCV, Caracas, July 1964. Obtaining a clear picture of the total financing of the peasant union movement would be a difficult and delicate task, because of its complexity.

14. For the Peasant Vocational Schools, see Powell, "Preliminary Report," pp. 23–27.

15. Address by Armando González at the Third Campesino Congress, at Los Caracas, Venezuela, February 10–12, 1967.

VIII. THE FLOW OF GOVERNMENTAL RESPONSES

1. Harold Lasswell, *Politics: Who Gets What, When, How* (New York: McGraw-Hill, Inc., 1936).

2. My thanks to Jorge F. Schuster, adviser to the vice-minister of agriculture, for pointing out the sources of this data. Schuster, who holds a doctorate in agricultural economics from the University of Wisconsin, is probably the most knowledgeable Venezuelan on agrarian reform.

3. The order of questions was: (a) "In your opinion, what is the greatest and most serious problem which confronts the members of your syndicate?" (Open-ended.) (b) "For the members of your syndicate, is (lack of land, inadequate housing, etc.) a grave problem, a minor problem, or no problem at all?" (A list of ten problems was mentioned individually.) (c) "In solving such problems confronted by your syndicate, has (the Administrative Committee, the MAC Extension Agent, etc.), been of much help, little help, or no help at all?" (Nine entities were mentioned.) In addition, respondents were asked, "Do other programs or organizations exist, not mentioned in the previous question, which have been of much help in solving the problems of your community? Mention them." It was found that there was no significant pattern of responses to this open-ended approach, and it was concluded that the earlier question had included all of the most relevant help-agents in the rural areas.

4. There were highly negative responses to items on the list as well.

The most negative response was triggered by the mention of "communism," 86.4 percent. Also prompting highly negative responses were "dictatorship," 85.6 percent; "latifundia," 72.0 percent; and mention of several well-known political leaders.

5 The initial findings of the agrarian reform evaluation study confirm that early in the program (1959–1961) the Agrarian Institute responded to the areas of intense peasant pressure but, after a period of reorganization (1962–1963), began to concentrate on geographic areas with relatively low population or organizational pressures (1964–1969). See Inter-American Committee on Agricultural Development, "Research Papers."

6. This seems to be a clear case of the operation of the "participation hypothesis," well-known in social psychology. The hypothesis suggests that work tasks are performed better and enjoyed more when the opportunity (or even the illusion) is provided of participating in setting goals and work norms. See Sidney Verba, *Small Groups and Political Behavior: A Study of Leadership* (Princeton: Princeton University Press, 1961), Ch. 9.

IX. THE POLITICS OF AGRARIAN REFORM

1. The FND minister of agriculture had replaced Alejandro Osorio, an independent closely identified with AD who had served as interim minister following Leoni's inauguration. After FND withdrew from the government, President Leoni formally appointed Osorio to the Cabinet position, thereby bringing all three of the principle agrarian reform agencies—the Agrarian Institute (IAN), Agriculture Bank (BAP), and Ministry of Agriculture (MAC)—under the dominant influence of the same party (AD) for the first time since 1958.

2. Fernando Núñez, *The Daily Journal* (Caracas), April 21, 1966, p. 1.

3. *El Nacional* (Caracas), March 19, 1966, p. 1. This was not the only occasion on which Villalba publically implied anti-URD discrimination in the agrarian reform program.

4. Interview with Eladio Reyes Henríquez, URD representative to the National Executive Committee of the Peasant Federation (FCV), Caracas, February 15, 1966.

5. Interviews with Jorge Pacheco, national campesino director of URD, his assistant Arturo Infante, and seven regional organizers, Caracas, April 20, 1966.

6. Interview with Manuel Alfredo Duplat, the COPEI agrarian secre-

tary, Julio César Vivas, the FCV secretary for labor affairs and COPEI's agrarian directorate, and Gastón Pulido, member of the same directorate and the FCV secretary of organization, Caracas, January 31, 1966.

7. National Agrarian Directorate (COPEI), "Movimiento Agrario Social Cristiano," typescript (Caracas: COPEI, May 1966).

8. Peasant Federation, "Reglamento: Procedimientos Electorales," mimeographed (Caracas: FCV, March 23, 1963).

9. National Committee of COPEI, "Reglamento Interno del Movimiento Agrario Socialcristiano," mimeographed (Caracas: COPEI, July 3, 1964).

10. A group of researchers from the Center of Development Studies (CENDES) of the Central University of Venezuela, and I attended the First National Assembly. Thirty interviews were obtained after drawing a random sample of delegates. After preliminary analysis, it was decided not to utilize the data because they represented such a specialized, highly specific leadership group, when compared with the national FCV sample data. The delegates to the COPEI convention represented a party organizational elite in terms of their education, occupations, backgrounds, and positions within the party structure.

11. Sanin, "The Parties in 1966: URD," *The Daily Journal* (Caracas), January 13, 1966, p. 4.

12. Interview in *El Trabajador* (Caracas), October 1965, pp. 8–9.

13. Interview with Eladio Reyes Henríquez, Caracas, February, 1966. On the basis of the estimates of other party leaders, and of the number of URD local leaders selected in the random national sample, most of these peasant unions are probably in the process of being organized, with perhaps some 200 fully functioning.

14. *El Nacional* (Caracas), March 19, 1966, p. 1.

15. *El Nacional* (Caracas), April 23, 1966, p. 1.

16. *El Nacional* and all other Caracas dailies carried the story on page 1 of their editions of April 27.

17. Fernando Núñez, *Daily Journal,* April 27, 1966, p. 1. Núñez, who seems to have excellent contacts within all of the major political parties, is a careful observer and political analyst.

18. Abraham Veitia, *El Mundo* (Caracas), April 29, 1966, p. 1.

19. *La Esfera* (Caracas), May 6, 1966, p. 2.

20. On July 1, 1966, Alirio Ugarte Pelay apparently called a news conference in his home to announce the formation of a new political party. While the newsmen were waiting in an anteroom, Alirio put a bullet through his head.

21. MIR later participated in the terrorist activities carried on prior to the 1963 elections, including assassinations, arson, and bombings, designed to bring down the AD government.

22. The Quijada affair coincided with the bolt of a small faction within AD nicknamed the "ARS" faction. For a detailed accounting, see Martz, *Acción Democrática,* pp. 273–286. In 1964 I visited the original headquarters of the FCV in an attempt to track down and interview Ramón Quijada. Though the pretense was still feebly maintained of being the one and only peasant movement, Quijada refused to make himself available.

23. This convention remains unnamed in order to protect my informants.

24. The principle asset of the alliance in these floor maneuvers was the desire of the AD peasant leaders to avoid embarrassment during the public sessions of the convention, at which the governor of the state and many newsmen were present. The combined COPEI and URD delegations comprised about one-third of all the delegates at the convention. Part of the skillful maneuvering by the alliance was to demonstrate to the convention managers that this one-third was potentially loud and aggressive in pursuit of its interests.

25. My thanks to John R. Mathiason of the University of Washington for the correspondence and news clippings on which this section is based.

26. For these internal party structures and their functions, see John Martz, *Acción Democrática,* pp. 147–161.

X. CONCLUDING PERSPECTIVES

1. Moore, *Social Origins.*

2. Hans Bobek, "The Main Stages in Socio-Economic Evolution from a Geographical Point of View," in P. C. Wagner and M. W. Mikesell, *Readings in Cultural Geography* (Chicago: University of Chicago Press, 1962), pp. 218–247.

3. Huntington, *Political Order,* esp. Ch. 1.

4. Charles Tilly, *The Vendée* (Cambridge: Harvard University Press, 1964).

5. See Marc Bloch, *Feudal Society,* trans. L. A. Manyon (London: Routledge & Kegan Paul Ltd., 1961).

6. Everett Hagen, *On the Theory of Social Change* (Homewood, Ill.: The Dorsey Press, Inc., 1962), pp. 110–111.

7. See Samuel L. Popkin, "The Myth of the Village: Revolution and Reaction in Viet Nam," Ph.D. diss., Massachusetts Institute of Technology, 1969.

8. The type of electoral system also affects the degree of fragmentation. See Philip B. Taylor, Jr., *Venezuela: Election Factbook* (Washington: Operations and Policy Research, Inc., 1963); Douglas Rae, *The Political Consequences of Electoral Laws* (New Haven: Yale University Press, 1968).

9. Huntington, *Political Order,* p. 77.

10. Huntington, *Political Order,* pp. 445–446.

11. For one attempt to construct such a perspective, see Robert Putnam, "Toward Explaining Military Intervention in Latin American Politics," *World Politics,* 20 (October 1967), 83–110.

12. See John Duncan Powell, "Peasant Society and Clientelist Politics," *American Political Science Review,* 64 (June 1970), 411–429. Alex Weingrod developed a similar approach in his "Patrons, Patronage, and Political Parties," *Comparative Studies in Society and History* 10 (July 1968), 377–400.

13. Tarrow, *Peasant Communism.*

INDEX

Acción Democrática (AD), 36, 37;
and coups d'état, 40–44, 65, 66,
85–88; internal crises, 193–196,
196–200, 206–211; in state Peasant Federation conventions,
200–205; strategic role in
Venezuelan development, 221–228
passim. *See also* Elections; Peasant-urban alliance
Agrarian reform: antecedents in
Venezuela, 69–73, 75–78, 90–94;
legislation, 79–81, 91–92, 106–
112; program, 163–181 passim;
role in political development,
212–228 passim
Agriculture and Livestock Bank
(BAP): history, 24–26; role in
agrarian reform, 106–112 passim,
163–165

Barrios, Gonzalo, 206–211 passim.
See also Acción Democrática
Betancourt, Rómulo: early
(pre-1945) political career, 28,
29, 31–33; in coup d'état (1945),
40, 41, 66; agrarian policies
(1945–1948), 69–71, 75–78;
elected President, 101–102; in
Acción Democrática crises,
194–196, 206–211. *See also*
Agrarian reform

Caldera, Rafael, 82, 101, 189, 190,
210. *See also* COPEI
Campesino Congress, 186, 187, 195,
196. *See also* Peasant Federation
of Venezuela
Coalition governments: origins, 100;
under Betancourt and Leoni,
101–103, 197, 198; role of issues
in performance of, 182–188. *See
also* Elections; Parties
Commercialization of agriculture,

10, 23–27; role in Venezuelan development, 212–226 passim
COPEI, 67, 68, 99; internal stability, 189–190; in Peasant Federation state conventions, 200–205;
outlook for, 226–228 passim. *See
also* Elections; Parties
Coups d'état: in 1945, 39–43, 44,
45, 65, 66; in 1948, 84–86; in
1958, 98–101. *See also* Acción
Democrática; Gallegos, Rómulo;
Pérez Jiménez, Marcos

Delgado Chalbaud, Carlos, 85–87

Elections: changing nature, 32,
66–68, 69; results, 36, 38, 67, 68,
100–102, 210. *See also* Coups
d'état; Parties
Escalante, Diógenes, 40, 41. *See also*
Coups d'état (1945)

Frente Nacional Democrática
(FND), 102, 183, 184. *See also*
Elections; Parties

Gallegos, Rómulo, 36, 41, 85–86.
See also Acción Democrática
Generation of '28, 27–29. *See also*
Betancourt, Rómulo; Leoni, Raúl;
Villalba, Jóvito
Gómez, Juan Vicente, 18–23, 30
González, Armando, 56, 96, 97; be-
comes president of Peasant Feder-
ation of Venezuela, 194–196; role
in Acción Democrática crisis of
1967–1968, 197–200, 202–205
passim
Guevara, Eustacio, 200, 209. *See
also* Acción Democrática
Guzmán Blanco, Antonio, 16, 17

Labor movement: origins, 31–34;
and communists, 35, 36, 62, 63;

DATE DUE

GAYLORD   PRINTED IN U.S.A.